LETTERS FROM VLADIVOSTOK,

1894–1930

THE ELEANOR L. PRAY COLLECTION

Collected and organized by Patricia D. Silver

Edited with introduction and notes by

BIRGITTA INGEMANSON

UNIVERSITY OF WASHINGTON PRESS

Seattle and London

LETTERS FROM VLADIVOSTOK,

1894–1930

Eleanor L. Pray

This publication was made possible in part by support from the Marianna Merritt and Donald S. Matteson Distinguished Professorship in Foreign Languages and Cultures at Washington State University, and by a generous gift from a private donor.

© 2013 by the University of Washington Press
Printed and bound in the United States
Design by Dustin Kilgore
Composed in Minion, typeface designed by Robert Slimbach
First paperback edition 2014
18 17 16 15 14   5 4 3 2 1

Letters from the Eleanor L. Pray Collection courtesy of the private collection of Patricia D. Silver.
Unless otherwise indicated, all illustrations are courtesy of Patricia Silver.
Maps by Kathleen M. Bodley.

The poem "Ancestry Dream" is reproduced by permission of Sophie Wadsworth, and was originally published in *Letters from Siberia: Poems by Sophie Wadsworth* (Syracuse, NY: The Comstock Review, 2004), n.p.

University of Washington Press
www.washington.edu/uwpress

Library of Congress Cataloging-in-Publication Data
Pray, Eleanor Lord, 1868–1954. [Correspondence. 2013] Letters from Vladivostok, 1894–1930 / edited with introduction and notes by Birgitta Ingemanson.
pages ; cm.
"The Eleanor L. Pray Collection collected and organized by Patricia D. Silver."
Includes bibliographical references and index.
ISBN 978-0-295-99453-6 (paperback : alk. paper)
1. Pray, Eleanor Lord, 1868–1954—Correspondence. 2. Americans—Russia (Federation)—Vladivostok—Correspondence. 3. Vladivostok (Russia)—Social life and customs—19th century—Sources. 4. Vladivostok (Russia)—Social life and customs—20th century—Sources. 5. Vladivostok (Russia)—History—19th century—Sources. 6. Vladivostok (Russia)—History—20th century—Sources. I. Ingemanson, Birgitta, writer of added commentary. II. Title. III. Title: Letters from Vladivostok, 1894–1930.
DK781.V5P72 2013   957'.7—dc23   [B]   2013015521

To dear Grannie Pray and Aunt Sarah, who always hoped that someone would be interested in these letters and would publish them.

To my beloved S. R. S., who did not think the book would ever be finished. —Patricia D. Silver

To the memory of Nils Åke Nilsson and Jan Olof Olsson, inspired writers who taught so well about Russian cities and culture.

In grateful and loving remembrance of Nina I. Velikaia (1925–2005), whose first five years in Vladivostok coincided with Mrs. Pray's last five.

To Gregory, in True Love. —Birgitta Ingemanson

Ancestry Dream

Through a narrow door I stoop
into the muslined room
of the dead   throw kerosene

flames snap   what to take
photographs and tintypes
the embroidered tablecloth

grandma's letters from Siberia
I hurry them under my coat
stumble over stubbled grass

flames break the window panes
mother father run down the road
no one sees me cross the furrows

slip into a circle of stones
smell of smoke   in the shade
everything left behind is here

books   wills   the tarnished ring
counted as lost   I gather them
into my hands   feel someone

watching me   ash-haired
is it you grandmother
holding the oval mirror between us

eclipsing your face
the glass   so bright
I cannot see

—Sophie Wadsworth

Contents

Photographs follow p. 102

List of Place Names

1. Amur Bay
2. Bay of the Golden Horn
3. Vladivostok city center
4. Egersheld, area southwest of city center
5. Tigrovaia Sopka, Tiger Hill (Danish House*)
6. Churkin, area south of Bay of the Golden Horn
7. Sedanka Reservoir
8. Novogeorgievsk Estate, with Irishain Beach along the west shore* (today DeVries Peninsula)
9. Pervaia Rechka, First River, area north of city center
10. Vtoraia Rechka, Second River, area north of First River
11. "Platform," 19th Verst (today Sanatornaia) Station
12. Okeanskaia (Ocean) Station
13. Ussuri Bay
14. Zoological Gardens* (general area)
15. Hippodrome*
16. Pokrovskoe Cemetery
17. Dry Dock
18. House of Lindholm
19. Admiral's House* and Garden
20. Railway Station
21. Cathedral of the Assumption*
22. Pushkinskaia, Pushkin Street
23. Kunst and Albers (today GUM)
24. House of Dattan
25. Alekseevskaia Sopka, Aleksei Hill
26. Sodomskii Pereulok, Sodom Lane (today Pochtovyi Pereulok, Post Lane)
27. Petrovelikaia, Peter the Great Street
28. Svetlanskaia, Vladivostok's main street

29. Aleutskaia, Aleut Street
30. Kitaiskaia, Chinese Street (today Okeanskii Prospekt, Ocean Avenue)
31. Borodinskaia, Borodin (today Pologaia) Street
32. Churin's store (today Women's GUM)
33. House of Piankov
34. Post and Telegraph Office
35. Dom Smith
36. Fernsicht
37. Lutheran Church
38. Narodnyi Dom (People's House), community center
39. Pekinskaia, Pekin (today Fokin) Street
40. Komarovskaia, Lieut. Komarov Street
41. Enlarged area with Dom Smith
42. Russian Island
43. Commercial Institute (today Far Eastern Federal University)
44. Admiral's Pier
45. Suifunskaia (today Uborevich) Street

*No longer in existence

Area Surrounding Vladivostok

Amur Bay
1

8

12

11

7

10

9

5   3
2
4   15
6
14

Ussuri Bay

13

42

N

KMB

Vladivostok Early 1900s

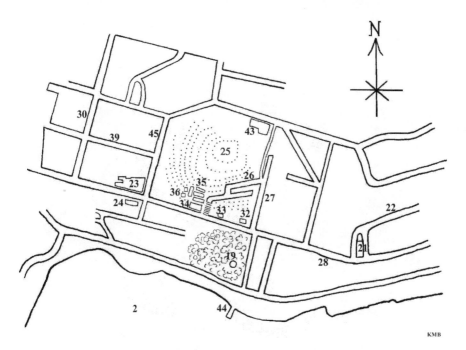

No. 41, Enlarged Area with Dom Smith

KMB

Introduction

Between the Two Bays:
Eleanor Pray's Vladivostok, 1894–1930

BIRGITTA INGEMANSON

CITIES, LIKE PEOPLE, ARE MUCH MORE COMPLEX THAN THE BOOKS and pictures that describe them. Certainly, a good guidebook will outline the history, architectural landmarks, and special events of any metropolis, and pictures such as Camille Pissarro's Parisian boulevard scenes and Alfred Stieglitz's photographs of New York offer vivid flashes of urban life. But take another look at those images. Although we are pushed straight into the noise and movement of Pissarro's street, just as the artist has intended—into "its jingling carriages and its throngs of people"[1]—there is a catch. We can go *to* the view, but we cannot be *in* it: the human mysteries of those captured moments cannot be revealed by a painting alone. Who are the passersby with their hats and umbrellas, and where are they going? How has the city shaped their lives? To answer such questions, we would have to follow these people to their homes, in the mad hope that they might open their doors and reveal their secrets. For to explore the character of a city, it is not enough to remain on the outside looking in; we must immerse ourselves in both its domestic and its public realms. This task requires more than the facts, more than the visual imagery and the fleeting testimony of tourists. In historian Lewis Mumford's words, we need not only "buildings, trees, gardens, but also men in action." As "a touch of actual life" he offers a scene glimpsed by Herodotus on a street in ancient Babylon: a father and his rebellious son in the midst of an argument.[2] There they are, universally human, adding vividness to an otherwise plain scene. Such personal vignettes are necessarily anecdotal and may be dismissed as insignificant, but they can both supplement and enliven the objective narratives of social historians, many of whom do recognize their value and "richness of detail."[3] If we are very lucky, private observations about a place—flashes of ordinary moments—may be found in individual residents' letters and diaries, allowing us to explore the human depths beyond the scholarly façades. Several writers portraying Russian imperial cities have achieved exactly this.[4]

And to explore the historical Pacific port of Vladivostok, there is no one better than Eleanor Lord Pray. Originally from Berwick, Maine, Eleanor Pray (1868–1954) arrived in East Siberia in June 1894 a starry-eyed, newly married member of the merchant family of Charles (1834–98) and Sarah (1858–1942) Smith, owners of the city's American Store.[5] She was destined to live in Vladivostok far longer than the five years to which she and her husband Frederick (1867–1923), Sarah's brother, had agreed, and, with great narrative acumen, transformed the good times and the bad of those years, 1894–1930, into an exuberant epistolary testimonial of interest, appreciation, and survival. Several days a week, and often several times a day, Mrs. Pray wrote diary-like letters on all kinds of stationery to numerous correspondents in New England, Europe, and China; some are two to three pages long, others average forty to fifty pages, altogether, she wrote more than two thousand letters numbering a total of approximately sixteen thousand pages. In addition, the Eleanor L. Pray Collection contains diaries from 1914–15, a calendar noting the birthdays of family members and friends, several scrapbooks, and a number of short stories, poems, and articles that reflect Eleanor Pray's life in Vladivostok. Furthermore, some twenty photo albums offer hundreds of striking scenes from "Old Vladivostok," often enhanced by precise annotations in the letters.[6] While this collection also includes letters written to Eleanor Pray (especially from Sarah), Mrs. Pray's own writings constitute its mainstay. Thanks to the immediacy and reliability of her observations—and to the loyal safeguarding of these written and visual memories by her correspondents and their heirs—the Eleanor L. Pray Collection is a significant source of primary information about bourgeois life in Old Vladivostok.

No other collection of letters pertaining to Vladivostok, with such a wide scope of chronology and contents as that of Eleanor Pray, is presently known. The city's repositories of history—including the State Archive of the Maritime Territory, the Vladimir K. Arseniev State Museum of Primorie (informally, the Arseniev Museum), and the Institute of History, Archeology, and the Ethnography of the Peoples of the Far East (Far Eastern Division, Russian Academy of Sciences)—suffer no shortage of historical documents, objects, or professionals to interpret them, but Eleanor Pray's contribution is unique.

Her faithful chronicle covers more than three and a half decades, through monumental historic changes; it consists of thousands of true eyewitness accounts, not reconstructed memories; and its clear, insightful prose and incomparable photos can reach and enlighten today's readers directly.[7] Here is a woman who welcomes us into her home and accompanies us out into the city and its surroundings. She portrays members of all social classes performing diverse tasks—servants, shopkeepers, officers, soldiers, sailors, construction workers, entrepreneurs, secretaries, salespersons, medical personnel, teachers, political activists, city officials, foreign officials, manual laborers, and peasants—yet her own sphere was that of a Victorian married woman who did not work outside the home. Mrs. Pray was secure in the knowledge that she and her Russian, European, and American friends were "ladies," and that her husband and their male friends were "gentlemen." For her, this identification had little to do with wealth (she became near-destitute in the mid-1920s) and everything to do with manners (dress code and social behavior). She used little slang and only a very occasional "d——n," but her beautifully crafted English reflects everything under the sun; she might agree that "nil a me alienum puto."[8] Although Eleanor Pray did not make history while living in Vladivostok (except for staying so long),[9] her name and testimony are being revived in the twenty-first century, like a cultural treat from the past that revolutionaries could not respect and dared not enjoy. An exquisite exhibit honoring Eleanor Pray's place in Vladivostok's history opened at the Arseniev Museum on 24 October 2008 and was reviewed favorably in the media, one critic calling it "a unique cultural project."[10]

Mrs. Pray loved expressing herself in writing, and, when not socializing, sewing, or sleeping, was constantly engaged with pen and paper. Her correspondence was a lifeline, a regular task that displayed and anchored the Prays' new life—in Mrs. Pray's own consciousness and in that of her family. She groomed her audience, humanizing what seemed like the wilds of Russia for "The Folks at Home" (her parents, her sister Clara, and her foster brother William McCue), her parents-in-law, and other relatives and school friends, and carefully adjusted her writing style and topics to the individual correspondents' personalities and interests. For instance, to Clara, who was perhaps envious and occasionally contemptuous of Mrs. Pray's adventures abroad, the tone is friendly but sometimes stilted or defensive; whereas to Sarah (who even after moving to Shanghai in 1916 remained Eleanor Pray's closest friend and mentor), the letters sparkle with heartfelt warmth and humor. Sarah appreciated every bit of Vladivostok news, and, although herself a somewhat reluctant writer, the supportive role she played by always offering an eager ear was considerable.

While Eleanor Pray named some of her writings "diaries," the letters were her true diaries, or, one might even suggest, her autobiography.[11] She recorded everything that seemed significant or amusing—minor events and great ones, joyous and sad, a "grab bag" of life-affirming moments. Here are household chores jumbled with births and deaths; tea-party conversations about clothing and baby care blended with politics. Considered as a whole, Eleanor Pray's letters form a streamlined, ever-widening portrait of concentric circles. In the innermost sphere we see the Prays, the Smiths, and their friends tackling their daily life (part 1, "The People"). Outside this calm but captivating setting of Victorian domesticity in Vladivostok, we visit the city's bustling streets and marketplaces, admire the spectacular natural vistas, and interact with well-known people and landmarks (part 2, "The City"). In the outermost circle (part 3, "The History"), we observe the often chaotic political events that befell Vladivostok—the Russo-Japanese War (1904–5), the riots of 1905–6, World War I (1914–18), the revolutions of 1917, the Russian Civil War, and the Foreign Intervention (1918–22). Against this diverse background, the city resembles a lively but dysfunctional theater, with the residents playing the actors, the authorities the frequently replaced directors, and the tourists and other short-term visitors the appreciative but often baffled audience.[12] Thanks to the location of her home overlooking Svetlanskaia, Vladivostok's main thoroughfare along the Bay of the Golden Horn, Eleanor Pray could watch both ordinary scenes and revolutionary dramas from her windows—and she understood what she saw.

Mrs. Pray was poignantly aware of the unusual character of her perch and of her own responsibility: she had to tell a truthful tale. While her background and personality prompted her selection of Vladivostok images, she was also guided by a quick mind that saw clearly, studied diligently, and reported fairly. She would state when an opinion was her own, or if she could not vouch for something she had heard. The information she gave that can be checked elsewhere is remarkably reliable; there are few discrepancies. When arriving in Vladivostok, Eleanor Pray was an educated young woman, but not about Russia, and she did her graduate research, as it were, with books and well-informed people.[13] She read voluminously on world events and the tsar's empire, devouring Russian, French, and English sources, local and international newspapers, and American and European magazines by subscription. With friends, she ventured into the multicultural stores of the

Millionka (the city's Chinese Quarter), photographed scenes in the Korean settlements, and explored the hills on foot or (from mid-1912) by streetcar.[14] In order to achieve all this, she had immediately to learn Russian.

Eventually, Eleanor Pray spoke Russian fluently, but (by her own account) with a thick American accent, for example, spelling and pronouncing the nickname for Pavel (Pasha) as "Parsha." Still, having studied French in high school, she enthusiastically plunged into her Russian studies and, fearless, soon engaged in numerous perplexing conversations, to the kind-hearted amusement of her family. Any language student will find the entanglements familiar. One day during her first Vladivostok spring, for instance, Mrs. Pray forgot her umbrella in a downtown store and went back to find it. Unfortunately, she had also forgotten the Russian word for umbrella, *zontik*, but was armed with the French word, *parapluie*. Just "Russianizing" this a little, she startled the salesmen with her question: Might they have seen her *parokhod* [steamship] anywhere? Undaunted by their confused reaction, Mrs. Pray continues, "They were polite enough not to laugh, so I went through the motions of an umbrella several times and then one clerk . . . exclaimed *Ponimaiu, ponimaiu*! (I understand), and immediately fished from under the counter a book of wallpaper samples! I left at once and was fortunate enough to find my umbrella at the Japanese shop" (29 May 1895 to Aunt Anna).[15] Through a mixture of happy everyday life and intriguing encounters, Mrs. Pray fell deeply in love with Vladivostok, and, despite the heartbreak of its violence and many misfortunes, ended up admiring its vivacious albeit dual personality.

Eleanor Pray's oeuvre displays Vladivostok as a composite of extraordinary ups and downs, of grief and joy existing side by side, which gradually blend into a vast, forever alluring, human mosaic that reflects life itself. The city is *real*: a beautiful, vibrant, but also flawed being, fraught with complexity and contradictions that usually support, but now and then destroy, human lives and dignity. While many of its nineteenth- and early twentieth-century visitors have noted only the absurdly stereotypical image of a gigantic fortress city run by wicked leaders,[16] Mrs. Pray shows a more authentic balance of positive and negative features, and, with some hyperbole, stresses her own "infatuation" with the very dichotomy: "Nobody ever loved this unkempt place as I do, I am sure. Everybody laughs at me for it but I can't help it. It is dreadful to think of living somewhere where I can't see one or the other of the bays" (6 June 1927 to Sarah). Early on, the breathtaking panoramas over the Golden Horn and Amur Bay offered not only joy but also spiritual sustenance in a life and a city distinguished by intense swings of fortune. Certainly, Mrs. Pray complained about this, but, as in a good marriage, she loved nevertheless.

Lidiia Ginzburg, a Soviet writer of profound insights, has pointed out the fallacy of judging any era only by its negative aspects, thereby ignoring a more holistic truth: "People are wrong to imagine the calamitous epochs of the past as totally taken up by calamity. They also consist of a great deal else—the sort of things which life in general consists of, although against a particular background."[17] While the fortress indicates Vladivostok's political and military purpose, this is only one aspect of the region. Its climate, natural features, and human culture are lit by startling contrasts, where, for example, autumn's typhoons yield to January's arctic blasts with brilliant sunshine, and where tigers, leopards, and ginseng live alongside bears, elk, and mountain ash. The absence of a local ice age allowed the flora and fauna of northern and southern climes to share the same habitat in a harmonious "weaving together," *perepletenie*, of opposites.[18] One might argue that the region is a fine example of unexpected, yet pragmatic Yin and Yang, where the convergence of diverse influences creates a natural balance. The city itself is Russo-European in Asia, settled by Russians, Germans, and Scandinavians, on land ceded only in 1860 from China. Like other discerning visitors to Vladivostok, Eleanor Pray, an irrepressible Victorian, and a conservative American in Russia, found stimulation in the dichotomy.[19] After describing anxious get-togethers with friends—someone was ill or the war atrocities were multiplying—she would add, completely unconcerned about the incongruity of the juxtaposition, "and it was very jolly."

At first sight, Mrs. Pray's letters and albums may seem quaint. Photos from the early 1900s show ladies playing tennis in heeled shoes and long dresses with belts. Pre-World War I dinners ended with the men retiring to billiards while the women did needlework. But peel away these external signs of culture, and universal emotions can build a human bridge between *then* and *now*, between *them* and *us*. We easily smile at young Günther Meyer, for example, who, not yet two years old in late 1906, "distinguished himself" during his sister's christening in the Lutheran Church. In the middle of the prayer, Günther, in his mother's arms, looked over her shoulder and caught sight of Mrs. Pray: "Very sweetly and politely he said 'Mund auf, Augen zu' . . . 'Mouth open, eyes shut'—his usual request for a piece of chocolate, a thing with which he always associates me. He said it in such a confident voice that

I nearly laughed outright" (25 December 1906 to Sarah; 26 December 1906 to Home). Mrs. Pray rouses our compassion when she describes a woman so thin that the American consul hesitated to invite her for a drive "for fear she would dissolve into thin air." But her condition was no joking matter: "She weighs only eighty-three pounds, and has run herself down from one hundred and forty, by taking [anti-]obesity pills, and it has ruined her health so she can't eat anything" (2 and 11 July 1907 to Sarah). Another lady may astonish us by proudly exhibiting a diamond "set in a crown over an eye tooth" (6 February 1915 to Home).[20] And a sting of stunned grief follows Warren Langdon, chief engineer on the USS *Albany*, who, on Russian Christmas night in January 1921, was fatally shot in the back by a Japanese sentry near the Nikolai Triumphal Arch. Mrs. Pray noted, "Had it been almost any other man on the ship we might have suspected him of coming home from a party with a little too much champagne, but Langdon is the only total abstainer in the lot of them" (9 January 1921 to Home). The human dimensions of Eleanor Pray's letters allow her facts to come alive, the outdated specifics receding from view. Although the past has been pointedly described (in *The Go-Between* by L. P. Hartley) as "a foreign country; they do things differently there," this intriguing point is, surely, distorted by cultural myopia. Yes, old-fashioned customs do recall a vanished world, but the human responses to what life brings, be it joy or sorrow, have remained equally light-hearted, indifferent, or despairing for millennia.

The question of censorship looms large in the study of Russian and Soviet life, and one wonders if Eleanor Pray could write what she wanted. She clearly understood the official rules and she tended, mostly, to follow them—such as not openly criticizing the city leaders or Russia's political path. She sometimes warned others not to raise political questions when writing to her, and her own outbursts of strong criticism are confined to a few letters hand-carried by trusted friends and posted abroad.[21] Yet her other thousands of pages do not give the impression that she felt suppressed or limited in her walks, meetings, conversations, and correspondence. She noted that the censorship had become more stringent in postrevolutionary times than under the tsar, but she found ways around this. For instance, several fable-like letters to her daughter Dorothy comment on the spread of Bolshevism through the symbol of a favorite dog: "I'm afraid—it is not quite nice perhaps to say it—that evil communications have corrupted Dicky's good manners and that he is rather inclined to the left, which is a great pity for a decent dog"

(13 October 1919 to Dorothy), and, just three months later, "Dicky has, one regrets to say, gone bolshevik and got the mange" (9 January 1920 to Dorothy).[22] Heeding her wish to live peacefully in Vladivostok, Eleanor Pray outwardly dealt with (rather than accepted) the political strictures, without inwardly succumbing to them.

After the revolution, the bourgeoisie was easily targeted for political attacks,[23] and little personal information about people outside the revolutionary movement survives from Old Vladivostok. Except for recurring invectives, everyday knowledge and documents about the tsarist-era middle class were mostly obliterated from the public sphere, hidden, or simply forgotten. In addition, the international investors who had helped populate and build the city came to be considered land-grabbing impostors, as a 1970 history textbook for teenagers made clear: "Foreign capital quickly permeated industry, trade, and agriculture, exploiting the population and rapaciously plundering the territory's natural resources."[24] By contrast, Eleanor Pray's letters allow prominent families such as the Bryners, the Dattans, and the Lindholms to regain a human face. Her closest friends were the wives of Vladivostok's entrepreneurs and officers, who in the sociopolitical turmoil after World War I lost both their status and their possessions. Still, Mrs. Pray kept writing her letters, describing life in her beloved Russian city, by then in Soviet garb.

With Mikhail Gorbachev's encouragement of *glasnost* in the late 1980s, the research climate began to change. Journalists and *kraevedy*, the regional history experts, including Larisa V. Aleksandrovskaia, Boris A. Diachenko, Tamara N. Kaliberova, Amir A. Khisamutdinov, and Nelli G. Miz, and historians, including Eleonora V. Ermakova, Ivan G. Striuchenko, and Elena V. Vasilieva, researched Vladivostok's previously suppressed merchants, academics, and cultural figures, confirming the contributions of many a persona non grata. Two such volumes are vividly titled *Forgotten Names* and *Pages of Forgotten History*.[25]

Similarly, the photos and letters of the Eleanor L. Pray Collection open the doors and windows into Vladivostok itself. Little-known in Europe or the United States, this former outpost seven thousand miles east of Moscow and sixteen hours ahead of Washington, DC, inevitably basks in the strange aura of being at "the end of the world." But such is the paradox that Vladivostok has always fostered and continues to enjoy long-term connections with international centers, including Shanghai, Nagasaki, and Hong Kong, and stands closer to Sydney and Los Angeles than to the Russian capital. Furthermore, while the city was settled to defend Russia against intruders, it also became the eastern terminal of the Trans-Siberian Railway which encouraged communication into and across the country. Thus, in Eleanor Pray's time, Vladivostok was a well-mounted gate—but a gate slightly, invitingly, ajar. Mrs. Pray's great achievement is to invite us into Vladivostok and to help us feel at home. Her letters replace the monotonously stereotypical and harsh images of Russian life with a blend of facts and feelings that, in addition to political shadows, includes human sunshine and engrossing aspects of everyday reality.

THE ELEANOR L. PRAY COLLECTION

That so many of Eleanor Pray's letters still exist has its own remarkable story. In the 1970s, Patricia Dunn Silver, Mrs. Pray's granddaughter, was startled by a seemingly innocent question from her mother, Dorothy Pray Dunn Barringer: "Would you like to see all these letters from Granny before I throw them out?" Mrs. Silver jumped at the possibility of learning more about her family's background in Russia, and spent years sorting, piecing together, and organizing this treasure. While Eleanor Pray had meticulously dated and paginated her letters, always stating the precise location at which she wrote— even on boats or in summer houses—the bundles that Mrs. Silver received were in great disarray. Often, she could assemble the fragile sheets of particular letters only by comparing their handwriting or the color and design of the stationery. In her research, Mrs. Silver also began to uncover the astounding path of her grandmother's weekly letters from Vladivostok to Dorothy and Sarah. Mrs. Pray joined her relatives in Shanghai in 1930 when she could no longer work in Russia, but after the attack on Pearl Harbor, the family was interned in a Japanese prison camp. When liberated in late 1943, they were ordered to take no personal documents with them. In righteous defiance, Eleanor Pray smuggled the cache of saved letters out in her corset, confident that the Japanese guards would not offend an elderly lady of majestic appearance with a body search. Without Mrs. Pray's extraordinary commitment to her correspondence, and the inspired and painstaking work by Patricia Silver, only a diminished assortment of Eleanor Pray's letters would exist today. Throughout my work on this book, Mrs. Silver has helped extensively and generously. Together, we discussed the ideas, outlined the research plan, and compared notes on the letters and on the city of Vladivostok itself.

The letters of 1894–1930 in the Eleanor L. Pray Collection were donated to the Library of Congress in 2012. Mrs. Silver had already given two photo albums to the Arseniev Museum in Vladivostok in 1995, from which, with kind permission, six photos scanned by Iraida N. Klimenko and Liudmila Kharitonova are included in this book. A third album was donated to the Library of Congress in 2002, and may be viewed, with explanations and complementary excerpts from the letters, at the library's web page "Meeting of Frontiers" under the name of Eleanor Pray (at frontiers.loc.gov).

NOTES ON THIS EDITION

Eleanor Pray's letters contain massive amounts of information from three and a half decades in Vladivostok, and an "edition" of such wealth must somehow be manageable. In this book I have chosen to highlight certain themes that the letters illustrate abundantly and well. With several assistants, I first transcribed extensive passages from every letter and compiled a database and reference guides on the people, places, and events described. This work took more than a few years, but that process also helped to identify thousands of pertinent "stories" for the different chapters. I selected the quotes according to three principles: They should (1) fit a chapter's particular theme, (2) be representative of Eleanor Pray's thoughts and ideas, and (3) read well. United by the overall goal of providing a portrait of Vladivostok "from within," the chapters are designed to be read one after the other, or separately. Each chapter is a unit unto itself, with the necessary background information available in its introductions and notes. All quotes are verbatim, but for the sake of clarity I have adjusted Mrs. Pray's flamboyant use of the possessive, added commas in long sentences, and standardized the spelling of the following words: amiable (from "aimiable"), bazaar (bazar), dacha (datcha), hawthorn (hawthorne), kopek (kopeck), ruble (rouble), though (tho'), today (to-day), and veranda (verandah).

DATES AND TRANSLITERATIONS

Because Eleanor Pray almost always wrote dates according to the American and Western European, that is, Gregorian, calendar ("New Style," NS), the dates in this book are predominantly in New Style. This includes most dates before 1 February 1918, when Russia still used the Julian Calendar ("Old Style," OS). In the nineteenth century, the Gregorian calendar was twelve days ahead of the Julian calendar, and in the twentieth century it was thirteen days ahead. Thus, the attack on Port Arthur, for example, which in Russian sources begins on the night of 26–27 January 1904 (OS), is dated 8–9 February 1904 (NS) here. Exceptions to the New Style usage include pre-February 1918 dates of Russian newspaper articles and letters by Russians, and will be pointed out in the notes and bibliography.

Russian words are transliterated according to the modified Library of Congress system, rendering a name such as Tyrtov different than it was (and is) written in English by the family, namely Tyrtoff. I have made three exceptions to the Library of Congress norm: (1) syllables with a consonant, a soft sign, and a Russian *e*, as, for example, in Arsen'ev, replace the soft sign + *e* with *ie* (Arseniev); (2) Aleksandr and Aleksandra become Alexander and Alexandra; and (3) the names of the composers Tchaikovsky, Rimsky-Korsakov, and Moussorgsky remain in these widely recognizable forms (rather than Chaikovskii, Rimskii-Korsakov, and Musorgskii). Soft signs are included in the notes and the bibliography, but not in the texts. All Russian, American, and European names that could be identified are spelled correctly, while Chinese and Japanese names have been kept as Mrs. Pray wrote them. A "Glossary of Uncommon Terms" listing foreign words frequently used by Mrs. Pray can be found after chapter 9; terms listed in the glossary will appear in italics when first mentioned. Brief identifications of the Prays' friends are in the appendix, "Biographical Notes," located after the glossary. Historical personages are identified within Mrs. Pray's texts or in the notes. Many of the streets and other locations in and around Vladivostok are on the city maps drawn by Kathleen M. Bodley.

LETTER RECIPIENTS

Aunt Anna Guptill, Mrs. Pray's maternal aunt

Clara Lord McCue, Mrs. Pray's sister (personal letters)

Cousin Clara Harrington, Mrs. Pray's cousin

Dorothy Pray, the Prays' daughter

"The Folks at Home," that is, Mrs. Pray's parents and Clara (family letters)

Mildred Pray, a sister-in-law, married to Sarah's and Ted's brother Moses

Sarah Smith, Mrs. Pray's favorite sister-in-law, Mr. Pray's sister

Frederick Pray, Ted, Mrs. Pray's husband

William McCue, Eleanor and Clara's foster brother (eventually Clara's husband)

In a few quotes from letters *to* Mrs. Pray, she is identified as Eleanor. In her family she was called "Roxy" (for Roxanna), but among Russians and others in Vladivostok, she was known in the Russian manner as Eleonora Georgievna Pray (including a patronymic in honor of her father, George Lord).

Biographical Sketch

The Smiths and the Prays

PATRICIA D. SILVER

CONNECTED BY FAMILY TIES, A SHARED PURPOSE, AND A DEEP, LOV-
ing friendship, Charles and Sarah Smith and Frederick and Eleanor Pray, all
originally from New England, made Vladivostok their home and became
eloquent witnesses to its character. Without these four people, the Eleanor L.
Pray Collection and this book would not exist today.

Charles Henry Smith and his brother Oscar first went to Siberia in 1858,
sailing around Cape Horn with a Captain Morse of the Boston firm Amos
Lawrence and Company. By the mid-1860s, the brothers were buying land
in the center of Vladivostok, which had been founded in 1860. As an agent
for the China and Japan Trading Company of New York, in the 1880s Charles
built his own house overlooking the city's beautiful bays.

On a home visit in 1880, Charles married Sarah ("Sadie," sometimes
"Sally") Elizabeth Pray of Great Falls (today Somersworth), New Hampshire.
After a few years in Cambridge (Massachusetts), they settled in Vladivostok
in 1886 and opened their own trading company, the American Store. First
located in part of their home, the store advertised the availability of a multi-
tude of goods for sale: hunting rifles and other guns; farming necessities such
as axes, saws, and seeds; mining and camera equipment; bicycles; gramo-
phones and records; typewriters; dried fruits and nuts; coffee; chocolates; and
canned foods. At the same time, Charles was buying furs from Russian trap-
pers and sending them to the New York and London markets. Through their
work, kindliness, and social skills, Charles and Sarah became close friends
with other merchant families, and saw their work prosper. By the mid-1890s,
extra help was needed in the store, and Charles asked his wife's younger

brother, Frederick, to come to Vladivostok to assist. When Charles died from a heart attack in 1898, Sarah became the owner of the store, and her brother and his wife stayed to support her.

Like his sister Sarah, Frederick ("Fred" or "Ted") Shenstone Pray was born in Great Falls at the family home, Echo Farm. Frederick was a gifted metal engraver and machine builder, but studied accounting and commercial practices in order to have steady work. When Ted graduated from high school on 17 June 1887, "after all the ceremony and congratulations," he accompanied his classmate "Roxy" Lord home and asked her to be his wife. Later she wrote, "And how happy I was, even if we did have to wait seven long years" (17 June 1929 to daughter Dorothy). They married in April 1894. Roxanna Eleanor Lord Pray had been born in Berwick, Maine, at Elm Wold, the Lord family home built by an ancestor in 1796 and still owned by the family today. Roxy's father was a judge and farmer who instilled in his daughter a deep love of knowledge.

In May and June of 1894, the Smiths and the Prays went to East Siberia together, traveling first by train across the northern United States to San Francisco, and then by schooner via Japan to Vladivostok. They shared a household, and Sarah and her sister-in-law Roxy became as close as sisters. From the very first day of their trip, Roxy wrote long letters, often sending scores of pages at a time, to her relatives and friends in New England. In 1906, Ted and Roxy's daughter Dorothy was born. Because Sarah never had a child, and because Roxy had suffered a miscarriage in 1900, this was a momentous event.

Dorothy was deeply loved by both her parents and by her Auntie Sarah, but 1916 was a wrenching year. The family decided to send Dorothy to the Shanghai American School, and Sarah went with her, finding a position as housemother there. Except for vacations (through early 1923), neither Sarah nor Dorothy was to live in Vladivostok again. This emotional hardship was alleviated by Sarah's and Roxy's weekly correspondence, a communicative practice that they had adopted when either had been temporarily away from Vladivostok: "Oh, sister Sarah, I do long sometimes to have a long talk with you, and especially after I get one of your letters. There are so many things I can talk over with you that I can't talk over with anybody else in the world with the same pleasure" (31 July 1905 to Sarah).

World War I made it difficult to bring merchandise into Vladivostok, and in early 1918, Ted closed the American Store. He was fortunate to have been offered a position as clerk at the US consulate in the city and would eventually become a vice-consul there. Despite political upheavals in connection with Russia's many revolutions, neither Ted nor Roxy considered leaving Vladivostok. They wanted to safeguard their home, and they had become used to their life and friends there. Even after Ted's unexpected death in April 1923, Roxy stayed. During the war, she had volunteered for the Red Cross; now she was hired as a translator and bookkeeper at the Kunst and Albers department store. She enjoyed this work, but by the summer of 1930, Kunst and Albers had to close its doors. This time, Roxy had no choice but to leave the city with its "blue water and beautiful far-off hills," writing aboard the SS *Gleniffer* with pain in her heart on the last day that she could glimpse Vladivostok: "Here I am, sailing on and on, every turn of the screw taking me farther from the loved home of thirty-six years" (8 December 1930 to Clara Lord McCue). Roxy settled in Shanghai, near Sarah and Dorothy, and took a job as a librarian and dorm mother at the Shanghai American School. Roxy returned to the United States in 1943 as a participant in an exchange of American and Japanese prisoners-of-war. She died in Washington, DC, in February 1954.

A farm girl from Maine, Roxy Pray lived through great events and had the wherewithal to record them. In Vladivostok, she learned to speak several languages, read voluminously, and led a vibrant, cosmopolitan life very different from that of her provincial origins. She met generals, admirals, royalty, and political leaders, and she danced to her heart's content aboard the warships in the harbor. She also saw the vast destruction of people and property during the political turmoil of the time, and lost everything that she held dear in Vladivostok except her memories and her pride.

The information in the Eleanor L. Pray Collection comes to us thanks to the Smiths and the Prays of Somersworth, New Hampshire, and Berwick, Maine. Charles Smith paved the way for these New Englanders to go to Vladivostok, and Frederick Pray good-naturedly accepted the challenge of working abroad in an alien culture. Their wives recorded their emotions and experiences on paper, reporting to their families at home and to each other, and chronicling history as it was lived. Today we can experience some of that world through their letters.

LETTERS FROM VLADIVOSTOK,

1894–1930

Part I
The People

CHAPTER 1

A Victorian Home in Siberia

THE FAMILY CALLED THEIR VLADIVOSTOK HOME "DOM SMITH."[1] A mixture of Russian and English, this name reflects the two cultures that the Smiths and the Prays not only inhabited but also wished to bridge. They were foreigners in Russia, brought up in the Victorian traditions of Europe and the Americas. Charles Smith had followed his brother Oscar to Siberia in the late 1850s, and after Charles and his wife, the former Sarah Pray, settled in Vladivostok in 1886, their American Store on Sodom Lane had sustained them well.[2] Russia, too, had begun to favor its growing entrepreneurial class, and Vladivostok's leaders offered privileges such as inexpensive land and a duty-free port to those who came and helped develop the city's commerce.[3] With his straightforward honesty, crisp intelligence, and warm humor, Charles Smith became a respected colleague among Vladivostok's merchants.

When Sarah's brother Frederick Pray and his wife Eleanor started their life in Vladivostok in mid-1894, its European colony was small, lively, and spread across several cultures. Some of its members, including German-born Adolph Dattan, had become Russian subjects, whereas most of the foreigners kept their native citizenships. Still, they all attempted to fit into Russian life, and the examples of cross-national contacts were well established. The Danes and the Swedes engaged in concerts and theatricals at the German-run singing club, the *Gesangverein*, and they often attended the annual "Blessing of the Waters" on 19 January. In respectable Victorian tradition, the merchant wives—whether Russian, European, or American—announced a *jour fixe*, the specific weekly hours when they kept an open house, and everyone participated in the "mannered domestic drama" of paying ceremonial visits to new acquaintances.[4] These ladies' get-togethers constituted an international marketplace where not only friendship but also useful information was shared: fashion tips from English and French magazines, ideas for home improvements involving Japanese furniture or the Chinese principles of feng shui, and health cures from both Europe and Asia. That many of the foreigners simultaneously used the Julian and Gregorian calendars created an annual swirl of double festivities: two sets of Christmas and New Year's celebrations, two Easters, and special holidays honoring both Russia and other countries. These families' social status, economic class, and openness to diverse cultures—rather than a single focus on their own geographic or national backgrounds—shaped their tastes and the everyday reality of their lives. Indeed, class united them more significantly than nationality.

The primary stage for Eleanor Pray and the women of her circle was the home, which they considered a sanctuary from evil. It was a private refuge of amenities and cozy relaxation that contrasted with the public sphere, that boisterous, noisy, and often dangerous world outside. With its beauty and well-ordered management, the Victorian home was supposed to offer an antidote to illness and stress, where men could engage in what we, today, would call networking, and avoid the temptations about town.[5] Mrs. Pray noted that "to entertain single men is a mission. They have no home here and if no one invites them, or if there is no house open to them so they can drop in any time, they are almost sure to get into very bad company. . . . Vladivostok has a continually changing population, so there are very few real homes here, and a much larger proportion of men than women" (14 August 1895 to Home). The home that Eleanor Pray came to love is on a large hillside lot above the Post and Telegraph Office in the center of Vladivostok. Here Charles Smith constructed several buildings: the main house, a smaller brick building (where the Prays lived for the first four years), the servants' quarters, and the American Store and its warehouse, along with walkways, lawns, and flower beds that for decades grew increasingly lush. Visitors would enter this world by a gate on Sodom Lane, approach the main door of Dom Smith—stylish with a wrought-iron portico and, later, a brass sign engraved "SMITH"—and then proceed into the drawing-room and sitting-rooms. Altogether, the property offered a soothing, pleasurable environment.

Far from fashionably idle, Sarah Smith planned and participated in all of the household chores, such as meals, gardening, and the massive semiannual housecleanings, together with her staff of servants, many of whom lived on the premises. Chinese men, known (in the language of the time) as *coolies*, served as cooks, members of the grounds crew, and night watchmen, and Japanese women, *amahs*, were maids, kitchen assistants, and nannies. Russian women were hired by the day for laundering, ironing, and sewing. The strictures and demands on Victorian middle-class women in Europe and the United States are widely recognized,[6] yet neither Eleanor nor Sarah seems to have suffered under a yoke of Victorian limitations. The former, with her joie de vivre and her "enthusiasm, intelligence, and sheer pluck," rode horseback, played tennis, and hiked vigorously, and was not given to "nineteenth-century feminine reticence."[7] Sarah, despite her inordinate load of housework, cherished her life in "the East" and compared its chores favorably to the much heavier (and more boring) ones of her New England home. The positive spirit of Mrs. Pray's letters suggests little similarity with the stereotype of the Victorian woman.

In fact, Eleanor Pray accepted her life in Vladivostok with ease, and missed it deeply when she and her husband visited their family in New England in 1902–3 ("Oh, for a corner of our V. paradise," 26 October 1902 to Sarah), but her husband had a harder time. Although Frederick Pray made friends in the city, including the American businessman David Clarkson, he did not thrive as did his wife. Able to display his true talent for engraving only as a hobby, and not taking a great interest in Vladivostok's history or special character, Mr. Pray began to exhibit failing health soon after they arrived in the summer of 1894. Within their first year in Russia, Mrs. Pray noted, "Ever since we struck this country he has been afflicted with boils in one place or another." She joked that this might be "a beautiful excuse for not making calls" (5 May 1895 to Home), a situation that strengthened Eleanor's primary purpose of giving her husband a comfortable home where the two of them alone, or with friends, could share peaceful moments. As she informed a cousin, "Fred is three fathoms deep in the *Youth's Companion* which came yesterday and it's of no use to interrupt him to send his regards, so please take the will for the deed. I wish you could step into our cozy little sitting-room and see what a nice little nest it is" (14 December 1897 to Cousin Clara). Sadly, the recurring boils eventually caused Mr. Pray's death by blood poisoning in April 1923, just two months before his fifty-sixth birthday. One of Eleanor's most cherished memories was their companionship by the fireplace: "I dread especially the few hours of Saturday afternoon more than all the rest of the week, for . . . I miss Ted more then than at any other time. So often on a Saturday noon he came home with a perfectly inscrutable face, and a little later, when a boy came from the florist's with a pot or two of flowers, of course he knew nothing about them. I would put the flowers in the window and with a fire on the new grate, the room would be so cozy and we would sit there the whole afternoon" (17 May 1923 to Sarah).

ELEANOR PRAY'S NEW LIFE

Mrs. Pray's letters reflect the delight and wide-open sense of discovery with which she embraced her new life. Sarah admired her sister-in-law's exuberance: "I oft-times think we are a decided contrast for I always take everything so calmly and quietly and she is all excitability and enthusiasm. She is a thorough child when anything pleases her, and it is a regular pleasure to see her enjoy things" (23 April 1895 from Sarah to Mildred). Like many newlyweds, Eleanor preferred modern furniture, but was not adept at cooking or other household tasks. She was inquisitive about Russia, observing the region's water shortages[8] and upside-down weather, and soon learning new words such as the British *tiffin* for "the midday meal," and Russian standbys—*pirozhki* (small, covered pies with savory or sweet fillings) and *zakuska* (appetizers)—before knowing how to prepare them. Uneasy during the First Sino-Japanese War (1894–95) and the Boxer Rebellion (1899–1901), and outraged by the attack on the USS *Maine* in Havana (1898), Eleanor followed all political developments closely. One is struck by her privileged station in this new stage of her life. As Mrs. Pray, she became a member of the well-to-do middle class, and, from the very first day in Vladivostok, she accepted and profited by its conspicuous benefits.

24 June 1894 to Home
After we came back from the Lindholms' yesterday, I unpacked my trunks and set things around. We have such a lovely room. It is on the front corner of the house. From the end window we see the upper end of the bay and the cathedral with the golden crosses, of which Sadie told you. From the two front windows (one of which is a glass door leading to a railed balcony), we see the entrance to the bay, the [Russian] Island and, beyond the hills, Peter the Great's Bay. It is such a pretty view, and it is lovely on the balcony in the evening.

3 July 1894 to Home
Fred and I had to stick out and make our calls after the Russian fashion. The stranger always calls first, and in full dress, too. A second call is of not half so

much account. Well, we dressed up in great agony, Fred in swallow tail and white kid [gloves], and I in my silk and new pair of gray kids that just matched it. I trimmed my black straw hat for the occasion with the feathers and ribbon from my velvet hat and some old rose chiffon like that on my dress. I assure you, I looked very swell indeed and so did my better half. When we had got primped up to our satisfaction, we sailed out, chartered a vehicle . . . and away we went. We had a white horse and a red horse, and the white horse, I am sure from the amount of real estate on him, was born and bred in Korea. He trotted and the other one galloped. Our driver wore the usual coachman's costume— a black . . . Russian blouse with turkey and red sleeves and a patent leather hat. . . . We called on Mrs. Dattan, Mrs. Hansen, Mrs. Lindholm, Mrs. Birk, Madame Bonsdorf and Mrs. DuBois. At the Lindholms' they insisted on our stopping for afternoon coffee so we were there nearly an hour. For all we dreaded it so much we had a very pleasant call everywhere and I shall be glad to see them again. Mrs. Dattan was not at home so we [have] not yet seen her. Sadie . . . herself is going to take me to call on the Governor's wife, and Fred is going with Charlie. Sadie and Charlie made thirteen calls yesterday afternoon and we came across them at Madame Bonsdorf's.

22 July 1894 to Cousin Clara
Aside from the weather, which can't last forever, I like Vladivostok. . . . These three houses along here have the finest view in Vladivostok. One of the others is in the same yard, a little higher up than this [main] house, and as soon as it is ready we are going to move in there. There are only two rooms but they are very large and pleasant. One will be a bedroom and the other a sitting-room, but of course we shall always take our meals in here [with the Smiths].

12 September 1894 to Home
Here I am in my new quarters and very nice ones they are, too. We finished moving yesterday. The house has been painted and has new matting so it is as fresh as can be. . . . There are double walls with two feet air space between so there is no dampness. Everything in it is of brick and cement but the doors and stairs, so it is absolutely fireproof. There is cement between the two stories, so no sound comes up. Downstairs there are work rooms and the furnace. I have nothing to do with them, but my trunks are down there. My two rooms are upstairs and from the windows I have a magnificent view of the harbor and bay. The windows are large and low, and have window seats about twelve inches [deep], which I am making cushions for.

17 September 1894 to Home
Fred engraved a solid silver cigar case last week that the officers of the *Nakhimov* presented to the first mate, on his name-day which was August 30th.
There was a long inscription, all in Russian, and Fred did it beautifully. The
officers were very much pleased with it, and it will be a first-class advertisement for Fred.

25 September 1894 to Aunt Anna
Do I not have a time of it? All I have to do is make my bed and take care of
my two rooms. I set my slop pail at the head of the stairs and a Chinaman
carries it down and brings it back. *Amah* brings my water, attends to the
lamps and candles, and sweeps my entry and stairs, and sometimes my
rooms. I was sweeping this morning when she came up and took the broom
from me and swept both rooms. She thinks Americans were not made to
work and I am quite willing she should think so. So, you see, about all I have
to do is enjoy myself.

30 September 1894 to Home
Charlie has had an invoice of household goods from San Francisco [for the
store], and Fred and I and Sadie went through the storehouse and tasted
them—jars of honey, . . . canned corn, canned tomatoes, peaches, pears, peas
and cherries, split peas, a large barrel of olives, two large barrels of cucumber
pickles, a barrel of hams, a barrel of pork, lard, beans, crackers, prunes, rai-
sins, dried (or rather evaporated) apples, pears, peaches and apricots, English
walnuts and almonds. Does that look as if we should starve this winter? He
also has some corn beef.

7 October 1894 to Home
Olga Kuster will begin soon to take English with me. She knows [it] well
enough for conversation now, but she will come for an hour a day for
practice—we shall read English together. I think we shall try *Kenilworth*
first.[9] The Lindholm girls, and Katherine Engelm, the admiral's daughter,
read with Sadie. I shall like very much to have Olga come to me for lessons,
for it will be a very easy way of earning a little money.

29 October 1894 to Clara
I have to put on my double windows this week. They go inside the others,
instead of outside as at home. First we stuff all the chinks in the outside win-

dows with cotton, pushing it in with a knife. Then a large roll of cotton is laid on the window sill, then the inside window is put in and strips of paper are pasted over the cracks so there is no possibility of taking cold by sitting near a window. There are upper panes in two of them that open with a hinge so that the rooms can be nicely aired. We have had an unusually warm and pleasant October and I do not need the windows yet, but Sarah says it is much better to put them in now than to wait until it is so cold.

31 March 1895 to Mildred
Charlie started this morning on his duck-shooting trip, and I wish you could have been here to hear the start—Sarah said the whole premises would be turned upside down when he started but I thought she stretched it a little, but now I know she didn't put it half strong enough. Yesterday everything was in an uproar all day, and this morning when we woke up the yard was full of Chinese and Russians, to say nothing of our own servants. The dog was about turning himself inside out at the prospect. Everyone was running hither and thither and in the midst was Charlie looking worse than any tramp you ever saw. He had on his old gray hunting suit lined with grass-green [material], and a hat to match. When he watches for the ducks he puts his clothes on green side out, so they will take him for a gooseberry bush. We told him the ducks had seen that suit too often, and would probably say among themselves, "There's that old grass-green duffer again, but we are too old to be fooled; guess we don't fly that way." He took two guns and shot, and provisions enough to last a year. Sarah says he will come home with the most of the shot, and a black and blue place on his shoulder, and think he has had a lovely time. He got away about eight o'clock and there has been a terrible quiet here ever since.

2 May 1895 to Home
[As war threatens between China and Japan] I look around my pretty home and wonder if it is fated to be destroyed by shot and shell, and wonder if in a couple of weeks I shall have to pack all my pretty things away and go into the interior. There is just enough uncertainty in the condition of affairs to make it extremely exciting, and it is our first experience in the probabilities of war.

10 November 1895 to Aunt Anna
I wish you could see our Compradore, he is the High Lord Nabob among the other Chinese on the place, and if he doesn't think himself fine, then never you mind. His name is Kow Lo Kin, but we call him Lo Kin. His business is

to attend to the Chinese part of Charlie's business—sell goods to the Chinese merchants, settle accounts, and look after any Chinese carpenters or masons employed about the place. . . . He wears a blue silk frock which comes far below his knees, and over that a black garment like a coat. His fingernails are an inch or more long, he wears a heavy gold ring on one of his slender fingers, and altogether he thinks himself a gentleman of great dignity. Like most of the other Chinese up here, his home is in Chefoo. Thune, our *manza* [Chinese person] who went down to Chefoo to be married last year, told Fred that while down there he visited Lo Kin's home, which was a very nice one— much money and three wives!

14 December 1897 to Cousin Clara
The gentlemen are playing billiards and I am trying to keep my eyes open till Fred comes home. Mr. Smith is very fond of the game, so when the new office was built, he built a second floor for a billiard room and ordered a table out from England. It was set up about four weeks ago and Fred has learned to play and likes it. I am very glad for his sake for it gives him a little amusement after the day's work.

23 January 1898 to Home
Sarah and Charlie are going South on the *Voronezh* which is advertised to leave next Wednesday. . . . Sarah does not care personally much about the trip, but she has urged Charlie to go on account of his health, for the cold weather takes hold of him and the Doctor says it is much better for him to go South where he can be out-of-doors more.

25 February 1898 to Sarah
Don't worry about us—we are all in good health and good spirits and everything is serene. The only thing that troubles me is the prospect of a duel between [our servant] Dou Kee and Omeya's husband, for the former is posing for a day widower and he flirts outrageously. It is evident that Omeya's plump cheeks have won his heart. Since the day when I saw him steal a real European kiss from her rosy cheeks . . . he hasn't wanted to look me in the face, and when I meet him he looks up in the sky. He sings now all the time, so is apparently in very good humor.

20 April 1898 to Home
The first rain came last night and it was delightful. Now we have plenty of soft water, and I shall wash my hands and face every time I think of it today.

7 May 1898 to Home

Four years ago today we left home and how quickly those four years have passed. I hope in another year we shall be preparing to come home.

9 May 1898 to Home

Last Saturday morning [7 May] at three we were awakened by a steamer which whistled and whistled until I fear some of the air around town was blue with the maledictions heaped on that noise. At day we saw it was *Khabarovsk*. Just before dinner, *amah* came to tell me that there were callers to see me in the other house. Well, you can imagine my surprise when the "callers" proved to be Charlie and Sarah who had come on the *Khabarovsk* when I expected them on *Tairen*. We were so glad to see them and I haven't stopped talking to them yet.

16 May 1898 to Home

How many things can be crowded into three days—it seems as if we have passed years since that horrible Friday morning three days ago.... When I came down to breakfast Friday morning it was nearly eight and I was astonished that Sarah wasn't down. Fred and Steve [the store assistant] sat in the veranda reading. A minute later Sarah came downstairs screaming for them to come because she was sure Charlie was dead. He was in his usual spirits, although he had not slept till toward morning, and at half past seven he awoke. He did not stop to dress but threw on his dressing gown and ran to the WC which is just around the corner of the house at the back. He was gone so long that Sarah went to look for him and there she found him fallen up against the wall, quite dead. He was hardly in the door when he fell and the rain was pouring in torrents. Sarah and I held the double doors open while Fred and Steve brought the poor body in and laid it on Sarah's bed.... Then she and Fred began working over him, and Steve and I ran for a doctor. We felt that it was of no use but at such a time one wants all the assistance possible. Poor old Dr. Berg was terribly upset but he said there was nothing to do. From the condition of the muscles, he says the shock must have been a very strong one and that death was instantaneous and painless. We sent for Mr. Clarkson and with his help Charlie was dressed, carried into the little sitting-room and laid on the couch there. Sarah did not want any strangers to touch him and it was much better so. He looked so natural that it was so hard to realize that he was dead. The room was not darkened much and the door into the hall was open all the time, so we could see him every time we passed, and it was less like death than a closed room. We went in and out and wrote notes there just as if he were only sleeping, so death had no horror at all. . . . The funeral was yesterday morning at half past eleven. There were prayers and singing here, during which we all stood around the casket. Then it was placed in the hearse and we walked behind it, Fred with Sarah, Steve with me, and a long, long irregular procession behind us, the carriages bringing up the rear. It was Sunday morning and the streets were crowded but not one person was in too great a hurry to stop and take off his hat, even to tiny little boys, and most Russians crossed themselves. We passed one carriage, whose occupant, a lady, stood up and bowed her head till we were past. Of all Russian customs, I find that is the most beautiful. At the cemetery there were more prayers, and then the casket was put in a zinc case and the case was soldered together. We stayed through it all till it was lowered into the grave. The zinc case was put inside a tarred wooden box, and the grave itself was bricked up. Sarah had the case made so she could take him home sometime—through forty years in a foreign country he remained a good American and, thank God, he will finally rest in the soil of New England. The bearers, who carried the casket from the house to the hearse and from the hearse to the grave, were Mr. Walldén, Mr. Clarkson, Mr. Dattan, Mr. Shulyngin, Capt. Brandt, Col. Chernoknizhnikov, Otto Meyer and Mr. Hansen, so no strangers touched the casket until it was lowered into the grave. Sarah bears her grief as only a true New England woman can, and as always, she thinks more of the comfort of others than of her own. . . . She says she has had eighteen years of such happiness as few people experience, and that she will thank God for that and try not to cry out because it has been so suddenly destroyed. . . . In Mr. Walldén Sarah has an old and reliable friend who knows Russian law thoroughly and who will save her all the annoyance he can. . . . In the funeral procession, one man (who is a little "off") walked near the hearse with a crooked iron cane and when he saw an unusually large stone in the way of the wheels he jerked it away. When we left the cemetery he came and shook hands with us all. He used to come to the office and Charlie had befriended him in many ways, so I suppose he did in his simple way what he could to show his sympathy. . . . Lo Kin came from Chefoo only yesterday afternoon, and when the poor fellow came in to speak to Sarah the tears began to roll down his face and that is a mark of very strong grief in a Chinaman. . . . When Dou Kee came in to see Charlie he tried to say something, but could get no farther than "*Madama, Madam*"—

and then he stood at Charlie's feet, clasped his hands and made a low bow in token of a farewell to his master. The house servants all cried, but not noisily, and all the servants on the place asked and received permission to follow to the grave. Cook kept as near his master as possible till the last and his eyes were at forty places at once. If anything was wrong anywhere, he was the first to see it and right it. Charlie was always good to him, as he was to everybody, and their grief is sincere.

27 May 1898 to Home
I am sure you at home are anxious to know what we are going to do, so I will tell you. Fred takes Charlie's place at the head of the business and for the present we shall continue with it, as it is a good one and not too large. . . . He often talked over his plans with Sarah so she knows what his wishes were in regard to the affairs.[10]

27 June 1898 to Home
We have been out shopping this morning and up to Mr. Clarkson's to look at some samples of bamboo furniture which he has up from Hong Kong. I ordered a divan, book case, and two small chairs which I think will make my sitting-room very pretty. I like the bamboo furniture very much, especially for such small rooms as mine. . . . Here it is expensive, but in Hong Kong it costs next to nothing and Mr. Clarkson has his own chartered steamers so the freight won't be so much.

22 September 1898 to Home
Today I am moving into the other house. No one knows how I hate to give up our dear little house, but it must be, and so I say as little as possible about it. It would be extremely selfish of me if I insisted on staying here, and leaving Sarah alone in that big empty house, where there is plenty of room for us all. For the first time I know what it is to break up a home that one has become attached to, and it is hard.

2 October 1898 to Home
I have now got my [new] room arranged and Lolla [Lindholm] says there is so much war there, that it must be a dangerous place to sleep in. Over the head of the bed is my flag, and on it, a picture of our *Maine* with the motto underneath, which no true Yankee ought ever to forget. Over my chest of

drawers is a silk handkerchief with a flag border, and (on this) Dewey's picture in a cherry lacquer frame. . . . On another wall is a place for my picture of the *Olympia* but I have not yet hung it up.[11]

14 May 1899 to Home
Housecleaning is finished, thank goodness, and I think I was never gladder to see a thing over with. As a rule, it doesn't trouble me a particle but this year we had such a general upset for ten days and so many Chinese workmen underfoot that it was enough to drive one mad. My room, the upper hall, the kitchen and dining-room had to be painted and white-washed, and the hall and dining-room repapered. Sarah wanted to get as much as possible done this spring so there would not be much for me to do in the autumn and next spring [when Sarah will be away]. The mattings were changed in four rooms so there really won't be much to do next housecleaning.

27 May 1899 to Home
Business has been so lively today that Ted has hardly had time to eat. This is the time of year that expeditions and engineering parties always start out and they all have to have firearms, ammunition, saddles, etc.[12] Ted sold eight saddles to one party and could have sold ten more if he had had a cheaper kind. We have never had saddles to sell before, that is, unless people especially ordered them, but these have gone so well, that Ted is sorry he didn't have three times as many. Expeditions are always striking out from here and the members are liberally supplied with money for their outfits, which is a good thing for us.

29 September 1899 to Home
I am turning the upstairs sitting-room into a little conservatory.[13]

6 October 1899 to Sarah
If you could but see the pretty rooms this morning, you would be charmed, I know, and I will photograph them by and by. . . . I had your desk brought down without the top and banished my writing-table so I have plenty of room for my dictionaries.

14 October 1899 to Sarah
It began to leak in the veranda about eleven o'clock and one couldn't blame it, for the wind is in the east and driving a very wet rain with terrific force.

The leaking stopped at noon and can you imagine that I *wondered* why, not at all taking into consideration the fact that it had stopped raining!

6 May 1900 to Sarah
I did a dreadful thing this noon time—I came into the veranda [room] quickly, and thought Ted sat there in a brand-new pair of trousers, so I gave him a slap on his leg. Can you imagine my horror when I raised my eyes to see Ted sitting on the other side of the room? It was Mr. Merritt [the new store assistant] I had slapped and I thought I should drop through the floor. As for that graceless husband of mine and Mr. Clarkson, they nearly burst from laughing.

25 May 1900 to Sarah
I do wish you were here to see how nice everything around the place looks. Ted has laid out flower beds the whole length of the other house and the *manzas'* quarters, with the exception of the corner by the store house. I have planted a single row of sweet peas which ought to make a pretty background for whatever flowers I fill the beds with. The space between the beds and the big plot is just wide enough for a *telega* [cart] to pass. Ted is in raptures over it all and he has taken such a lot of pleasure in getting it ready.

26 June 1900 to Sarah
[The Boxer Rebellion against Western influences in China has turned many Vladivostok residents against the Chinese.] One rather lively officer [visiting the American Store] had a gun go off in his hands and the bullet went straight through the window and flattened itself against the telegraph wall. Ted will devote his time tomorrow to making dummy cartridges to fit all the guns. Another one, after buying a gun, pointed it at Jan and said to him that it was a very good gun to shoot *manzas* with. Noble-minded, was it not? The Chinese have nearly all cleared out of the bazaar and there is absolutely nothing to be had.

6 August 1900 to Sarah
Saturday evening Mr. Clarkson gave a dinner party, at which we enjoyed ourselves very much, but the greatest fun of all was that coming home we were stopped by the guard of the house next ours as suspicious characters! I was driving Mrs. Ivy and we were stopped in the glare of an electric light and asked our business. I said we wanted to go home and as that didn't suffice I

explained in my sweetest meekest voice—"We are only two ladies, we are not *hoong-hoozi*" (Boxers) whereupon we were allowed to proceed. I do not know if [these guards] expect the Boxers to appear disguised in pink satin dinner gowns, but, from that, I should fancy they did.[14]

20 July 1905 to Sarah

Quick, quick, let me record my virtue before it escapes my memory—what do you think—I've actually done a two weeks' wash today—it is the first time in my life that I ever seriously washed, and I'm not dead, and I haven't yet burst from pride. There were ninety-four pieces; I left the bedding, stockings and Ted's starched things but washed everything else—eighty-seven pieces, and the boy washed the seven towels. We put the tub there between Wang's little gate and the water barrel where it was nice and cool, I washed the things out, Ted boiled them, he, the boy and I, rinsed and wrung them out and I hung them up. . . . We got them all out on the line before *tiffin* and now they are dry, and I have taken them in and begun to iron. There are 3 blouses, 1 table-cloth, 18 napkins, 12 tea napkins and doilies, 8 undervests and under-drawers, 4 pair drawers, 2 pair stockings, 25 handkerchiefs, 1 sideboard cover, 3 corset waists, 2 night dresses, 3 fancy collars, 2 shirts and 7 towels. Do keep this letter to show my grandchildren! . . . You should have seen me. I had on an old linen skirt without a petticoat, a blouse with the sleeves cut off to the elbows, and Ted's white hat—I was that fetching!

13 August 1905 to Sarah

This afternoon Ted took his typewriter on my sewing table up in the back-yard and we did have such a cozy, pleasant afternoon and no one came to disturb us. Part of the time I sewed and part of the time I read off numbers to Ted, for him to write, and then we had tea up there.

10 October 1906 to Home

When I came home Saturday afternoon, I found a beautiful new gramophone on a black wood stand of its own, with a cupboard underneath for the records, all of which, Ted informed me, was a present to me.

1 March 1907 to Mildred

I had a brilliant idea strike me the other day and have just carried it into execution. We have a small empty room in our Chinese quarters which Ted has just had painted and papered, and I proposed to the seamstress Nastia that she take that room and work for me two weeks of every month in payment. She was delighted because the only room she could get in town would cost her twenty-five rubles a month, and I am delighted because I can find plenty of work for her.[15]

25 July 1907 to Sarah
Our telephone was put in yesterday and will be connected in a day or two. Ted had it put in the cook's room—he thought it would be less disturbance there than anywhere else in the house. I absolutely refused to have it in [our] part of the house. It will really be a great convenience if it works properly, and the charges are only seventy-five rubles a year.

24 January 1909 to Home
The biggest piece of news on our premises is that Dou Kee has a son—he is forty-three years old and this is his first child, so you can imagine that he is on the verge of bursting with pride. As he lives somewhere in the interior of China, the news only reached him a few days ago, the child being already two months old. You know it has always been said that the evil wind which came down the lane prevented anyone on this place from having children—no child had ever been born here, and no child had ever been born to any of our servants during the time that they worked here, and the Chinese firmly believed that it was the "Feng shui" . . . which caused this state of affairs. Four or five years ago Churin's [department store] began to build in that lane, putting up several large buildings which do a great deal toward protecting us from the East wind—since then Dorothy, a little Molchanov boy, and Tussie Tyrtova have been born on the premises, and now Dou Kee has a son, so the "evil wind" was evidently to blame before![16]

5 November 1909 to Home
For two or three months I have been inquiring for a Russian nursery governess, but could hear of no satisfactory one. Finally I asked Nastia, never dreaming that she would consent, but on the contrary she was very glad to and we were all so pleased. She is a good girl, and has always made Dorothy mind, besides being an excellent seamstress.

4 January 1911 to Home
[At four and a half years old,] Dorothy has a good memory, for she will repeat, word for word, the tales which she has heard oftenest. Today Nastia

was lying down with a compress on her nose, and Dorothy sat down beside the couch and began to read to her. She went through the whole tale of *Red Riding Hood* in Russian—several pages there are—without a halt, and never failed to turn the page at the proper time. One could have sworn she was reading, she did it so nicely and with such good expression.

1 January 1912 to Home
[Our *amah*] Kiku has gone to Japan for two or three months, and the kitchen without her loud smile is like a receiving tomb. She is such a good faithful soul and laughs from morning till night no matter how hard she has to work.

6 November 1916 to Sarah
Just fancy, late last evening we suddenly remarked that the onyx clock was merrily ticking away, and our attention was called to it by its striking the hour. It is at least four years that it has stood still and the *amahs* say they did not touch it excepting to move it when necessary, and one can't imagine what has got into it.

17 May 1923 to Sarah
[Frederick Pray died on April 2, 1923.] This morning He Fa has been getting out the window screens, and I have cried my eyes out untying with my awkward fingers what Ted tied up so carefully and marked for the rooms where each belonged—"until next summer"—and that next summer has come and he is not here. No one will ever put them away so carefully again.

20 July 1923 to Sarah
I took my time about coming home and actually went into one of the confectioner's and had a cup of tea and a cake—or rather I went in to buy bread, and everything looked so clean and nice that I was tempted into the above. If I give up housekeeping I shall do that every day probably like dozens of other lonely women here.

RITUALS AND CELEBRATIONS

Eleanor Pray was eager to participate in all manner of Russian traditions, and both her sister-in-law Sarah and Nathalie Lindholm (1848–1920) became her guides in this endeavor. Mrs. Lindholm and her husband Otto (1832–1914), the prominent Vladivostok merchant, were Swedes born in Finland, and thus

Russian subjects.[17] Mrs. Lindholm was known for her quick wit, sharp tongue, and impeccable manners which, however, might be flung aside in the various amusements enjoyed in their social set. Old friends with the Smiths, she invited the Smith-Pray family for lunch on the first day that they stepped ashore in Vladivostok, and Mrs. Pray was impressed with the elegant home: "They have such a lovely house. . . . Their summer dining-room is a veranda with plants and shrubs around it, very nice and cool. . . . After lunch, Mrs. Lindholm and the girls showed us many beautiful things which they had picked up in China and Japan while they were there last winter" (24 June 1894 to Home). Mrs. Lindholm and daughters Natalia (Tullie, sixteen years old), Helen (Lolla, fifteen), and Aina (ten) "adopted" Mrs. Pray into their family, and through their many years together they shared conversations and confidences, warm merriment as well as searing pain, and always wonderful Russian food. While Eleanor did not embrace the Russian cuisine at once, her tastes soon developed, and on the way back from New England, in 1903, she asked Sarah to have all kinds of favorite dishes ready: "My soul and the more mundane parts of me as well yearn for a pheasant jelly with slices of lemon all around the edge, a *kisel* [boiled-fruit dessert], either apricot or *brusnika* [bilberry], some *bolshoi* [big] chup-chup, fried pheasant served with rice and thick gravy, a shrimp salad with the shrimps chopped up so you can't tell them from lobster, an apple tart and some cheese toast, some bazaar black bread and boiled salt salmon—there, that will do to begin with, and I can already feel my forlorn skirt bands tightening" (1 February 1903 to Sarah).[18]

6 January 1895 to Home
[For years, the Smiths and the Prays celebrated Russian Christmas Eve with the Lindholms.] The tree was all decorated with tinsel, glass balls, colored candles, etc. The gifts are not hung on the tree, but placed under it, as the German fashion is. It was the prettiest tree I ever saw for it was loaded with ornaments to reflect the light, and sifting all down through it were tiny bits of white cotton that looked like snow. At five Lolla and her father and Sarah and I all went to the Lutheran church. The service was printed, and I could follow the words in many places. Then we went back to the Lindholms' and Charlie and Fred and Herr Pastor Rumpeter came. We had tea, cakes and fruit in the dining-room, and a big Swedish cake which all Swedes have on Christmas. While we were at the table, the tree was lighted, and when we came back into the sitting-room, a circle was formed around the tree and they sang a Swedish song. Then each person made a dive for his or her pile of

presents and such a hubbub as there was! Everybody was reading poetry and screaming with laughter.[19]

16 January 1895 to Mildred
Such fun as the masquerades here are. Parties in mask go around the town and call wherever there is a social evening, whether they are acquainted with the people or not. Masqueraders are supposed to act the worst they know how, and once Mrs. Lindholm, at a masquerade, climbed on the back of Pastor's chair and jumped whack over his head, on to the floor in front of him, and everybody thought it was a man dressed up for a woman, until she unmasked.

23 February 1895 to Home
We got home at one o'clock last night and consequently, we feel stupid this morning. The dinner was a much bigger affair than I thought.[20] Besides the Lindholms there were nineteen guests, and . . . dinner lasted nearly two hours. There were all sorts of cold dishes, baked fish with delicious cabbage salad and egg sauce, roast pheasant, potatoes and peas, asparagus, ice cream, and all sorts of sauces, apple, etc. While we were at dinner the naval orchestra came and after dinner we danced until twelve o'clock.

10 April 1895 to Cousin Clara
Fish and all kinds of game are very abundant here. From October till March we had so many pheasants that I am heartily sick of them. Wild ducks, geese, venison and boar . . . are very plenty in their season, also salmon and many other nice fish. From January to April we have crabs, with meat very similar to lobsters. They are bought alive and their body, aside from the innumerable legs, is larger across than a large dinner plate; they are ugly-looking customers and when Cook buys them I give the kitchen a wide berth until they are safely boiled. They cost only ten cents apiece. Now we can get twenty herring for a cent, good-sized ones, and I think no one ought to starve when food is so cheap.

6 May 1895 to Home
I have seen slurs in some of the papers about the Russian soldiers having only black bread and soup as if that were scant rations, but when one has once tasted a common Russian soup, one almost envies them, for it is the most delicious soup you can imagine. It has all kinds of vegetables in it and huge

chunks of meat, and it is good enough for a king. After the soup is eaten, they eat [the] meat with a little mustard. Black bread is also very nourishing.

29 November 1895 to Home
The prettiest dish [our Japanese cook] fixed last night was the smoked salmon. It is deep red in color and was sliced in thin slices a little larger over than a silver dollar. These were lapped, one over another in a circle around one of my cake plates. In the center was a hard-boiled egg cut in the shape of a flower, and a sprig of green in the center. Outside the slices of salmon was a bank perhaps an inch high of hard-boiled eggs, chopped very fine, and outside that a border of [green fern], and I think I have never seen a prettier dish.... The Japanese do such things as that very nicely and they enjoy it and take pride in their work.

10 February 1898 to Sarah
My dinner was a great success, so much of a one that I can hardly realize that it was of my own engineering.... Immediately after *tiffin* I cut and arranged the flowers, there were enough for the two little vases ... and they looked very nice. Then I arranged two dishes of salted almonds, a dish of olives and a small dish of pickles. As soon as tea was over I put on a clean cloth and laid the table myself, not making any very great mistakes, with the exception of forgetting the glasses and getting the knives on one side of the table on the wrong side of the plate.... I ordered dinner at quarter past seven ... and when at twenty-five minutes past no one but Mr. Rodgers had appeared, I began to get nervous, and I was afraid if I kept them waiting in the kitchen, there would be discord there, so Fred put the clock back twenty-five minutes. Soon after, O Sok-san came in her most dignified fashion to say *gotovo* [it's ready]—when half-way across the dining-room she looked at the clock and went back to the kitchen chop-chop. The Hansens and Mr. Clarkson came at half past and we sat down at once. The *zakuska* consisted of caviar and a crab salad. Nearly everybody had two helpings of each so I think they were good. Then came a boiled tai (I think) and then the roast mutton with asparagus. The mutton was just like that nice one we had four weeks ago, as tender and juicy as it could be and *how* people enjoyed it.

6 January 1899 to Home
Russian Christmas. Yesterday ... the tree was lighted and we circled around it singing the usual Swedish song, and then everybody grabbed and kissed his next-door neighbor. There was mistletoe hanging everywhere, and Mr.

Lindholm, Capt. Brandt and Fred took ample advantage of it to say nothing of the others. Lieut. Stark made a very laughable mistake—he got the word "kisseltoe" instead of "mistletoe," supposing it took its name from the kissing that takes place under it! ... After admiring our gifts a couple of hours, we went out to [be seated at] dinner. I went with Mr. Stark and Fred with Tullie, and we all sat together at the lower end of the table. It was a very lively dinner and just at midnight Mrs. Lindholm told each gentleman to kiss his lady and then clear out for there was nothing more to eat. Most of the gentlemen took advantage of it, but Mr. Stark, being a bashful young officer, pretended he didn't hear. Tullie at once repeated it for his benefit and told him it was his duty to kiss me, and Fred gave him full permission. He is not the young man to shirk a duty, but he still had some doubts upon the subject, so he asked me if he might, and I told him very severely that if he did, I would stand him in the corner the next time he came for his [English] lesson. Well, you should have seen the "God bless you" look in his face, when he found out he hadn't got to—it was so funny that we all screamed.

1 January 1901 to Home
Our guests have gone and before going to bed I want to add just a line to my letter, to wish you all a Happy New Year and an auspicious beginning for the new century. We were eleven at dinner tonight—Mr. and Mrs. Lindholm and Tullie, Mr. and Mrs. Hansen, Messrs. Walsham, Meares and Merritt and we three here. It was a full-dress affair and if I do say it, we looked very nice. . . . At midnight, we had champagne, and three cheers and a toast for the new century were given just as the clock struck.

8 April 1906 to Home
This year [for Easter] the tiny charms in the shape of eggs were for sale here for the first time, and . . . Ted gave me a beautiful red one, Sarah a gold one, Tullie a green one and Mrs. Hunter a pink one—which with the two I had before make quite a lot, and I wear them on a gold chain as an Indian does a string of bear claws. They are very pretty but it is only the custom to wear them at Easter.

4 December 1906 to Home
I have begun an "at home" day or *jour fixe* as they call it here, and I am at home Sunday afternoons from four till six and anybody who comes gets a cup of tea, cake, sandwiches, a little music and conversation.

9 February 1908 to Sarah

Last Wednesday evening I had the bridge here and, as I expected only the three Hansens and the Kizheviches, I told Cook to have soup, cold fish, chicken fricassee, and *kisel,* and I said one chicken would do. At noontime I invited the Newhards, thinking the chicken could be stretched a little. When I came home at six o'clock, imagine my horror to see the table laid for eleven people, as Ted had invited Mr. Smith and Mr. Szentgali. I gasped, knowing that the chicken was not of India rubber. Cook added a salad and some cold tongue to the table, and will you believe me—there was enough fricassee off that one bird for us all, and the following day four people lunched off it and three people had supper off it—one chicken for seventeen people! I am proud of the cook.

1 May 1910 to Home

Sarah and I went to the Cathedral to hear the [Easter] midnight mass and the glorious anthem "Christ is risen." . . . We went to the Cathedral about eleven o'clock and worked ourselves in until we were quite near the altar. I can't describe the crowd, but I realized for the first time what it meant to be a sardine. There wasn't room for a flea to hop, and to wipe one's own nose was a luxury not to be thought of. One swayed with the crowd, no matter in what direction. You may imagine the pressure when I tell you that when the people had to fall back to let the procession down the center, I was so squeezed that the whole five clasps on my corset, one after another unfastened—did you ever hear anything so ridiculous? Shortly before midnight a coffin was carried out of the Cathedral, after which a procession of priests, led by the bishop, came out from the holy of holies, and, headed by seven or eight standard bearers, marched the length of the church, out at the main door, and around the church, many people falling in behind and marching with them. The first two carried huge lanterns on poles—looking something like an abducted street lamp; then came four or five huge banners, evidently of gold filigree work, each containing a portrait of a saint, and each having three standards, with a man to each standard; then another man carried a cross; they formed in the center of the church, and when the priests came out, the march was taken up, chanting going on all the while. The Cathedral up to this had been very dimly lighted excepting around the altar, but as the procession began, the great chandeliers with dozens of huge candles were lighted and the electric lights turned on. Behind the altar, on the partition to the holy of holies, lines of small red and blue lights were placed, with most gorgeous effect. Let us hope no conservative old saint will object to such an innovation. The people were listening intently to the chanting outside, watching for the words "Christ has risen," and then they began to light the tapers they held in their hands, and candle grease began to flow. The procession returned to the church and the mass went on, both choirs participating and the priests chanting. The music is beautiful. . . . Outside were hundreds of people and it did look so pretty—the whole enclosure around the Cathedral, perhaps an acre or more in extent was hung with ropes of colored lamps and decorated with flags, and three powerful search lights from the men-of-war in the harbor were thrown on the Cathedral, making it as light as day—a most beautiful sight. On the way home we met hundreds of people hastening to the church with huge *kulichi* [Easter buns] . . . to have them blessed by the bishop.

14 February 1912 to Aunt Anna
This is carnival week and consequently people are eating pancakes and caviar. I wish I wasn't dieting, for I do love that indigestible mess of buckwheat cakes, sour cream, caviar and raw fish—you can't think how good it is. One doesn't mind six weeks of fasting after such a good feed.

27 October 1923 to Sarah
[Sarah turned sixty-five on this day.] This afternoon in the quieter moments I have thought so much of the old jolly birthdays before Charlie left us—that excitement there always was and how many secrets between Tullie, Lolla and myself, and how everyone came to tea, and then some of them to dinner, and the fête was something to look forward to for weeks and look back on weeks after it was past. Ah, well, those days have gone forever but it is precious to have such memories and you and I have so many of them.

CHAPTER 2

Women's Work and Leisure

MOST OF THE WOMEN IN ELEANOR PRAY'S PREREVOLUTIONARY circle—merchant wives in Old Vladivostok—had no professional training nor salaried positions in commercial enterprises. They were wives and mothers, homemakers and hostesses, and their customary freedom from financial hardship allowed them to volunteer in charitable organizations or spend their time leisurely. It is tempting to consider these women frivolous, their lives seemingly so carefree. Imagine calendars chock-full of tea parties, formal dinners, and intricate menus that you simply order from your kitchen staff. Servants keep your rooms clean and cozy, and you always wear white in the summer. Imagine never fetching the water for your bath, and almost never washing your own dishes, bedding, or impressively designed clothes. The sleeves and the skirts of your dresses expand and contract according to fashion, and you go nowhere without a hat. But now also realize that this picture is poignant only by its selectivity, for it reflects neither Mrs. Pray's and her friends' variable reality before World War I, nor their far more complex existence in Soviet times. By the late teens and early 1920s, their easy "antebellum" comforts had been drastically reduced.[1]

The tea party was these women's central meeting place. Started as a social gathering of foreign ladies, Marie Dattan's particular group thrived in the 1890s and early 1900s, and by June 1901 its members decided to memorialize their friendship, as well as their pretty gowns, in a photo. Arranged elegantly before a professional photographer are Mrs. Dattan, her sister Anna Cornehls, Wilhelmina (Minni) Langschwadt, and Sophie Wohlfahrt (all connected with the German trading house of Kunst and Albers, or K&A);[2] Eleonora

Hansen (wife of the director of the Danish Telegraph);[3] and Sarah Smith and Eleanor Pray (from the American Store). Russian ladies were also invited, including Mrs. Bushueva (wife of Ivan Bushuev, a public prosecutor and member of the circuit court), and Tullie Tyrtova (née Lindholm, wife of Konstantin Tyrtov of the cruiser *Russia*). They drank tea, coffee, or hot chocolate and ate light refreshments—pastries, slices of cake, or small open-faced sandwiches—while discussing diverse topics, such as city news (with its inevitable gossip) and recent art events. Not infrequently, they also helped each other overcome the human anguish that monetary security does not control and cannot soothe: that children often ail and sometimes die, that friends suffer, that violence may strike in our midst. The Wohlfahrts lost several babies during these years; Paul Dattan (born in 1891) was chronically ill; Minni Langschwadt died from diphtheria in November 1902; and Mr. Bushuev was murdered on the Isle of Askold in 1897.[4]

The tea circle thus served as a support group, its moods ranging from light-hearted and giggly to somberly compassionate, its philosophy neatly illustrating Horace's idea of mixing *dulce et utile*, the pleasing and the useful. The "pleasing" part was the atmosphere of comfort and care in the members' homes, contrasted with the often unsettling conditions outside: "It was a stormy day and I strayed into [Sarah's] house and we talked of home as we worked all the afternoon. The storm was something terrible, fine snow, accompanied by a whirling wind. One could not see ten steps ahead" (2 February 1895 to Mildred). The "useful" part was the empathy of trusting friendships, as well as a more tangible contribution: the women's work. Trotting off to their meetings, they took along basketfuls of assorted sewing jobs, from small to voluminous. Sewing proficiency was expected of all married women, its products benefitting both their families and others. "Allegri," charity bazaars, were held regularly, serving worthy causes often sponsored by the local Philanthropic Society.

During the political upheavals that started in 1914 and continued through the mid-1920s, most of the foreigners left Vladivostok, and those who stayed, including Eleanor Pray, were uprooted from their former mode of living. Forced by the necessity of survival, her final decision in the fall of 1930 to join her family in Shanghai led to much bureaucratic wrangling, and, mitigated by sweet nostalgia, put into bright focus the rise and fall of her economic fortunes as reflected in her clothes: "As I neared the [visa] place, I wondered what hitch there would be, but couldn't even guess—I soon found out. They had no blanks—please come again tomorrow! . . . Outside I sat on a curb stone for at least half an hour, and no one seeing a neat but shabbily dressed *burzhui* [bourgeois person] sitting there in the dirt, would have dreamed that she once (perhaps twice!) trailed silken raiment across highly polished parquet floors" (9 October 1930 to Sarah).

CLOTHES AND HOME DESIGNS

During their voyage from the United States to Vladivostok in the spring of 1894, Eleanor, Sarah, and their husbands stopped in Yokohama, an event that vividly illuminated Mrs. Pray's new status as a married lady. She could shop for any fabrics and fashions that she wanted, and her husband always encouraged her to dress elegantly (6 January 1908 to Aunt Anna). Far from abusing this privilege, Eleanor Pray selected her colors and patterns carefully, much like an artist, and immediately recorded some of her first impressions of married shopping: "Our tailor and dressmaker is Chang Chow Esq., and a very polite Chinaman he is, too. I brought a yellow cotton crepe from home, which he is making with narrow black velvet ribbon, and I shall buy one or two new dresses here. We went to a place where they make hats, yesterday, and I ordered a white sailor to be made as soon as possible.[5] The Jap[anese milliner] said he had six to make for the Emperor of Japan, and as soon as he finished those he would make mine. This is the first time I ever came in second to such an important dignitary and I assure you, I feel quite set up. In my wildest flights of fancy I never dreamed of a royal hat-maker, who blinks his eyes when he looks at you as if the light of your countenance dazzled him" (6 June 1894 to Clara).

In addition to ordering clothes by mail, many of Vladivostok's merchant wives sewed both their families' wardrobes and the decorative items for their homes themselves. Excepting the heaviest pieces, such as winter coats and men's suits, they made curtains and drapes, bedclothes and rugs. They embroidered dainty napkins and elegant pillowcases; stitched handkerchiefs and tablecloths; and, sometimes with the help of local seamstresses but often alone, designed and produced their own clothes: blouses and waists (tops of two-piece styles), skirts and dresses, underwear and baby clothes. Before the world war, Vladivostok's Kunst and Albers and Churin's stores carried materials and notions but few ready-to-wear outfits, and Mrs. Pray and her friends shared patterns, pored over the dress plates in magazines, and showed great ingenuity in cleaning, repairing, and modernizing their clothes.[6] The intricate fashions of this era—often using ten to twelve yards of fabric for one dress—required both creative talent and professional competency, especially when these well-off but frugal women economized by "making over" outmoded styles into updated ones. Working with natural fabrics such as silk, cotton, linen, alpaca, and wool, they might replace their dresses' sleeves or skirts, and refresh them with new collars, ribbons, or dyes. Blue, black, or brown serge—a fine wool tweed used for both jackets and coats, and dresses and skirts—was especially popular because of its longevity and reliable shape; long-worn coats and skirts of serge could easily be remade into, for example, a "home dress." This was Eleanor's favorite material: "In thirty-four years I have not known what it is to be without a blue serge dress any length of time" (11 November 1928 to Clara).

As members of "polite society," Eleanor Pray and her friends considered it necessary to change clothes several times a day, even if they owned just a few outfits. A "morning dress" was worn until *tiffin*; a suit or dress with a jacket was required for afternoon visiting; and a formal, low-necked gown sparkled at fancy dinners in the evening. Eleanor wrote, "My garnet dress has been lengthened and white satin put in in front and . . . it is just what I need for afternoons" (13 March 1902 to Sarah). Thus, in one swift image, the glimpse of a fashionable lady walking into Kunst and Albers or riding along Svetlanskaia in a carriage quietly testified to the mind-boggling skills and care behind her costume.

31 July 1894 to Home
As soon as it is a little cooler I shall go to work on sheets and pillow cases. I am going to make some of linen if we can get it cheap in Shanghai. I want a couple pair of linen pillow cases and a couple of sheets to hemstitch.

30 September 1894 to Home
When you [write] in February, send the March fashion plate, if it is out, and it probably will be. I want to send down [to China] for new summer dresses by the steamer that the mail comes up on. I am going to have some thin silks. They are cheaper here than cotton, wash fully as well, and do not need starch. Does it not seem strange to be where silk is cheaper than cotton?

3 March 1895 to Mildred
I may have a pongee silk morning dress—thin pongee is as cheap as anything and is very serviceable. When we go bathing it is a lot of work to take off and

put on a skirt and shirt waist with necktie, belt, etc., so I want a simple dress, skirt and a basque that buttons, so I can get in and out of it lively.[7]

29 March 1895 to Mildred

Yesterday and day before I worked on my garnet and white dress. I took out the old sleeves and put in short puff sleeves of the garnet, then I took the lace off and ironed it and when it was back on, the dress looked as good as new.

20 June 1895 to Home

Tuesday it poured all day and Sarah and I took that time to rip up our blue serge skirts, sponge and press them and make them over without a lining. Now they are quite ready for the summer.

24 November 1895 to Aunt Anna

I intend to be sick for the next two or three weeks, in fact till my box from Shanghai comes, for I am in very straitened circumstances as regards clothes. I am reduced to putting on a silk dress as soon as I have swept and dusted my rooms every morning, and as I haven't been accustomed to silk very long I feel decidedly uncomfortable at having to put it on so early in the day. My everyday clothes are in shreds and if I put on one of my nice wool dresses, I must change it if I go out-of-doors, because the sleeves are too big for the sleeves in my old coat, and only the silk sleeves can be squeezed in, and there I am.

1 January 1898 to Home

[Charles has given Eleanor a Russian *bashlyk*.] This is a kind of hood which all Russians, little and big, rich and poor, wear over the cap in the winter. It is made of felt with long ends that go twice around the neck and a peaked crown. I have wanted one ever since I came here.

19 April 1898 to Sarah

A week ago last Saturday, I got caught between two carts (. . . they were crossing the sidewalk and I couldn't go either way) and a horse kicked mud all over my gray skirt and you should have seen me! Of course I had to have the skirt washed but it was some time before a suitable day came, and *then* in spite of the soft water which I collected from the barrels, it shrunk half-way to my knees and I have to put a band of something around the bottom.

14 July 1899 to Aunt Anna

I was at the Lindholms' yesterday afternoon when the dressmaker sent home their new ball gowns and they were too lovely for anything. Each had a white crepe trimmed with chiffon and lace. Then Tullie had a cream lace over yellow silk, and Lolla a violet lace over silk of the same color and trimmed with ribbons. Of course, the girls are very disappointed that the balls they intended them for are not coming off on account of the death of the Crown Prince.[8] I told them it was very inconsiderate of the Prince to die at this time of year, when, as he has been sick so long, he might have died at Lent when there was nothing going on.

2 August 1899 to Home

Yesterday and today I have rushed through a tremendous amount of work and now, I am happy to say, it is finished. Yesterday I made three dozen menu cards for the bazaar, and in the evening I made myself a hat of which I am inordinately proud, it is such a success. . . . The frame is covered with white silk, trimmed with white lace and red and white roses in great profusion. As the whole business only cost me the price of the canvas, wire and white silk (a ruble and thirty kopeks), I think I have the right to be proud of it and Mrs. Hansen says if I advertise it as a twenty-five dollar Shanghai hat, no one will dispute me.

21 October 1899 to Sarah

I was upstairs in K&A's with Miss Morphew when Mr. Stechman the younger came along and asked if I wouldn't come in to his department and see the nice new things. I had long ago hunted there for a jacket and they told me they had received all they should so I haven't been there lately. Can you imagine my delight at finding a French seal skin coat, just my size, for fifty rubles? I wouldn't believe Mr. S. when he told me the price, but then I saw it was French seal which didn't trouble me a bit as long as I liked it and the price was within our reach. I had it sent up, put it on and then paraded into the office to surprise Ted. He was almost as far off his head as I, and since supper—to please him—I have tried it on three times.

29 November 1899 to Sarah

Mrs. Boesch was dressed to kill—a black chiffon, fluted skirt which lay an inch or two on the floor all around and which we all took turns in stepping on, and an overdress closely fitted to the knees, of pale blue brocade trimmed with blue net and black sequins. I think she is about my age—but Mr. Clarkson says I am young and innocent.

30 April 1900 to Sarah
Tullie and Lolla have been to make a fashionable call this afternoon and they looked so nice. They had gray gowns trimmed with cherry color, and a cherry colored velvet turban with gray feathers, quite unlike anything they have ever had before, and I thought it very becoming. Lolla said the turbans were very fashionable, but she hadn't yet got over feeling like a Sikh policeman when she looked at herself!

5 July 1900 to Sarah
Ted has two new suits of white clothes and I wish you could see how nice he looks in them. I really can't say who is the most pleased with them—he himself, I, or Dou Kee. The latter walks around him in admiring circles every time he appears in them, and the other day for fear I hadn't seen them, he called to me to look at "Master's new dress"!

22 February 1901 to Home
This is my time of year for making underclothes and I have a good big pile cut out to go to work on, and next week I am going at it in real earnest. When I begin machine work I like to be able to keep at it.

13 May 1901 to Home
The tea party was at Mrs. Behn's Saturday afternoon and it pretty nearly developed into a bargain sale, much to our profit and delight. She and Mr. Behn are leaving for a six months' trip to Germany, day after tomorrow, and she has recently got a box of hats and gowns which she has not been able to wear. We told her it was of no earthly use to take them home with her for she could get new ones there and *we* couldn't very well get new ones here now there is such a fearful duty, etc.,[9] and the end was that she let us have them like the dear little thing she is. . . . I got a red velvet hat, just the color of the one I had when I left home, and a whole cloth suit of heavy cadet-blue material, skirt and coat quite plain, tailor made, and the bodice with a vest of pale pink and blue Dresden velvet, edged with white and silver braid. It is perfectly lovely and could not have fitted me better had I been measured for it.

31 January 1902 to Home
I am staying in the house these days, thanks to a piece of unparalleled stupidity on my part. I insisted on having my new serge skirt pressed *on me*, and the result is a blister nearly as large as the palm of my hand, and my corsets irritated it so much that I am obliged to go without them till it heals.[10] . . . Did you ever hear of anything so ridiculous? I wish Mr. Bok of the *Ladies' Home Journal* would try the advice he allows to be published, before giving it to the world!

4 November 1904 to Clara
I am so shabby and old-fashioned that I have been obliged to order myself some clothes from Petersburg, and Tullie has been kind enough to send my measure to her dressmaker there. I am going to try an afternoon dress and a blouse and if these are satisfactory I shall order more. Once my measure is there, I can easily order by telegraph (only ten kopeks a word) and in five weeks one has the things.

29 May 1906 to Home
[Plans for Baby Dorothy:] Now everything is ready, excepting the bed and basket. Mrs. Hansen is going to line the latter for me, with my blue satin ball dress.[11]

6 January 1908 to Aunt Anna
I haven't any new dress this winter for it seemed a sin to order them when I had so many such nice ones, so I put some new lace on my blue broadcloth instead of the tassels, so that it would look a little different in the eyes of my lord and master, and am wearing it for a calling dress, although this is its fourth winter.

22 March 1913 to Home
I've sworn off taking tea this week, or rather off the cakes that accompany afternoon tea, and I'm sure no monk in a hair shirt ever felt himself more of a martyr. Why, oh, why, was I not born with a tendency to thinness instead of corpulency—when I see the spread of cakes wherever I go, I almost envy Miss Sarjeant, who resembles nothing so much as a clothes pin. She can have all the cake she likes—but she doesn't want it.

24 June 1914 to Aunt Anna
Another glorious day, but not so warm as yesterday. I have earned my night's repose, for I have been at the machine practically all day, and Sarah has sat beside me helping manage the things. We had to make two new awnings—one 2 1/2 × 3 3/4 yards and the other just a little shorter, and pieces of that size are not easy to manage on a hand machine, so it took both of us.

23 September 1917 to Sarah
Well, we have some new people [renting] your room—a Mr. and Mrs. Jackson—very pleasant people with grown-up children. She . . . had on a skirt which would frighten a motor-car out of the road. In all my life I have never even seen curtains of such a loud pattern and it had a white groundwork. She said to me that for some reason or other her husband wouldn't allow her to wear it on the street here. I gasped at the very idea, but she, luckily, didn't see me.

17 October 1917 to Sarah
Nastia is just finishing such a nice, one-piece dress for me of that dark gray check, like my summer costume. There will be one or two fancy collars to go with it and I'm sure it will be a very useful morning dress this winter.

12 November 1917 to Sarah
He Fa just brought a Chinese to look at our old furs and he bought my squirrel lining and black hat for sixty rubles, and Dorothy's old white coat and muff for forty. I couldn't get him to take my sealskin because he didn't understand it, but he promised to send a more experienced man.

2 May 1922 to Sarah
This morning, having outgrown my everyday shirt waists, I went to Churin's for some material and ran across a piece of gray and white seersucker from the Amoskeag Mills. It was only sixty kopeks an *arshin* [Russian measure of length, almost thirty inches] and I simply couldn't resist buying a dress length. Churin's have heaps of goods from different New England manufactories, and they are not at all expensive.[12]

3 February 1930 to Sarah
Such a piece of luck this afternoon. Vera Georgievna, the dressmaker, has been promising to come to me for a long time, and I was afraid she wouldn't

get around, but this afternoon she was waiting for me when I came out of the office, to ask if I could have her, as Mrs. Christensen, for whom she was working, was ill and couldn't have her. Of course, I *was* pleased—it just looked like Providence. All I want is a dress made out of that black costume B[elle] B[reck] gave me so many years ago, and the sleeves in another dress made long which ought not to take many days.

CHARITY BAZAARS

Eleanor Pray and her friends in the tea circle regularly donated hand-crafted items to the lotteries at the various charity bazaars, such as doilies, purses, and belts. They might also lend cups, saucers, and chairs for the tea pavilions, serve the tea, and help keep track of the accounts. It is not clear how truly useful these arrangements were for the needy of Vladivostok, but Mrs. Pray and her friends took their tasks seriously and worked with good will and astute organization.[13]

27 July 1899 to Home
I have had a great surprise as well as a great pleasure today and I am sure you could never guess what it is. The charity bazaar here is one of the great events of the season, and the most select part of that is the tea house. I have never been asked to assist before and never dreamed of such a thing, but this year the new [Military] Governor is arranging the bazaar and I—humble person that I am—have actually been invited to assist in the tea house. I haven't gotten over the shock of it yet and I am meditating on whether or not to accept. Mrs. Knorring has charge of it and her other assistants are Miss Chukhnina (the Admiral's daughter), Tullie, Lolla, Mrs. Skorupo (Mr. Stark's sister), and one other whose name I have forgotten. I have plenty of gowns to choose from but no white hat and unless I am able to scrape one together I shan't go.

22 August 1899 to Aunt Anna
The charity bazaar came off day before yesterday and was a great success, especially our tea pavilion. We had a tent about sixty feet long and twenty wide, the inside walls of which were draped in pale blue and pale yellow—the Governor's own colors. We had eight bamboo tables and, at each, four bamboo chairs, each table being separated from the others by groups of potted palms. . . . At the back was a long counter where the money was received and where the cakes were also given out. The first of the afternoon I tended the

flower booth, and almost my first sale was to the Governor himself. I got quite confused, blundered in my Russian so that His Excellency began to speak French to me. . . . Just then Miss Chukhnina came along, and hearing her speak English to me, he followed suit. I sold him two miserable little boutonnières for fifteen rubles, which I considered as doing very well. . . . At the end of the day we had seventeen hundred and odd rubles, which surpassed our wildest expectations. It could easily have been twenty hundred, if we had had more flowers, sweets, etc., but everything but the tea was cleaned out before six o'clock. Last year the tea booth only brought five hundred rubles and the year before twelve hundred. . . . Yesterday morning I went to the garden with Mrs. Knorring and helped sort out and send home the chairs, tables, etc., and then she gave me the money to go around to the shops and settle the bills. In the afternoon I brought the receipts to her and found her washing up the dishes. They were all of K&A's best china and she would not trust them to the servants.

9 October 1899 to Sarah
[That fall, another bazaar was held.] The Allegri is over, thank goodness, and I've had enough of it for I never in all my life came so near freezing to death as I did in that tea house. I wore my black serge skirt, pink silk blouse and a Parisian creation of black and pink (which I created the night before) on my head and felt very fine until I found that Mrs. Levitskaia was to serve with me and she looked so lovely that I was not in it. She was dressed in black, and her hat was a picture in itself with its black plumes and violets. Had we only been stood on our heads, I should have been the belle of the outfit, for Mrs. Levitskaia, with that lovely hat and gown, wore a pair of brown and white *canvas* tennis shoes! She looked so lovely and was altogether so nice that I longed to offer her my shoes.

10 October 1899 to Sarah
Now I must tell you what Lolla did at the Allegri. She was selling billets when a small boy came along and bought four, paying for them with nearly all the money he had. He was a poor boy about seven years old and he was terribly disappointed to find only blanks. Lolla had thirty rubles' worth of billets and had drawn sixteen numbers, so she gave four of them to this boy because he was so disappointed. Well, those four billets drew a gold watch, a silver watch, and a sewing machine [that] we gave, and the cash prize of a hundred rubles! Wasn't that small boy in luck, thanks to Lolla's kindness?

5 August 1901 to Home

The bazaar came off yesterday and there were crowds of people there. . . . The booths were very prettily arranged, especially the tea house, the ladies in charge being Mrs. Osipova, Mrs. Konstantinovich, the two daughters of Gen. Linevich-Pekinskii and another lady whose name I do not know.[14] There were several officers from the battleship *Petropavlovsk* to assist, and sailors from the same ship to wait on us, for which I was very glad, for we only had to take orders and money and need not get our gowns spoiled by tea, coffee, etc. The sailor appointed to stand at my elbow was a cure, and I did laugh inside at some of his remarks. For instance, along came two sailors from *Navarin* and asked, "Have you lemonade? If so, we will take a bottle." The idea of a common sailor like himself being so extravagant was too much for the *Petropavlovsk* man so he sidled up to Navarin and said, "It is *very dear*." "Never mind," said the Navarin, in rather a lordly voice. "We can pay whatever it costs!" "Oh," said Petro, greatly awed by such wealth, "perhaps you would also take some cake?" "Oh, yes," they would take some cake, and presently the cake and lemonade were set out for them on a table where they proceeded to enjoy themselves. When they called for their account Petro said to the sailor whose duty it was to collect it, "Don't you give them a kopek of change no matter how big a bill they give you." Evidently he did not intend them to get off too easy after scorning his advice! Then a military officer came along but said he did not care for anything, when I asked him if he would have some tea. As soon as his back was turned the sailor said to me in the most scornful way, "They are not like *our naval* officers—they are a poor sort of men," which of course amused me very much. Fancy a sailor regarding a military officer like that! About eight o'clock, I thought I was tired enough to come home and the streets were so crowded with people that I knew I should be quite safe in coming home alone instead of waiting for Ted to come for me. Everybody stared at me for of course a lady alone in a white silk dress can't go along unmolested but nobody interfered with me. When I got up to K&A, "Teeth" with four of his small friends was sitting on the steps and he evidently thought I needed an escort which duty he and his friends took on themselves, marching along beside me, a self-constituted bodyguard which amused me immensely.[15]

SPORTS

For the summer and fall bazaars in Vladivostok's parks and gardens, the urban landscape became a barely hinted backdrop, whereas for the women's sports activities the hills and the sea were centrally important. They swam, skated, and paddled, often in the two bays, and although their athletic clothing may seem constraining from today's uninhibited point of view, we can empathize with the joyful camaraderie and well-being created by those lively hours spent in motion.

Swimming

17 July 1894 to Home
Mrs. Unterberger is very nice, she takes Sadie out bathing with her every morning across the bay. I do not go for it is really swimming instead of bathing and I have not the courage to learn.

2 September 1894 to Aunt Anna
I am learning to swim and a nice time that I am having of it too. I never knew how much like bullfrogs we were built until I saw the other ladies swimming. We wear short pants and a waist made all together and buttoning on the shoulders. Mine are wide blue and white stripes and I can dance . . . in them beautifully. We have the use of a bathing house and go every day.

10 August 1922 to Sarah
The swimming here in town is simply glorious—I go every morning and stay in the water about an hour. There is a rope to hang onto while one rests, so my feet touch nothing and that is why I like it so much. There are sights there to make the angels weep and I usually bring enough tales home to entertain my family at *tiffin*.

Horse-Riding

28 October 1894 to Clara
Last Wednesday Olga Kuster loaned me her saddle horse for the afternoon and what a glorious ride I had. I rode about a mile before it struck me that I could neither stop nor start the horse, so I walked him way back to her house to ask how to address a horse in Russian. You say "purrr," rolling the "r," to stop him, and *poshel* [let's go] to start him, but he understood the whip in English as well as any horse. I took tea with the Kusters and did not get home till dark, and . . . it was so nice to be on a horse's back again.

Tennis

24 August 1894 to Home
Next Thursday the First East Siberia Tennis Tournament will take place at
Mr. Lindholm's. The first prize is a solid silver cup which Fred is marking.
We shall have a fine time there, for it will last all day and all the evening.

22 September 1895 to Home
The *Azov* tennis party came off yesterday and we really had a delightful time.
The day was perfect, no wind and just warm enough. We went to the Admiral's Pier at half past two, and there Lieut. Ivanov met us with a large man-
of-war boat, manned by sixteen sailors. . . . It took only a short time to cross
the bay [to Russian Island], and on reaching the tennis court we were wel-
comed by the officers of the *Azov* and conducted to a tent, in which were
plenty of seats overlooking the court and tables, loaded with cakes, candies,
etc., and one table where tea and *stronger* drinks were served. Soon after our
arrival Mrs. Lindholm and the girls and Miss Korn came in another *Azov*
boat, and then the playing began. A band was stationed just outside our tent
and the music was beautiful. The first game was between Tullie and Lolla, Dr.
Parenago and another officer. Just as the game was fairly begun, Dr. Popov,
the head doctor of the fleet[16] . . . appeared around the corner of the tent, leading his small brown bear Misha, who was tugging at his rope with all his
strength. Misha was at once the center of attraction. He is only three months
old and like all small bears has a head several sizes too big for his body, and
is such a clumsy little beggar! After the doctor got his breath, he went to the
refreshment table, filled a bottle with milk for Misha and poured a glass of
beer for himself. Then Misha sat on his haunches facing the doctor, and they
clinked glasses and drank to each other's very good health. Misha's pint
bottle of milk disappeared very quickly and then he began to politely beg for
some of Dr. Popov's beer, and Doctor told him, if he would turn three som-
ersaults, he might have some. So, Misha turned three in less than no time,
and Doctor poured some of his beer into the bottle. Misha took one drink,
and then like a sensible bear poured the remainder on the ground amid the
shouts of the spectators. After half an hour or so Misha and Doctor went back
to the *Azov* much to our regret and then we gave our undivided attention to
the playing.

18 July 1899 to Home
Yesterday afternoon for the first time this year we played on our own court
[at the Danish House] and it was so nice to have the Knorrings there again.
Now, when the weather permits we shall play every day. I have engaged two
small Chinese to pick balls for me[17] and they are to be on duty every day from
four till eight for which they are to receive three rubles each per month. I
bought them each a suit of clean clothes which is to be kept here, and Dou
Kee is to see that they wash every day before they put them on. Each suit cost
a ruble and twenty kopeks which I thought was cheap enough. Sarah is going
to buy them shoes and stockings so they will be real little dudes.

Paddling

12 July 1895 to Home
Yesterday afternoon after tea we went out for a drive and as usual, hauled up
at the Lindholms'. We all went down to the tennis court, Mrs. L. and I to look
on and the others to play. Soon Mr. Igoni came over and asked me if I would
not like to go out in one of the canoes and of course I said yes at once, for I
have wanted to try it for a long time. Mrs. Lindholm and Aina went down to
the beach with us, and the *manzas* brought down two canoes. I went in one
and Mr. Igoni in the other and Mrs. L. sent a boat to follow us in case of an
accident. How I liked it! We paddled out on the bay for half an hour or more
and I enjoyed every minute of it.

12 September 1895 to Home
Now mother and father—I can see by Clara's letter that you are worried about
this canoe business, but I don't want you to be, and at the same time I do not
want to promise you, as you ask, to give up such a healthy exercise. I wish I
had not mentioned it at all. . . . You may be very sure Mr. Lindholm would
not allow the girls to canoe if he thought it in the least dangerous. They have
canoed for three years now and have never had any kind of an accident.

1 September 1913 to Home
Every morning now [in the country] I go out at a little before seven for exercise in rowing and I enjoy it very much. Usually I row for half an hour, but
this morning I went to the other side [of the bay] and back which took me

fifty minutes. On the way back I heard what sounded like a locomotive blowing off steam which I couldn't account for and it came nearer and nearer, so at length I found it was in the air and . . . sure enough, there was an aeroplane, the first I have ever seen, sailing along over my head and looking like a toy two feet long with a Teddy Bear riding on it—I couldn't distinguish anything but the thing in front, which must have been a man, and the long tail with a propeller on the end of it, and presently it grew so small that I could scarcely see it and disappeared behind the clouds on the way to Vladivostok.

Bicycling

9 July 1898 to Home
I went up to the Lindholms' [yesterday]. The wind blew a hurricane but they were all down on the tennis court to watch Tullie, Lolla and Aina learning to ride a bicycle. It was great fun and the girls were wild over it. . . . When their father came home, there was one wild rush at him with petitions for him to immediately order three wheels (it was Sarah's they were learning on), and although he did not promise there was a twinkle in his eye which meant "yes."

Skating

3 December 1894 to Home
Christmas afternoon Sarah and I went up to Lindholms' and after tea we went skating. That is, I did, and the others came to see the fun. Mrs. Lindholm sat down in their sledge chair, and acted as ballast for me. I kept a firm grip on the back of it, you may be sure, and ever and anon, when my feet flew out from under me, I hung up on the back of it. The first time I did it, I expected to see the chair come over backwards, and Mrs. Lindholm go flying over my head, but the chair was too heavy for that.

20 January 1895 to Home
The skating rink is very nice; it is in front of the Naval Club and is about half an acre in extent, which is kept clean by coolies. It is fenced in and has a house on each side where you can go in to warm, and to get hot tea. Near the entrance is a bandstand where the band plays twice a week. Season tickets are five rubles, and a single entrance fee twenty kopeks.

21 January 1895 to Mildred
Yesterday, Sarah and I started for the rink about half past two, Fred absolutely refusing to accompany us. Mr. Klepsch, Mr. Stockman and Mr. Otto Meyer met us at the entrance and Mr. Klepsch asked me if I would go to ride on the ice. Of course I said "Yes" and he brought up such a nice horse and sleigh, which he had borrowed of Mr. Cornehls. The other day he heard me say that I had not driven any since I came here, so he planned this. He gave me the reins, and [we spun] up and down over the ice. It was bitterly cold, but the fact that I was once more holding the reins kept me braced to the cold, and how I did enjoy it. The ice is smooth and hard and the roads over it are beautiful sleighing, far ahead of the city streets.

6 March 1895 to Home
[An ice carnival has been held.] The Rink was beautiful—from the street above it looked like fairyland, it was all illuminated with strings of colored lanterns, and now and then a naphtha lamp. The band played and a lot of people were there. In spite of the warm weather the ice had been scraped until it was as hard and smooth as glass. I had no trouble skating at all, and didn't I enjoy the evening! . . . They danced the Russian quadrille on skates and it was so pretty; of course, no one took part but good skaters and they did it very nicely.

Golf

26 November 1900 to Home
Mr. Walsham, Mr. Merritt and I had the honor yesterday of laying out the first golf links in East Siberia and of playing over them. We found a splendid place up the back of the hills and I think we shall enjoy the game very much.

22 May 1901 to Home
This is the end of one of the loveliest May days I ever saw in this land of fogs and we have improved it to the utmost, as it luckily was a big holiday. . . . We went on the hills about half past ten this morning, a party of seven of us, Mssrs. Walsham, Fisher, Merritt, Brown, Ted, Mrs. Crompton and I—six to play and Mrs. Crompton to look on. My two tennis Koreans—"Microbe" aged nine and "Teeth" aged fourteen—trudged on behind with the lunch baskets and they had the picnic of their lives. It was pretty warm playing so I stopped off after the third hole, and Mrs. Crompton and I with the two

coolies skirted the hill between holes five and six and found a nice place to lunch in. We had to wait about half an hour for the crowd to finish six and then we lunched very comfortably under the trees. Cook had given me all the scraps of bread and tongue left from trimming the sandwiches for the coolies and after they devoured that—there was about a pound of it—I gave them each a small loaf of bread and a glass of orange fizz which they enjoyed immensely. At the end of their feast "Microbe" took the tin the tongue scraps were in, climbed a tree, and carefully fixed it there for the birds—rather thoughtful of the little monkey, was it not?

Part II
The City

CHAPTER 3

Vladivostok Scenes

ON 16 AUGUST 1929, ELEANOR PRAY WROTE TO HER SISTER-IN-LAW Sarah Smith in Shanghai that yet another couple of friends were about to leave Vladivostok. Both women knew well that, for many of the foreign residents, this was a place of transfer—into Siberia to explore its natural wealth, or out via China and Japan, to escape—as well as a step on the promotional ladder in international corporations seeking Russian trade. But Mrs. Pray then noted her own dissenting opinion: "Sometimes I long to get away from here and be done with all the worries and vexations of everyday life . . . but deep in my soul I know I shall never be as contented anywhere else as in this beautiful unkempt place, for the best part of my life has been spent here." In the words of the marriage vow, Eleanor Pray loved the city and her life in it—"for better or for worse."

A spectacular embrace of hills and sea creates Vladivostok's natural relief. Of striking shape and importance, the L-shaped central harbor, the Bay of the Golden Horn, is protected from the south by the massive Russian Island, dominating the horn's lower prong like an old-fashioned lock. To the west, off the Egersheld Peninsula, glitters the grand Amur Bay, and to the east of the whole city, Ussuri Bay. The prerevolutionary panorama of Vladivostok's man-made landmarks, looking north from the Golden Horn, was appealing. Old photographs show, on the west side of town, the famous railway station, the Danish Telegraph, and, later, the lovely art nouveau mansion of the Bryner family;[1] in the middle the bustling marketplace on what is today the central square, near the stately trading house of Kunst and Albers (K&A); and, not far east of the city center, the Admiral's House, the Nikolai Triumphal Arch,[2] and the Cathedral of the Assumption. Toward the end of her residency in Vladivostok, Eleanor Pray fondly recalled this vista: "Thirty-six years ago today I made my debut in Vladivostok and . . . I remember asking [brother-in-law] Charlie what the old Kunst & Albers building was—being quite disappointed to hear that it was only a department store, when it looked like a palace" (23 June 1930 to Sarah). If one scrutinizes the old photos carefully, Dom Smith, with its large second-floor veranda, may also be discerned somewhat to the northeast of Kunst and Albers, from 1899 on fronted by the impressive Post and Telegraph Office on Svetlanskaia Street.[3]

History's preferences, often narrowly political, have wreaked havoc with the seafront, and the cathedral was brutally razed in the late 1930s.[4] Still, while the architectural plans for Bolshoi Vladivostok (Greater Vladivostok) in the 1950s and 1960s called for massive, prefabricated housing developments, efforts were made to capture in iron and concrete the shape of the *sopki* [cone-shaped hills]—to create the effect of an amphitheater or "a kind of gigantic staircase, on which the rows of the houses will alternate with the rows of greenery."[5] Many of these terraced apartment blocks seem to cascade down, draping, as it were, over the hillsides.[6]

Few visitors can remain unmoved by Vladivostok's natural beauty. When Anton Chekhov visited in the fall of 1890 on his way back to Moscow from Sakhalin, he relished a scene very similar to that which was to impress Frederick Pray a few years later. Eleanor recorded, "Fred just came tearing upstairs, for me to look out of the window—there were three whales in the harbor and it was such fun watching them blow" (27 April 1895 to Home).[7] In 1913, Fridtjof Nansen, the explorer, found the combination of sea and hills picturesque, comparing it to Naples.[8] Walks in central Vladivostok can be veritable feasts for the senses. One article is titled simply "Listening to the City," and a former sea captain describes his own lyrical connection thus: "You can hear the rhythms of time through bells and fog-horns from the ships, and if you touch the old brick walls, you can feel the warmth of past years."[9] Eleanor Pray, too, was inspired by the very sensuality of Vladivostok's sights and sounds, enjoying, for example, the bugle calls from the anchored ships at sunset (29 September 1895 to Home); pieces from Russian "grand opera" interpreted by a young man in the next building—"as long as the weather is warm enough to keep the windows open, I shall have the pleasure of it" (31 August 1929 to Sarah); and splashes of bright color against a lowering sky from "the blaring red of the boxes of strawberries being carried along the Svetlanskaia at the ends of poles on Chinese shoulders" (17 July 1926 to Dorothy). Eleanor regularly extolled the fantastic formations of the sunsets, as for example one fall afternoon in 1922 when, hurrying to a friend, she simply had to stop and absorb the vision: "To the West, over Tigrovaia [Tiger Hill], there was a thick, black smoke cloud, through which the sun shone, a dark red ball, with a reflection on the bay like that of a forest fire, cutting through the smoke. To the East, a full, round moon pale as silver was about the same distance above the horizon as the sun, and a little farther to the South the crosses of the cathedral stood out, [the] blue of the sky lighted by the sun" (5 November 1922 to Home).

Despite the grandeur and historical interest of Vladivostok, visitors have often proved unwilling to accept its sharp contrasts, recalling the residents' own complaints even at the beginning of the nineteenth century: the sea is everywhere, but the city has no municipal waterworks; the local physicians are good, but hospital care can be inept; the volunteer fire brigade uses fancy costumes but shows little speed or ability in its work.[10] The very idea of a city being a fortress alarmed many Westerners, who could find nothing positive in the fact: it was a "desolate" place, crushed by military strictures and far from civilization (1904), with "secrets hidden in the slopes of the hills" (1943).[11] And then there was the weather, not merely unpredictable, but seriously topsy-turvy, as an Australian businessman wrote in July 1913: "We are now past mid-Summer and have had no Summer yet. We have only seen the sun about five days at the most during the last two months or more; we have had rain rain rain rain fog fog fog fog and damn it all rain rain rain rain fog fog fog fog fog."[12] While Eleanor, too, complained about these phenomena, she found the inherent contradictions fascinating; to her, they were an energizing part of the Vladivostok package.

NATURAL BEAUTY, PICNICS, AND EXCURSIONS

For excellent reasons, Vladivostokians love to show their city and its stunning surroundings to newcomers. Soon after the Prays arrived in June 1894, the Smiths' close friends the Lindholms generously began issuing invitations to afternoon teas, tennis parties, and, best of all, Sunday outings on their boat, the *Siberia*. They went south to Russian Island, west and north into Amur Bay to Sedanka, and (for instance, in 1895, 1899, and 1901) east to the Lindholms' summer house at Nakhodka. These nature excursions with friends recurred to the very end of Eleanor Pray's Vladivostok life, always offering a heady infusion of well-being. Despite the frequently tumultuous forces of wind, snow, and rain, walking in Vladivostok invigorated her, and her determination to persevere through the weather disturbances came to powerfully symbolize both the hardship and the pleasures of her Russian life: "The wind was something awful and the bits of fine snow and sleet were like needles when one had to face it. I waited, without success, some fifteen minutes for a tram or a bus—and then started home on foot. The wind was behind me and I enjoyed every step" (13 December 1923 to Sarah). Even during Mrs. Pray's hardest Vladivostok years—as a widow from April 1923 on— she considered the colors and textures of the city a "tonic" (30 August 1927 to Sarah): "It makes me sick every time I think of [leaving]—saying goodbye to so much that I love and may never see again. The Amur Bay this morning, after the rain, is like a bit of Heaven on earth, blue as blue, with just a narrow bank of fleecy clouds on the Western horizon. The harbor is like a gray-green mirror—Shanghai with all its comfort has nothing like that to offer" (16 September 1930 to Clara).

24 June 1894 to Home
There are three Russian men-of-war in the harbor and last night at sunset we went out on the balcony to hear the naval band play the Russian national prayer as the colors were hauled down. It was a beautiful thing and I hope some time to get the music of it to send home.

20 May 1895 to Home
We started at six o'clock yesterday morning—Charlie and Sarah, Fred and I, with Cook and Thune along for servants. The *Siberia* stopped just off the Admiral's Pier and we went out to her in a *sampan* [small, low-lying boat]. On board were Mr. & Mrs. Lindholm, Tullie, Lolla and their *amah*, Mr. Igoni and Mr. Izakovich. Soon came Mr. & Mrs. Rasmussen, baby Axel, and two *amahs*. Then we were off. It was as beautiful a morning as one could ask for, as clear as a bell, and the sun was very warm, but we all wore our winter coats as it is always cold on the water this time of year. The *Siberia* was very clean and nice, the sailors all had nice new caps and uniforms and everything was as fine as could be. It was a little rough rounding the point out here, but otherwise very comfortable. How I did enjoy it! I sat quite still drinking in every bit of the air and scenery I possibly could, without speaking to anyone. The water was so blue and the air so clear and I couldn't take in half as much air as I should have liked. We reached Sedanka at nine o'clock. There is no settlement, simply a small river which winds in and out among the hills.[13] We went ashore in the *Siberia*'s boats and then went up the post road over a mile and turned into the

woods, where we found a delightful little camping-place beside the river. The gentlemen each took a bite of something and started off. We spread comforters on the ground to sit down on and then spread the food out and had a good substantial breakfast, with hot tea and coffee. In a little opening close on the water, Cook and Thune built a fire and hung the tea kettle, and then they built a small stove of stones preparatory to frying fish. They had a stump to wash dishes on, and that was the kitchen. About two *rods* [old English measure of distance, one rod equaling 5 1/2 yards] farther away into the woods was the dining-and-sitting-room and a couple of *rods* beyond that, the *amahs* fixed a nice bed for baby, and that was the bedroom. We strolled around and picked flowers and what a delight it was to be in the woods again. . . . About two o'clock the gentlemen sent a lot of trout down, and Cook built a charcoal fire in the stove to cook them over, so we had an impromptu dinner of fried potatoes and fried fish and all sorts of other good things. . . . When we reached [the seashore, going back], we found quite a stiff breeze blowing. The sailors brought the boat onshore for us and we started for the *Siberia* which was half a mile out. . . . We reached home about seven o'clock, tired out, but feeling wonderfully free and happy after a whole long day out-of-doors.

27 May 1895 to Aunt Anna
We left the Admiral's Pier at one o'clock yesterday afternoon. The party consisted of the Lindholms, Mr. & Mrs., Tullie, Lolla and Aina, Peter, Gori and Mania Unterberger, the Governor's children, with their governess, Miss Hirsch, Charlie, Sarah and I. . . . In less than an hour we landed on Russian Island, where Dr. and Mrs. Gustafsen met us on the beach. As soon as we reached the house we had some cake, cheese and coffee, and then we all started over the hills. We found very few flowers on the Eastern slope but on the Western slope for acres and acres it was one mass of lilies-of-the valley in full bloom. Positively you could not keep from walking on them. I picked all I could hold and everybody else ditto, and then I sighed because I could not take the whole hill home to Fred. You can imagine what a delicious scent the air had from such quantities of the sweet-smelling flowers. They grow wild in great profusion all over this part of Siberia, and now you can buy as many as you can hold, on the streets, for three cents or so.

2 July 1895 to Home
It is cold enough to freeze and I really wonder why we were foolish enough to take our double windows out. Fur coats and flannels would be none too

warm today. This is the most beastly climate I ever saw. In June and July when civilized places are having summer we are having nasty raw East winds and everything else that's disagreeable.

2 December 1895 to Home
Yesterday Fred, Sarah and I went for a long walk over the hills—we climbed the twin peaks at the upper end of the bay and it was a good stiff climb I can tell you. From the summit we could see the whole length of the Golden Horn, the [Egersheld] peninsular separating the Harbor Bay from the Big Bay, Russian Island, and the entrance to Novik Bay, and farther to the West, the whole extent of the Big Bay as far as the mouth of the Suifun River. Back of us were the hills, and in the valley we could see the Convict Settlement at First River. It was a magnificent view and we lingered on the peak as long as we could, but the wind began to freshen up so we turned toward home.

5 July 1898 to Home
After supper Mr. Clarkson came and at nine o'clock the evening was so lovely we took two *sampans* from the Admiral's Pier and were rowed up the bay. . . . There is a full moon and the water was like glass and it was delightful. The Chinese kept the boats moving but that was all, we were on the water nearly two hours.

15 January 1899 to Home
The coldest day of the season so far—it was twelve below this morning, and is, I think, even colder than that now. Isn't it strange, this particular week every year is the coldest of the whole winter. Everyone can remember it, because it is the week between New Year's and the Blessing of Waters.[14]

25 March 1899 to Home
This morning I walked up to the Lindholms and back directly after breakfast and I did enjoy it, because there was a cold East wind and a wet snow. [The icebreaker] *Duchy* was waltzing in the ice up by the dock, quite without difficulty, and in the course of the forenoon she "quilted" the whole bay and now the ice is floating out in huge chunks. This end of the bay is quite clear for the ice near the shore went out last night, taking with it a lot of frozen-in *sampans*, the Chinese owners of which jumped in and went too, and now they have managed to get their boats free of the ice, and are paddling back from Russian Island.

1 January 1910 to Home
Last night we had the biggest snow storm for eight years—over a foot fell, and as there was comparatively little wind and not very cold, there is magnificent sleighing and Dorothy does enjoy a spin up and down the Svetlanskaia—the horses simply can't go fast enough to suit her, and she is always wheedling her father to give her fifty kopeks so she and Nastia can have a drive.

26 March 1918 to Sarah
The storm kept on all night and isn't quite over yet—the streets are piled with snow and everything is coated with it. . . . I have never seen Vladivostok more beautiful and it was so nice to go out and breathe in double lungfuls of such clean air. I waddled down to Tkachenko's for some sweets and enjoyed every step of the way.

2 April 1922 to Clara
It is a glorious spring morning and only people who live near an ice-bound harbor can understand the joy of seeing the blue water glitter again.

CITY LANDMARKS AND MAN-MADE ATTRACTIONS

The hills rising around central Vladivostok invite the perception of the center as a vast stage. Urban "props" of the 1890s—the railway station and the Post and Telegraph Office, the Admiral's and the Governor's Houses—furnished this stage, and the everyday needs of its "players," the residents, were met in the stores of Kunst and Albers and Churin's, at the markets, and in the myriad specialty shops, pharmacies, cafés, and restaurants along the main streets and in the Chinese Quarter. Against this impressive backdrop, Vladivostok hummed with confidence. Parades moved along Svetlanskaia; the new establishment of higher education, the Eastern Institute, was officially opened with blessings in 1899; and historic Russian battles against foreign invaders, including Napoleon, were celebrated: "Today is the centenary of Borodino and there was a big review in the town, about forty thousand troops participating" (8 September 1912 to Home). For the bicentennial of the defeat over Sweden at Poltava, the commemoration showcased the dramatic element of special costumes: "A salute was fired from every battery of the fortress, and a big review of the troops was held at the race course, a few of the soldiers in each regiment being dressed in the uniforms of Peter the Great's time" (14 July 1909 to Home).

Not only historic personages but also contemporary artists graced Vladivostok's scene, and in 1899–1901 alone, Eleanor Pray watched many pleasing stage productions, for example, Gogol's play *The Inspector-General*; popular operas by Rossini, Bizet, and Verdi; *Faust* by Gounod, and concerts of Russian romances. For Mrs. Pray, living in Vladivostok meant not only admiring the city's natural beauty but also exploring its alleys and public places, in order to learn about Russian life and culture.

12 August 1894 to Home
[Mr. Lindholm has invited the Prays to a train excursion on the brand-new Ussuri Railway.] The railroad is very nicely built, and has cost a great deal of money. There seems to be no chance left for any kind of a wash-out. The banks on each side of the track, whether they go down or up, are paved in [a] diamond [pattern] and grass grows in the diamonds. The beds and sides of each small brook are paved for quite a distance each side of the track. They have as yet no first- or second-class cars, so we went in a third-class one and it was very comfortable and clean; it was divided into six compartments with two seats in each, and the passage-way along one side. The partitions between the seats went to within three feet of the roof, then there was an open space of about a foot, then a shelf above that, that reached each side of the partition. This space gave a lovely chance to peep over and reach the nose of the sleeper in the next seat with a branch!

14 October 1894 to Home
Sadie and I have been to the Lutheran Church this morning. . . . It is so small that it is more like a chapel than a church. The pastor himself looks after it, and always sees that the grounds are nicely kept, and that there are lovely plants and flowers in the church, to make up for the bare walls and wooden seats.[15]

19 December 1894 to Home
Yesterday after tea, Tullie, Lolla, Sarah, Fred and I went around to all the Chinese shops to see what they had for Christmas. I enjoy poking around in those small out-of-the-way places very much.

9 June 1895 to Home
The Governor General has just struck the town and we have been watching the parade from Sarah's windows ever since lunch. There was a continuous

line of soldiers from Gov. Unterberger's to the depot, more than a mile by the road. First came a Cossack rider and the chief-of-police, Petrov, both in gorgeous uniforms; they cleared the road from everything but the soldiers. Then came a beautiful carriage drawn by a troika of beautiful gray horses, with harness glittering with blue and silver. The driver wore a black velvet coat with blue sleeves. In it were Gov. Unterberger in his full gray uniform with red sash, and the Governor General in blue uniform.[16] Then followed the carriages containing the town officials, etc., in full uniform. As the G. G. passed, each company saluted and after he reached the Gov.'s House they began to sing. I like very much to hear the soldiers sing, as they nearly always do when they march.

30 April 1900 to Sarah
Ted took Mr. Merritt to the Moscow [Hotel] this noon and arranged for him to have his meals there. He has to pay thirty-five rubles a month and Ted says everything there was immaculate. If that were my opinion, it wouldn't go for much, but you will understand that Ted knows an immaculate thing when he sees it. Mr. Merritt said the food was very good indeed.

9 February 1901 to Home
Last evening we went to the opera, as guests of Mr. Taylor, to hear *Il Trovatore*. Mr. Clarkson was also of the party, and we had the lower box opposite that of the Governor. The opera began more than half an hour late the reason of which was that they were waiting for the Governor's party which included General Linevich, the commander of all the Russian forces in the Orient, who has just returned from Peking.[17] A clash from the orchestra heralded his arrival and everybody in the house arose to greet him, a compliment which he acknowledged with a bow and a military salute. It was something worth seeing though of course the whole thing was over in a few seconds.

19 June 1907 to Sarah
Where do you suppose we went last evening? To hear Mikhailova and Labinskii! It seemed too absolutely good to be true that they should come all the way out here from Petersburg though it has been told here for three months. But they actually came and are booked for two concerts, one last night and one tonight and the town gave them a royal welcome I can tell you. The house was packed and they got such applause that they sang three and even four encores to each song.[18]

22 January 1909 to Clara
Sunday [January 24] the new Lutheran church is to be dedicated. We are to
gather in the old church, where a short farewell service will be held, then to
march in a body across the garden to the new church, where the dedication
will take place. The new church is of brick and is a very pretty one, making a
big addition to that end of the town.

15 November 1910 to Aunt Anna
Today Vladivostok is celebrating its fiftieth birthday[19] and there has been a
mass in the Cathedral, a big parade of the troops and fire companies, and this
evening some of the largest stores are illuminated. We took Dorothy out to
see it and she found it very nice indeed.

27 October 1920 to Aunt Anna
There was a terrible railway accident ten days ago, near Pogranichnaia [Sta-
tion], when . . . two heavy, mixed passenger and freight trains collided with
such force that one lot of wagons jumped clean over those of the other train.
It was on a heavy down-grade, the train coming up had two locomotives and
the engineer, seeing the danger, stopped and began to back to lessen the force
of the inevitable collision. The other train, both engineer and fireman dead
drunk, was going down-grade at eighty miles an hour so the crash can be
imagined. It was shortly before dawn when most of the passengers were
asleep, and fires broke out at once so there was no chance for them to save
themselves. . . . Most of Dolin's old and well-known theatrical troupe was on
board and all but four were killed. There was a big funeral here yesterday and
five coffins, carrying the bones of fourteen people of the troupe, were buried.
Mr. Merriam, coming through from Harbin on the first train to pass after
the line was cleared, said absolutely nothing remained of the cars but twisted
iron work.

STREET VIGNETTES AND HUMAN INTERACTION

On 16 February 1929, Eleanor Pray took in Verdi's opera *Rigoletto* from the
fourth row of the balcony at the main theater on Svetlanskaia. She liked the
performance, but better yet were the intermissions: "I amused myself listening to snatches of conversation around me—nearly all of which were not on
the subject of music or acting, but of the staff of life" (17 February 1929 to
Home). This "staff of life" was Vladivostok's gift to Mrs. Pray: situational

glimpses as precious as bread and as varied as the faces of humanity. Like photographic stills, the bits of conversation that she overheard on streets and in train cars created an urban mosaic of rare power. Showing the drama of human life directly performed on the city's "stage," they are poignant, heartwarming, and often amusing.

27 January 1895 to William

Yesterday, just as the *Kostroma* was starting, Mr. [Charles] Smith thought of a letter he ought to write, so he wrote it as quickly as possible, and sent for a carriage to chase the steamer down the harbor. Fred and I went with it, and when we left the house, the ship was nearly half a mile off, but going very slowly indeed on account of the narrow channel and the solid ice on each side. We drove onto the ice at the foot of the hill and didn't we fly! We caught up with the ship when she was off Goldobin Point and I sat in the sledge while Fred went to mail the letter. He had tied it securely to a long cord and tied a bit of lead on the other end; he ran beside the steamer and called until he attracted the attention of a sailor, who stood near the rail to catch the letter. The first time he threw, the cord got caught on his buttons and only went a few feet, but the next time he came pretty near throwing it over the main mast, so the letter was quickly drawn on board.

6 March 1895 to Home

Now [that] it is Lent, we see constantly battalions of soldiers coming across the bay to church. Each company has to come to church morning and evening for three successive days, before receiving communion. The soldiers on the farther batteries are hurrying up matters, for if they wait until the ice is cut, they will have to march five miles each way, and across the ice it is not more than a mile. They all come to confession during Lent and it must make things lively for the priests when there are so many thousands of soldiers to be pardoned for a year's sin each.

29 November 1895 to Home

Everybody here is laughing over a little episode that took place last Sunday. There is a small merchant here named Shkolnikov, a widower upwards of sixty, and his daughter and her husband, Mr. and Mrs. Biurgen, live with him. Mr. Sh. took it into his head to marry again, and his wedding was set for last Sunday afternoon and he did not tell his daughter of his plans until the last moment. Well, the joke was, when the ceremony was over and Sh.

took his wife home, Madame, the bride, found herself grandmother to Mrs. Biurgen's small daughter, who was born while the ceremony at the Cathedral was taking place. They say the bride was disgusted for she had not reckoned on being a grandmother. Shkolnikov's friends, of course, are joking him unmercifully about it.

5 December 1899 to Sarah
I'd have given anything to have got a snap-shot at something I saw this afternoon. Evidently an *izvozchik* [coachman] was drunk and a policeman had taken him in charge, put him on the seat of his own carriage, sat flat down on him and drove off, the *izvozchik* arguing meanwhile with all his might. I met them near Terentiev's, and Mrs. Hansen met them near the church, and she said the driver was still arguing. Evidently the policeman was a good driver for he managed both horses and man.

9 January 1900 to Sarah
Last night there was a fire out in *Slobodka* and I had an opportunity to see how the alarm was given to the volunteers. I heard the fire department go out, and about five minutes after, someone leisurely climbed the stairs to Fernsicht and announced in a carefully modulated voice, *Feuer!* adding as an afterthought *Pozhar!*[20] . . . In about the length of time it would take to change a suit of clothes, give the brass helmet a rub or two and blacken the boots, the volunteers began to come out and they didn't hurry either. What happened to the house meanwhile, we have not yet heard!

10 January 1900 to Sarah
Doctor Birk came yesterday and gave me a full account of the fire which did me more good than any medicine I've had so far. It was a *godown* [storehouse] beside his stable and had in it goods to the amount of eighteen thousand rubles, belonging to the man who rents the lower part of his house. Of course everything was destroyed. In the middle of the excitement a very pompous policeman came up to Dr. Birk, carefully saluted, and said, "Your Excellency, I have to inform you that the building next your stable is burning." "Is it?" said Doctor, "I've known that for an hour!" Then finally they concluded to take Doctor's horses out of the stable and either a fireman or a policeman was detailed to help him. Doctor put a bag over the head of the first horse and led him out without any trouble. The man put a bag over the

head of the second one, then took the horn that hung at his side and gave two long toots. As a natural result the horse stood straight up in the air and then the idiot gave two more toots presumably to bring him down! Of course the horse refused to budge an inch and they had an awful time getting him out. Mrs. Hansen, who was here at the time, and I laughed till we cried to see Doctor act out the performance.

5 March 1901 to Home
How little we can tell what is before us—at the Lindholms' silver wedding, ten days ago, Mr. Shulyngin sat opposite me at table, a strong healthy man, just in the prime of life—ten minutes ago I watched his funeral pass in the street below us. He is a well-known man in town and his death, from congestion of the lungs, has been a great shock to everybody.

19 March 1901 to Home
We passed a very pleasant evening with the Hansens, but of course it was more or less shadowed, unavoidably, by talking over the horrible, horrible thing which happened the night before, when Gen. Keller, the head of the railway, was burned to death in his private [rail] car between here and Nikolsk. He left here at midnight, quite alone, and early in the morning, just before reaching Nikolsk, his car was discovered to be in flames and as yet we have heard nothing of the details. He was not more than forty and received the rank of Major General some few months ago on account of his services guarding and repairing the railway at Tientsin during the [Boxer] trouble. . . . At the Lindholms' silver wedding, less than a month ago, Gen. Keller, Col. Chernoknizhnikov and Mr. Shulyngin sat opposite me at dinner, and now two of the three are dead. If I were Col. Chernoknizhnikov, I should tremble literally for fear my turn would come next. I remember so well how each of the three drank to my health and touched glasses with me when the health of the ladies was proposed that evening.

16 November 1903 to Home
A week ago Sunday, while Sarah, Mr. Zellers and I were walking, I found a horseshoe—the first in my life and I was very proud of it, so the next day, when I went with Dr. Stein, I hoped to find another, but instead of that lost the road (and my reputation as a guide also) and got quite frightened, for we did not get home till after dark. Wednesday I went with him again and what

do you think we found—nothing more or less than a dead Chinaman sewn up in a sack and lying close beside the road! That is a happy custom the Chinese here have of throwing out their dead bodies to save burial expenses. On our way back we met a policeman, two Russians and a cart to take the body away so someone had evidently reported it. . . . Now Ted laughs at me and asks what I am going to find next time.

23 February 1908 to Sarah
Day before yesterday . . . Wanda [Newhard] took me for a long [carriage] drive over my beloved haunts—in a way I enjoyed it, and came back feeling like a new person, but it is sad to see how everything that was pretty and restful has been spoiled. There is not a tree, either on the hills or the whole length of the valley road, and where we took our long delightful walks are now hundreds and hundreds of cottages.

8 August 1915 to Home
Being too thrifty to pay the higher priced post-train ticket I took a third class as I often do but the time was not lucky, as there were only four wagons of that class on the train and they were packed full. I had two large square parcels so, with these for a seat, I established myself on the platform of a car filled up with Chinese, and in the next car were twenty-five soldiers . . . evidently going off to war. One of them looked so forlorn, I called a *baba* [woman] who was peddling along the platform, and bought two packets of cigarettes from her, giving one to him and one to another one, and soon after, I heard the other one say a few words in English, evidently, just to show off a bit. "Go ahead, Johnny—all right. Do you verstehen?" so I asked him where he learned English, and he told me that he had been two years in America. . . . [H]ow I enjoyed myself—the soldiers were all men between twenty and thirty—nice, sturdy lads, good-natured and full of fun. It made one sick to think of what probably awaited them. I told them what our papers and the English ones were saying of the bravery of the Russian soldiers, which of course pleased them. . . . At Sedanka we passed a trainload of raw recruits, probably coming into Vladivostok to be whacked into shape and they were sitting in box cars, singing at the top of their voices. My soldiers shouted to them as we passed to ask what province they came from, and they shouted back that they were from the Amur region—*Amurtsy* they called themselves—youngsters, probably, but it was too dark to see much. . . . I wouldn't have missed that trip for anything.

10 December 1916 to Sarah

Last Monday a woman was instantly killed, while walking along Svetlans-kaia, not far from [the store] Treugolnik, by a piece of stucco from a balcony of the second story falling on her head. Was that not fate? Now all those balconies are being inspected and several of them pulled down.

27 December 1917 to Sarah

Arrived back in town [by train from the country], I was too tired to walk home so I sat in a tram for over an hour, waiting for the current. As usual, I amused myself very well indeed. After the first class passengers . . . [gave] up in disgust and climbed out, I became aware of the fact that something inter-esting was going on in the second class, so I got as near the dividing door as possible. . . . The second class was crowded and a man sitting in a corner was making a speech but there were so many others lipping in that the effect of the whole was something like the quartet from *Rigoletto*, this speechmaker being the accompaniment for he didn't once stop to take breath, and rarely either raised or lowered his voice. Evidently there were bolsheviks [members of, or sympathizers with, the communist party] and mensheviks [opponents of bolshevik ideas; social democrats] and Heaven only knows what else and I had vain hopes of their coming to blows, but no such luck. . . . The car was practically dark, excepting for the street lights, and the frost on the windows was something wonderful.

5 January 1918 to Sarah

Mrs. Reuben [Smith] had her pocket picked in a tram yesterday—in her purse were coupons for a hundred and thirty rubles, and a twenty-ruble bill besides. This morning she went to the bank to hand in the bond numbers and there, at the window, stood a young man trying to cash them! He was promptly arrested and the coupons returned to her. That was one chance in a thousand.

9 February 1918 to Sarah

The other night there was a round-up at a boarding house on Pervaia Mor-skaia and some *moshenniki* [swindlers] broke through the line and ran the militia after them, some toward Egersheld and some down the hill to the sta-tion, and both parties were shooting. I don't think you know Mr. Barrett—he is a tall, elderly Englishman, with plaid trousers and a monocle who looks exactly as if he had stepped out of *Puck*—altogether a quaint character, and, being a little round-shouldered he carries his head exactly like a hen about to pick up something. He came around the corner by the Grand Hotel just in time to meet this procession, and promptly flattened himself against the wall to diminish the chances of stopping a bullet, but he couldn't flatten his head back. The last militiaman caught sight of him and went for him, thinking he was one of the robbers, but Barrett was the quicker of the two: in a flash he had covered the militiaman with his revolver and had politely said in his funny cracked voice, "One step nearer and I'll blow your damned head off." This was enough for the militiaman and he turned back to join the pursuit, leaving Mr. Barrett to continue his way home unmolested. It is a pity that the man, who probably grasped Mr. Barrett's meaning, couldn't have understood English well enough to appreciate the purity of the diction.

12 February 1918 to Sarah
Do you remember the time you and I went to the *Kaznachei* [treasury] to pay seventy-five kopeks on your passport and what a dull time we had during the long wait there? Now one is simply racking one's brain for an excuse to go there because there are most exciting scenes every day. Newhard-san was telling us of one he was let in for this morning and which he enjoyed more than anything he had seen for years. It seems an order has gone forth from these —— (make it as sulphurous as you choose)[21] that pensions must be paid in Khabarovsk, which is one way of robbing widows and orphans, for who is going to pay fifty rubles' [train] fare each month to draw forty rubles or less pension? One lady, evidently an officer's wife, had come to draw hers and, being told of this new crazy or rather scoundrelly regulation, high words ensued and when her voice would go no higher, she snatched off one of her overshoes and flung it at the head of the commissar. It hit someone else however, who flung it back at her, but hit instead a lady who had accompanied her and who promptly fainted! Of course there was a great hubbub and the arrest of the lady of the galoshes was demanded, but by this time she, in her turn, was in hysterics and some level-head suggested that she was not responsible for what she did and that it would be wiser to give her a glass of cold water than to arrest her, which was done. She took the water in at a gulp, turned and, like a Chinese laundry-man, "exploded her face" [i.e., screamed and yelled, perhaps even spat water] over the lady who had fainted.

1 May 1918 to Sarah
A day or two ago some of the fire brigade removed the eagles from the Nevelskoi Monument and the Nikolai Arch.[22] When, after some difficulty, the

eagles fell from the arch onto the pavement, the workman who had accomplished it acknowledged the "hurrah" of the bystanders by raising his cap and crossing himself three times—and it is more than likely, in his superstitious ear, he prayed "God forgive me."

25 October 1920 to Aunt Anna
A horrible thing happened at the foot of our lane Friday [22 October] morning, about eleven o'clock—Mrs. Startseva, a newly married young woman, was walking down town and the man she had been engaged to but threw over for Alexander Startsev about a month ago, shot her from behind and then shot himself; he died instantly but she lived for a few minutes; there was a horrible pool of blood there even when we went down the stairs at four o'clock.

11 June 1922 to Sarah
It was hot and uncomfortable on the train but I amused myself very well knitting and listening to six little hooligans (probably beating their way) making each other's acquaintance, or rather sizing each other up. . . . We had five sacks of things and I deemed it wise to sit on them as they were in the corner close to the wide-open door. Just as we entered the tunnel, one young hooligan clinging to the door rail lost his hat, which accident gave him a certain distinction, and also furnished the lot of them with a lively topic of conversation till we came to Second River, the destination of the hatless one, who spent the time telling how he would recover his lost cap if he saw it on the head of any Chinese or Korean. After his departure the others began to talk of various things and there was great excitement when it became known that among them were an eight-year-old uncle and a nine-year-old nephew. The uncle was greeted with a cheer of derision and the query "What kind of an uncle are you?" "Only eight and your nephew nine, fie!" "He lies," cried the offended uncle, "he's only seven," but his voice showed where truth lay, so no one took his refutation seriously. The nephew, who was certainly the older, gave him a look which promised a lot when they were in a less dangerous place than the door of a moving train.

CHAPTER 4

Historic Names

FROM ITS VERY BEGINNINGS, VLADIVOSTOK HAS HOSTED NUMEROUS
prominent visitors. Before the Trans-Siberian Railway functioned regularly
in the late 1890s,[1] transport from Saint Petersburg and Moscow to East Siberia, while not impossible, was achieved in three complicated ways. One
could travel eastward along the old prisoners' track and the rivers of southern Siberia; westward and south by ship from the Baltic Sea, around Europe
and Africa (or, from 1869, through the Suez Canal), then east across the
Indian Ocean and northward around Southeast Asia; or by ship due west
over the Atlantic Ocean, then by train and ship across the United States and
the Pacific. To those living in the Russian capitals, Vladivostok seemed situated in another world.

But to those undertaking the immense journey, the Far East offered alluring prospects. East Siberia's vast natural resources beckoned, and the new
telegraph and steamer lines—including the Volunteer Fleet, which from 1879
offered regular runs between Vladivostok and Odessa—encouraged both
Russian and foreign entrepreneurs to venture into the region. Thus aided by
modern communications, Vladivostok was becoming the hub of diverse
projects with a corresponding enhancement of its status: appointed the home
of the Siberian Flotilla in 1873, it was upgraded to the status of city in 1880,
and to fortress in 1889.

Prominent entrepreneurs settled in Vladivostok, began to develop additional resources for the city, and also built their own fortunes, for example,
in shipping (Iulii Bryner), retail commerce (Gustav Kunst, Gustav Albers,
Adolph Dattan), and the navy yard, with its wharves and dry dock (Otto

Lindholm). Eleanor Pray mentions Governor-General Chichagov's proposal to beautify the messy streets: "He called a meeting [of] the principal merchants and asked them to undertake the contract, and it was awarded as follows: from Aleutskaia [Street] to the railroad crossing, Skidelskii; from the crossing to Toong Lee's, Langelütje; from Toong Lee's to Startsev's, Dattan; in front of Startsev's, Suvorov; and then Dattan as far as the admiral's, I think. Naturally there will be a sharp competition as to the quality of the work and . . . it would be safe to bet on Mr. Dattan's part" (24 April 1900 to Sarah).

Other historic personages came just to visit, look around, and move on. Their appearances amounted to a form of guest roles on a provincial stage, but in a theater providing the appropriate props and a keen audience. Mrs. Pray enjoyed a view, live, from the gallery, of one leading actor: "Yesterday the tea party was with Mrs. Rasmussen, and we spent a very pleasant afternoon on her veranda which overlooks the Aleutskaia. We saw the Bourbon prince, who is, I believe, a son of Don Carlos, and who is one of Alekseev's suite.[2] He had on such an amazing pair of red trousers that I forgot to look at the man himself. Consequently I have no idea what a Spanish Prince looks like, but I should recognize those trousers among a thousand" (28 August 1904 to Clara). Supported by city leaders committed to trade, and twelve foreign (including honorary) consulates by mid-1909,[3] both visitors and residents with political, military, and mercantile connections explored new opportunities in Vladivostok. A Republican to the core, Eleanor Pray had never assumed that her life would include royalty, and she was particularly impressed with the humble demeanor of a relation of Prince Petr A. Kropotkin, the anarchist: "I wonder what you at home would think of an advertisement there was in the paper this morning to the effect that Prince L. A. Kropotkin, a repairing mechanic, was ready to do anything in his line, etc., etc. This is a prince of a very old and high Russian family. Fred knows him and his work, but I never happened to come across his ad before" (24 January 1899 to Home). Instead of being off the beaten track, Vladivostok was a vibrant center in the Far East.

MAGNIFICENT SHIPS

In the 1890s and early 1900s, the impressive warships of Russia's Pacific Fleet regularly visited the Bay of the Golden Horn, immeasurably exalting "the season" with their beautiful lines and nattily attired officers. Focusing on entertainment along with their maneuvers, these summer guests were considered "better" than those of the army, and their presence at tennis parties, elegant picnics, and sumptuous balls added substantial glamour to Vladivostok's high society.

Imbibing this hospitable, opulent atmosphere, Eleanor was exhilarated, as well as initially anxious: "Life here is very easy and very gay it seems to me, but as I am a 'down Easter' I have never seen much of society" (22 July 1894 to Cousin Clara). Her rural background had not prepared her for the big world, but guided by the Lindholms and her own inquisitive mind, she entered it relatively easily. She grew fascinated with the cruisers of the Vladivostok Squadron—the *Bogatyr*, *Gromoboi*, and *Rurik*, often accompanied by the *Russia*—and made friends with several officers on the *Gromoboi*. She loved the sound of the cannon salutes from one ship to another that greeted official visitors, Sarah explaining, "We have an Italian gun-boat here with a Prince on board and yesterday some of the Russian ships came; two more are expected today. . . . There was a lot of saluting yesterday and Roxy was in her element. She calls it gunpowder politeness." Sarah then adds that Vladivostok's charm increases with these ships and the festive atmosphere that they bring: "It makes a great difference when the fleet are [sic] here. You can already hear the difference in the streets. The carriages go faster and oftener, and there seems to be a general commotion all around" (14 July 1895 from Sarah to Mildred).

17 July 1894 to Home
We went to the Peter and Paul ball . . . in a carriage to the Admiral's Pier, where a steam launch was waiting to take us on board the flagship *Admiral Nakhimov*. We were received by Captain Lavrov and Admiral Tyrtov. Well—one could never imagine that the ship was built for bloody war, for it was decorated until it looked more like a palace than anything else. The afterdeck was covered with three awnings so no rain could possibly get in. This was the space used for dancing. . . . It was shaped like a tent, and in the apex of the tent was a large mass of green branches, concealed in which were about fifty small incandescent lights. The tent itself was formed of alternate stripes, blue and white. Starting at this cluster of lights and reaching to the edges of the tent in every direction were heavy festoons of green leaves, and, at intervals of about three feet, incandescent lights with paper shades of different colors that nearly covered them. They looked like so many flowers among the green.

A platform was built up over the big guns, and the sailors' folded hammocks formed very comfortable lounges all around it. It was all covered with rugs and draperies, so you would never mistrust what you were sitting on. This platform was about eight feet above the deck, so it was a nice place to watch the dancing. . . . Below-stairs the ship was beautifully decorated. A garden about 40 × 40 was arranged with rocks and bushes and ferns and two beautiful fountains. How they could make such a wild, cool-looking place on ship I cannot tell. . . . Back on the platform . . . was the Russian double-headed eagle made of the sailors' knives and revolvers. It was so nicely put together that you would look a long time before you noticed how it was made.

18 August 1894 to Cousin Clara
They had torpedo practice in the harbor Wednesday night and such fun as it was. Of course, it was all play but it was very exciting. We could see it all from the upper veranda. Two small torpedo boats were trying to approach the *Kornilov* and the men on the *Kornilov* were hunting for them with their two electric search lights. The boats would dodge hither and thither and when the search light fell on them, the big guns would blaze away at them, but before the smoke cleared away the torpedo boat would be out of sight. Once it stole up under the very bows of the *Kornilov* before it was discovered, and then such a blazing as there was, Gatling guns and all.[4]

19 August 1894 to Home
The French admiral's ship [the *Bayard*] came in this morning at sunrise. I heard the sunrise gun from the guard ship and Fred said, "Here comes the Frenchman." . . . It came slowly on until it came to an anchorage near the *Kornilov* and directly in front of us. . . . At eight o'clock, [the French admiral] made his bow to the battery with twenty-one guns that echoed and re-echoed from the hills like a perfect pandemonium. The battery returned the salute with twenty-one more guns. Then the Frenchman saluted the admiral on board the *Nakhimov* with fifteen guns, and of course the *Nakhimov* answered with fifteen more. Then simultaneously the French ran up their flag aft, their band playing the "Marseillaise," and the Russians ran up their flag, their band playing "God save the Tsar." Then the French ran a Russian flag . . . and the band played "God save the Tsar," and at the same time the Russian ships all ran up the French flag and played [the] "Marseillaise." Then there was a cessation of politeness for a while and I had some breakfast.

During his trip around the world in 1890–91, then Tsesarevich Nikolai Alexandrovich Romanov reentered his native country from Japan by way of Vladivostok.[5] In early July 1891, he placed the founding stone for the soon-to-be-admired railway station, and was honored with the dedication of the Nikolai Triumphal Arch in the Admiral's Garden. From Vladivostok, the Tsesarevich traveled north to Khabarovsk, where he continued westward on the Amur River. Among the staff on the river trip was captain Nikolai Merkulov, of the Amur Steamship Company, who was invited to engage in conversation with Nikolai Alexandrovich. The latter wished to learn about East Siberia's salmon fishing and whaling, as well as about the lives of the sailors. In gratitude for a safe trip, he gave Merkulov a ring studded with emeralds and diamonds.[6]

Alexander III's unexpected death in 1894—from kidney disease at age forty-nine—plunged his eldest son into a position for which he was ill prepared. The precipitous change at Russia's helm alarmed both the participants and the onlookers, and was considered a bad omen for the future. Nikolai II was never to visit Vladivostok again, but his and the Imperial family's feast days were faithfully celebrated, until the February Revolution of 1917 erased the Romanov glory. Vladivostok's festivities in May 1896 for the coronation of Nikolai and Alexandra were memorialized by Eleanor Pray with an article published in the United States, and by a friend of the family with two impressive photos of the decorated city.

While not to be compared with Moscow's dazzling coronation week, Vladivostok's arrangements were grand, both sites using electric lights to impress the spectators. A biography of the empress describes the beguiling finale of Coronation Day, 26 May, in Moscow: "Alexandra was handed a large bouquet of roses on a silver tray; when she picked up the flowers, she set off a hidden switch which sent a signal to the Moscow Power Station. At once, thousands of tiny electric lights all across the city—lining streets, surrounding windows and doorways, creeping across rooftops and the onion domes of churches, sparkling in the spring foliage of the trees—flickered on."[7]

21 October 1894 to Home
Dr. Liepke took tea with us Friday [19 October] and he says the Emperor is in a very critical condition with very little hope of his recovery. . . . There were

special services on board all the ships Friday, and, today in the Greek Church,[8] prayers for his recovery. His name is on every lip and it seems here like those months while our [President] Garfield lay at the point of death. There is the same anxiety, and the same eagerness for telegrams of the Emperor's condition, which come two or three times a day.

2 November 1894 to Eleanor's Mother
At ten this morning the *Nakhimov, Kornilov, Zabiiaka* and the *Razboinik* each fired the Imperial salute of 101 guns and the spars on all the warships were tilted, so from the front they look like great X's. At noon there was another salute, which I think must have been for the new Emperor. "The King is dead, long live the King." You probably knew this at home as soon we did here. The hearts of the people are all turning toward their widowed Empress in her bereavement; it is a well-known fact that the Emperor and Empress were just such a devoted couple as Prince Albert and Queen Victoria.[9]

26 November 1894 to Home
Only three weeks ago Friday that the Emperor died, and then it was bang, bang, bang, flags at half mast and faces as lugubrious as possible—the next two days, it was bang, bang, bang for the new Emperor. Then everything went back to half mast again, for two weeks—and today it is bang, bang, bang, and the whole city painted red for the new Empress, for today the Emperor Nikolai and Princess Alix of Hesse are married. It is only a week ago today that Emperor Alexander was buried, and it strikes me that their wedding and funeral come very near overlapping.[10] The telegram announcing that the wedding was to take place reached here only yesterday. One member of the city government forgot and flew his flag at half mast in celebration of the wedding, much to the amusement of everyone who saw it.

2 November 1895 to Home
This is a big holiday, everybody has a flag up and the ships are decorated from stern to stern, and there has been a salute which satisfied even me. There was the royal salute of one hundred and one guns from each the *Nikolai, Kornilov, Nakhimov, Monomakh, Ostrazhnyi*[?], *Kreiser,* and the fortress, in all 707 guns and some of them very heavy. It is a year today since Emperor Nikolai took his seat, and yesterday all the officers shed the crepe bands which they have worn on their arm a year for Alexander III.

10 November 1895 to Aunt Anna
Everybody who can is leaving here for Europe so as to be in Moscow in May
for the Tsar's coronation. The Governor and his family, the Mayor and the
Head of Police are among the magnates who have left on the last two or three
steamers.

8 May 1896 to Cousin Clara
All we are thinking about now are the festivities of the approaching coronation, less than three weeks away. There is to be a grand illumination here,
balls, afternoon dances, and I don't know what all. Besides the entire Russo-
Asiatic squadron, there will be a great many foreign men-of-war here, and it
does my soul good to think what a lot of gunpowder will be used on the great
day.

15 May 1896 to Cousin Clara
The Tsar's birthday is next Monday and the festivities will begin then. They
have cleaned the Public Garden and laid out some flower beds in it.

3 June 1896 [from Eleanor's article]:[11]
[These] were days long to be remembered in Vladivostok. Every house in
town, large or small, was gaily decorated with flags and festooned with evergreen and bunting. Twenty thousand flags, at the very least, were flying on
those three days. At several points along the main street, arches covered with
bunting and evergreen and ornamented with flags were erected. The most
noticeable of these was the one built by the Japanese in front of their consulate, which was about forty feet in height. It was supported by four octagonal
pillars which were covered with closely clipped evergreen branches; sus-
pended between the cross-bar and the keystone were the letters N. A. (Niko-
lai-Alexandra), surmounted by a crown. At a short distance these letters
looked like burnished gold, but when close to the arch we discovered that
they were made from small oranges nailed to strips of wood. Every ship in
the harbor, man-of-war or merchantman, was gaily dressed with flags, and
from some of them were displays of fireworks. But as beautiful as were the
decorations, the illuminations far outshone them. Vladivostok is peculiarly
well situated for anything of this kind, as the harbor is nearly surrounded by
hills, so that, seen from the bay, the illuminations appeared to be in terraces.
Each side of the main street, for more than one and a half miles, was festooned with Japanese lanterns, of which more than fifty thousand were in

use. The houses and business blocks had various fanciful arrangements of colored lanterns, and everywhere was the monogram, "N. A." Large bonfires of tar barrels were lighted on ten of the surrounding hills, and the harbor was gay with colored lights. Each Russian man-of-war had the masts and spars outlined in incandescent lights, and each also had the monogram and crown arranged with lights of different colors to represent jewels. . . . Foremost among the shore illuminations were the house and grounds of Admiral Engelm, the commander of the port. Each line of the house was traced with incandescent lights, and on the water front was a huge monogram. The multitudinous paths of the extensive gardens were edged on both sides with colored glass lanterns, which, seen through the trees, gave to the whole the aspect of a fairyland. About ten thousand lights were used in these grounds alone. A naval band, stationed near the house, played the various national airs of Russia, and once in a while we were greeted by the familiar strains of "Hail, Columbia, Happy Land!"[12] . . . Across the bay, on the side of a hill, lanterns were placed to trace the words "God Save the Tsar."

LINDHOLM CONNECTIONS

Thanks to Otto Lindholm's astute business sense, his family attained an exalted position in Vladivostok society, leading a comfortable life that sparkled with amenities unimaginable for most people around them. The Lindholms' mansion on Shefnerovskaia Street featured an impressive *salle* or ballroom with potted palms, a grand piano, and a large fireplace; a "Red Drawing-Room" where one might take tea under portraits of the emperor and empress; and flower gardens, a tennis court, and the private "Lindholm Pier" on the shore of the Golden Horn.[13] The family regularly visited Japan, other parts of Asia, and Europe, and, like the Romanov grand duchesses, the Lindholm daughters kept deer for pets; spoke Russian, English, and German; and owned fabulous gowns and jewelry. The Lindholms met the Tsesarevich on his visit to Vladivostok in 1891, and they attended the 1896 coronation in Moscow. In January 1907, Aina married Lieutenant Alexander Butakov, one of the officers on the tsar's yacht, the *Standart,* and thus became a member of the imperial circle.

Such privileged beginnings do not ensure unblemished happiness. In the workers' riots of November 1905, which ravaged much of central Vladivostok, the home of the Lindholms was severely damaged.[14] The rebuilding took several years, and meanwhile the family rented an apartment in "Sollogub's

House" on Pushkin Street by the cathedral. From here they watched the celebration of the Romanov tercentenary in 1913, the last imperial show of tired brilliance before Europe fell apart, and the following year, the family was struck by a numbing double blow. Within just two days, Otto Lindholm, the patriarch, and Aina's husband, nicknamed Sashik, died. The tsar himself grieved over Lieutenant Butakov's death in a private letter to the empress on 15/28 December 1914, announcing that "our dear Butakov had been killed—it is too sad, that kind good man, loved by all. How wretched his little wife will be, she who is only one bit of nerves already. Another one of our yacht friends gone already, how many more will this terrible war yet claim!"[15]

6 March 1913 to Home
We are just home from seeing the sights and I want to tell you about the day before I go to bed. Three hundred years ago today Mikhail Fedorovich Romanov was elected Tsar of Russia, and today all over the Empire they are celebrating the tercentenary of the House of Romanov. . . . As all traffic on the Svetlanskaia ceased from ten o'clock in the morning and one could not get through the lines without a special permit, we turned out at half past nine and went up to the Lindholms' which is just opposite the Cathedral, and from there we could see the regiments as they came up, the standard bearers all going into the Cathedral close, and the regiments remaining below in the Svetlanskaia. A nasty raw wind came up, and we nearly froze to the marrow, watching the affair, and after all, it wasn't up to much—not nearly what it could have been had it been better arranged. The big shops and the houses of the officials were decorated, and in the evening there was a grand illumination.

29 December 1914 to Home
[9.30 AM] This terrible war—it has come home to us now as the news came last night that Sashik Butakov, Aina's husband, had been killed [27 December] in some of the fighting around Warsaw—such a clean, honorable, good-hearted man, of a type all too rare in the service. Poor little Aina, left a widow after less than eight years of married life. He was a naval officer and from being *revizor* [inspector] on the Tsar's yacht had been promoted to chief officer on the Dowager Empress's yacht. Of course yachts don't go to war, so when the call came, he volunteered in the infantry and this is the lamentable result. We can think of nothing this morning but his invalid mother, Aina, and her little six-year-old son. Sashik had been brought up at court as his mother was a lady-in-waiting, and since he came back from the East, the Tsar

has taken a great fancy to him and often had him in to spend the evening, when at the palace in the Crimea.

[Later] Mr. Lindholm is lying at the point of death, and Mrs. Lindholm is holding him back by the sheer strength of her love for him—at least, so it seems to me. Tullie and I decided not to tell her of the telegram [about Sashik] because the news of Aina's grief would upset her terribly.

31 December 1914 to Home
Mr. Lindholm died Tuesday noon [29 December] at quarter to one—very peacefully, and Sarah closed his eyes. Only then did they tell Mrs. Lindholm of Sashik's death and like the wonderful mother she is, she forgot herself for the moment and thought only of Aina's young, hopeless grief. They have been married almost thirty-nine years and have had such a happy life, the only real grief being that their eldest child, a son, was still-born, and the loss of a little two-year-old girl, between Lolla and Aina—over thirty years ago. Sunday morning about four o'clock, Mr. Lindholm stretched out his arms to her and pressed her to his breast, although he could say nothing, and we all think that it was his goodbye and that he knew then that he was going. Ted and Mr. Walldén, his life-long friend and for many years business partner, came at once and helped lay him out.

1 January 1915 to Home
Mr. Lindholm's funeral was yesterday—Sarah stayed with Mrs. Lindholm, and Kostia [Tyrtov] stayed at home too, because he got a nasty cold the first day and Mrs. Lindholm begged him not to go, as he was the only man left in the family who could do anything. . . . Admiral Schultz took Tullie and his sister; Admiral Rimskii-Korsakov, Ted; and I came next to them.[16] It was over two miles to the cemetery but the walk did not tire me at all, and Tullie left a motor for us to come home in, as Ted and I stayed till the grave was quite filled in. Tullie wanted to stay but we insisted on her going home—it is awful to see and hear those clods of clay tumbling on to the box with its awful, hollow sound, bad enough, even for an outsider to hear. A great many people attended the funeral as Mr. Lindholm had been in this country sixty-four years and was well-known.

24 January 1915 to Aunt Anna
Aina hasn't written yet to her mother or Tullie, but one of her cousins-in-law wrote, and then there was a long account of Lieut. Butakov's funeral in the

Novoe Vremia. The Tsar himself sent a huge white cross and his two daughters, the Grand Duchesses Olga and Tatiana, went to the funeral. The Empress-Dowager, the Queen-Dowager of Greece, and the Tsar's two sisters were also present, and two or three very high civil officials.[17] Of course all this won't bring Sashik back, but it must be very gratifying to Aina and her poor old mother-in-law to know how much people loved him, for his rank, that of a lieutenant in the navy, wasn't enough to call for the presence of any one of them, and they only came because they all knew him personally and were fond of him.[18]

12 March 1915 to Home
Poor Aina came [to Vladivostok] this noon—I dread seeing her—what can one say to such a terrible grief as hers? We are going up there tomorrow afternoon.

15 March 1915 to Home
We went out to have tea with Mrs. Lindholm Saturday [13 March]—Sarah, Dorothy, Ted and I. Aina has grown older, of course, but hasn't changed as much as I feared she had—she is thinner than she was as a girl, but the moment she begins to talk, it is the same Aina, only one mustn't look for the old, glad light in her blue eyes. . . . Aina talked very freely of Sashik and said that even now she couldn't realize that he was dead and not in the thick of the fight around Kovno.[19] He was shot in the stomach and lived about twenty minutes, fully conscious to the last and able to talk—broken-hearted at the thought of leaving his dear ones, but glad, even in that moment, to die for his Sovereign and for the honor of the Butakov family, which is a very old one. The Empress, with her own hand, wrote Aina a letter of four pages, which Aina let us read. It was written in English, and was the most touching expression of sympathy I have ever read—neither flowing nor stilted, but straight out from a heart full of sympathy for Aina in her loss . . . a letter that any woman of deep feelings might write, but that few can. Well, she is Princess Alice's daughter and a woman before she is an Empress—though one involuntarily thinks of that sort of people in crown and robes of state.[20]

4 April 1915 to Home
This week I have been helping Aina mount photos—she has brought quantities with her and they are so interesting—those I mounted were nearly all snapshots taken at Livadia by the Empress herself and given by her to

Sashik. Then there are Sashik's own snapshots of their delightful life there—walks, tennis, etc., etc., with the Tsar and all his family—such a pleasant cozy life they seem to lead, both there and in Finland (where they spend the alternate summers). The Empress is so different in these snapshots to what she is in the published pictures—she has such a nice smile. Best of all I like a photo of her sitting in a corner of the deck on the royal yacht *Standart* crocheting, while the Emperor sits on something near, with one of the daughters lolling over him. . . . The new palace at Livadia is beautiful—roses everywhere, and at the ball Aina went to last year, the dining-room was all decorated in roses and violets, and for confetti and cotillion favors the same flowers were used, the little Prince driving his donkey straight into the ball-room with cartloads of flowers.[21] Then Aina had some interesting photos of Kamenka, the Davydov estate near Kiev, which belongs to Sashik's Mother's brother—an old man ninety-eight years, and with him lives a sister also over ninety.[22]

GRAND DUKE KIRILL VLADIMIROVICH

Kirill Vladimirovich (1876–1938), first cousin to the tsar (their fathers were brothers), arrived in Vladivostok in the summer of 1898 to the delight of the society ladies who found him dashing, albeit ineligible. Confirming nine-teenth-century royal traditions, yet also scandalizing the family, in 1905 he married within close royal circles: his bride was Victoria Melita, the divorced former wife of empress Alexandra Fedorovna's brother Ernest, grand duke of Hesse. This was a more than usually convoluted example of the complex relationships among European royalty, for Victoria and Alexandra were first cousins, granddaughters of Queen Victoria, as were Victoria and both her husbands as well. The continuous inbreeding caused many medical tragedies, including the spread of hemophilia into European royal houses—but not to grand duke Kirill Vladimirovich. He eventually left Russia and, in 1924, declared himself emperor, in exile.

27 May 1898 to Home
Wednesday morning the *Russia* came in, and . . . [on board] as a midshipman is the Grand Duke Kirill Vladimirovich. In honor of his coming, the town was decorated Monday, Tuesday and Wednesday. . . . Yesterday was the anni-versary of the Coronation and last evening there was a fine illumination. Both Kunst & Albers and Churin had nice electric displays.

5 June 1898 to Home
The Grand Duke is being entertained in good shape here, and they say he is very handsome. At the Admiral's ball he showed Tullie great attention, danced with her several times, and to the amazement of the ladies whose rank entitled them to expect it, he danced the mazurka with Tullie and ended by taking her out to [the] supper [table]. He danced with Lolla once, and she says he came down on her toes so she will have an imperial corn to remember him by.

23 June 1898 to Home
The Grand Duke gives a ball on board the *Russia* next Monday, and Tullie and Lolla have lovely gowns to wear, white silk crepe with a pale blue sash in white lace and flowers. Mrs. Knorring also has a lovely toilette for that occasion, a white velvet trimmed with pale blue and pale pink, with butterflies appliquéd on it of black lace over pink, edged with black beads. . . . She is so proud because she made it herself from the gown she had for the Coronation Ball.

29 June 1898 to Home
The ball given by the Grand Duke was a great success and again he honored Tullie with the Cotillion which made at least one lady in town tear her hair. . . . The *Russia* leaves today for Yokohama and then the town will be quiet for a while.

PRINCE HEINRICH OF PRUSSIA

10 September 1898 to Home
Mrs. Wohlfahrt was here this afternoon and she told us all about the Prince's visit to the Dattans', Thursday evening. He asked to come to dinner informally, and there was no one to meet him but the Dattans, Wohlfahrts and Messrs. Klepsch, O. Meyer, P. Meyer, Suhr, Behn, Appenroth and Wedekind. Mrs. Wohlfahrt said she got quite pale when the Prince came into the room, but he was so everyday-like that everyone soon felt at ease. He asked to see the children, so Sasha, Pasha, Gori and Adi came in. [Eight-year-old] Sasha addressed him as "uncle" at first until his mother corrected him and told him to say "your royal highness." Today, by his invitation, Mr. and Mrs. Dattan, Sasha and Pasha, lunched with him on board the *Deutschland*. He is to live

on shore for the next few days in a new house belonging to Mr. Dattan, and Mrs. Dattan is fixing up the rooms and fitting them out with her and Mrs. Wohlfahrt's things. Neither of them had a nice tea strainer so Mrs. W. asked us to lend one and I sent my lovely enamel one for the use of his royal highness.

12 September 1898 to Home

Yesterday about four I went down to call for Mrs. Wohlfahrt and she proposed that we stay on her veranda a few moments until the Prince passed on his way from the Singing Club to the Allegri. Mrs. Langschwadt with her two little boys was also there. Before long the Prince passed, driving with Mr. Dattan, and when the latter bowed to us, Prince Henry bowed also and touched his cap. . . . He looks like his brother, the Emperor, only without that disagreeable, imperious expression which is always in pictures of Willie, the High Flier. Then we went to the garden, and in the crush we saw him twice, once at the champagne tent, and once at one of the lottery booths. . . . Once I was so close to him I could almost have touched him and I must say racing around to see him was just exactly like running after a circus procession.

ISABELLA BIRD BISHOP

In the fall of 1894, a most unusual woman appeared in Dom Smith. Isabella Bird Bishop (1831–1904), the writer and world traveler, was researching history and contemporary life in China and Korea, and would publish three books based on this material: *Korea and Her Neighbors* (1898), *The Yangtze Valley and Beyond* (1899), and *Chinese Pictures* (1900). Mrs. Bishop carried letters of introduction and was received politely as an honored guest, but Sarah soon invited her to stay at Dom Smith, and she became a dear friend to the family.[23] The three women settled into several weeks of pleasurable company, and Eleanor Pray was pleased to be asked to trim a hat for "so distinguished a lady." In her usual fashion, she created something new "out of an old [silk] petticoat, an old veil, and an old dress" (8 December 1894 to Home).

Isabella Bishop inspired Eleanor Pray. Here was a woman of sharp intellect, indefatigable curiosity about life in all its variety, and vast factual knowledge about the geography, history, and culture of diverse regions. Her standing in the world was impressive: the first female member of the Royal Geographic Society, Mrs. Bishop had just witnessed the political upheavals in

Korea that led to the First Sino-Japanese War (1894–95) and the destruction of Korea's independence. Like Mrs. Bishop, Mrs. Pray loved to go horseback riding and hiking, dressed "properly" out-of-doors, yet with comfort—and suffered no fools. The two women also shared an interest in poetry, photography, and serious writing, and Mrs. Bishop's example of using her home letters as a foundation for her books may well have stimulated Eleanor's never-realized hope of writing publicly about her Russian life.

While in Vladivostok, Isabella Bishop became familiar with Anne E. Ivy's panoramic photos of the city, and a year later in Shanghai met Mrs. Ivy herself (29 November 1895 to Home). One of those images appears in *Korea and Her Neighbors*, titled simply "Wladivostok." It is a wide view from Tiger Hill northeast over the city center, with the Cathedral of the Assumption, Kunst and Albers, and Dom Smith clearly visible. The book does not show the provenance of this photo, but Mrs. Ivy was its author.[24] Biographies of Isabella Bird Bishop include some of the details mentioned in the following excerpts, for example that she carried two cameras and was amused by the song-bird participants in the Chinese campaign, but the material in Mrs. Pray's letters adds fresh, personal color to the official portrait of this formidable woman.[25] Mrs. Bishop left Vladivostok on board the *Tokio* on 10 December 1894.

12 November 1894 to Home

Today Mrs. Bishop showed us what photographs she had with her, and they are very interesting, all in China and Korea. She has two cameras, and has taken over five hundred photographs. . . . Her mother's family is one of the seven families in England who hold the same home [Aldborough Manor] that they did at the Norman conquest. She has a house in London but she likes better her home on the Island of Mull, off the NW Scotch coast. She was up here [in the Prays' apartment] an hour and a half this morning, and looked over my books and things. She was much interested in Miss Powers' poems, and asked me, as a great favor, if I would copy for her, on the typewriter, one called "Supplication" and "The Prairie Land." The former, especially, she liked very much. In 1858, she spent a week with Longfellow in Cambridge, and . . . although Longfellow was a dear personal friend, she likes Whittier's works much the best. Her favorite among them is "Andrew Rykeman's Prayer." She was also much pleased with *The Christian's Secret of a Happy Life*, which Mr. White gave me. She wrote down the name and the publishers for future reference.[26]

24 November 1894 to Home

The *Tokio* will be about a week late, so we shall have Mrs. Bishop with us some time longer. Her company is such a pleasure that we would gladly keep her all winter. Talking with her is like reading a very interesting book of travels, and she is so very unassuming. . . . She was telling us this afternoon of her first, and her last, sight of Queen Victoria. She had no brothers, so her father took her with him when he rode, and taught her when only six years old to ride on a huge carriage horse. Her grandmother lived only seven miles from Windsor and once while visiting her, [Isabella's] father took her to Windsor. They knew the Queen rode each day at a certain hour, so they waited near a place where she would be sure to pass. Quite a crowd of people had gathered there, but [the girl] and her father stood their horses in the front row. Her father's hair was long and snow white, so he was a gentleman that would be noticed in a crowd, and he remained bare-headed from the time the Queen came in sight until she had passed. The Queen came riding down the avenue in a carriage with Prince Albert driving—she was then twenty years old. When she saw this white-haired gentleman she nudged the Prince's arm, and then bowed very low to Mr. Bird, the Prince doing the same. . . . The last time Mrs. Bishop saw the Queen was when she passed through the streets of London on her way to the wedding of the Duke of York, an old lady, seventy-four years of age, seated in the famous glass coach, and wearing a diamond crown.[27] Mrs. Bishop has of course seen her many other times, but she recalled to us only the first and last.

30 November 1894 to Home

[Mrs. Bishop's mother's family] own another property, called Boroughbridge Hall in Yorkshire, which is about four hundred and fifty years old. This is where Mrs. Bishop was born. . . . She says her maternal grandfather refuses a peerage. He said his family had always been honest Saxon squires, and squires they would remain. She says a peerage is thought less and less of in England every year, and now it is nearly always called the "Beerage" because so many wealthy brewers have been made peers.

1 December 1894 to Home

Mrs. Bishop said she saw the Chinese troops when they left Mukden for Korea, in their right hands they carried a spear, and most of them had in their left either a birdcage or a bird chained to a small pole for camp amusement—Warlike implements, are they not?

4 December 1894 to Home

Last evening Mrs. Bishop read a paper on Tibet before the German Singing Club, in their Club room. It was a delightful paper, and written in such simple language that it was easily understood. One thing she said amused the audience immensely—it was this: "You know it is said that England has a finger in everybody's pie—and the Tibetan pie is no exception—an Englishman supposed to be there for the purpose of protecting the traders is in reality put there to watch Russia, which you all know is to England a great big bear." You may be sure there was a good laugh over that. . . . It was so strange to be the only one in the audience, born to the language of the speaker. The theme occupied an hour and a quarter and then we spent two hours more in social conversation, and tea and cake was served. Mrs. Bishop says she never read before an audience who asked such sensible questions; in all the conversation not one silly question was asked.

19 April 1895 to Home

Sarah had a letter from Mrs. Bishop written at Swatow.[28] She has been in Seoul a month since she left here and has had four personal interviews with the King and Queen of Korea, and they gave her permission to photograph the throne and many other Royal fixings and palaces. She says she has worn the hat I trimmed for her many times, especially while in Hong Kong.

RICHARD THEODORE GREENER

Richard T. Greener (1844–1922) had a remarkable life. The first African American to graduate from Harvard College, in 1870, he earned a law degree from the University of South Carolina in 1876, and worked as a professor, librarian, and lawyer before entering Republican politics. He participated in the 1880 presidential campaign for James Garfield, and was a personal friend of general, later president, Ulysses S. Grant. After President Grant's death in 1885, Dr. Greener served as a trustee of the Grant Monument Association in New York City. In 1897, president William McKinley appointed him US commercial agent to Vladivostok, and Dr. Greener arrived in March 1898. Although never recognized with the title "consul," Dr. Greener used his status to perform consular duties, such as providing civic documents (including the death certificate for Charles Smith in May 1898) and arranging exhibits of Americana. His official dispatches to Washington, DC, are full of precise information and are very read-worthy.[29] During the Russo-Japanese War, Dr.

Greener represented British and Japanese interests, helping to repatriate 1,500 Japanese citizens stranded in Vladivostok. After leaving Russia in 1905, he returned to the United States, where he made his home in Chicago. This man's life and work represent an important part of African American academic and diplomatic history, a fact also noted in Vladivostok.[30]

Eleanor Pray's letters and those of Richard Greener to the State Department illustrate a clash of cultures between the public official, with his immense "energy and ambition,"[31] and some of the other Americans. A handsome and flamboyant man, "an intellectual giant of the era," Dr. Greener enjoyed deservedly high opinions of himself and his US connections, but showed little knowledge of Russian life and customs. He attempted to work with a set of conservative Americans whose tolerance for flamboyance was low. He dressed in pink shirts, carried ostentatious business cards, and was not averse to heavy drinking—neither diplomatic nor useful, but, as he himself stated, "The world I love, and all its life/Solitude I abhor."[32] Despite their differences, Mrs. Pray records many successful social gatherings of the American colony with Dr. Greener, and her albums contain two unique photos of him, at a picnic and on a boat excursion.

11 October 1898 to Clara
The crowning stroke came last Friday—there was a long article in the *Dalnii Vostok* about this same Mr. Greener, a regular cheap politician's puff, which could have been dictated by no one but himself! Such a thing is unheard of in Russian papers, for whatever their faults, you never see in them cheap personalities or puffs, so the consequence of this remarkable article was to set everybody laughing at the new American consul and with very good reason. It made us *rage* and it is a shame for our Country to be represented by a man who is so lacking in self-respect, to say nothing of the respect due to his position. Among other things in this article were the facts that he was a *close* personal friend of both McKinley and Day. Nice recommend for our President and Secretary of State? . . . He is also foolish enough to talk about the information he is gathering to send to the State Department concerning the fortifications here! Of course we know all consuls do those things, but they ought to know enough not to talk about it.

21 October 1898 to Home
He informs everyone he meets that he speaks several languages, and then to back up his statement, he usually drags in some French phrase. As it is the

exception here to find an educated person who does not speak French fluently, these boasts of his are absurd. He goes swelling around town with a flag, about four inches long pinned with an eagle to his waistcoat, and a flag pin in his tie, so of course everybody knows who he is.

19 February 1899 to Home
I really wonder what [Mr. Greener] will do next. His chief diversion is playing poker and it's a wicked shame the way he and Bechtel are ruining that young Newhard.[33] The poor little fellow lost forty rubles playing last week with them and he never thought of gambling when he came here, and now they are at it at least four nights out of seven.... Last week that *man*, the representative of our Nation, was at a Chinese dinner and got as drunk as a fool!

4 September 1899 to Home
We had a lovely day at Sedanka yesterday and enjoyed it so much. There were eight of us—we four here [including Dr. Ivy], Mrs. Hansen, Miss Morphew, Mr. Davidson and Mr. Greener, with Dou Kee and a boy to attend to the luggage. I can't tell how we passed the day—doing nothing mostly, with the exception of Ted and Doctor who caught enough [fish] for today's lunch.... Miss Morphew and Mr. Greener talked literature, and I accused Mr. Davidson, who was lying down under a sun umbrella, of snoring in the midst of an animated discussion of Ruskin's *Sesame and Lilies*, whereupon Mr. Davidson retorted that it was perfectly justifiable to snore when that old sinner Ruskin was mentioned for he would sacrifice the well-being of the world to art.[34]

23 October 1899 to Sarah
Yesterday afternoon I went to Miss Morphew's Marie Corelli tea party.[35] ... Mr. Greener was there and we really had a very pleasant tea. I read four choice selections from Marie C. which were without doubt beautiful. One was a poem called "Lotus Lily," then a poem "The Voice of the Beloved," afterwards a selection from *Aidath* where the lady melts away from earth, and the last letter to Thelma from her father.... We spent a most delightful two hours and I hope to repeat them some day.

11 December 1899 to Sarah
Mr. Greener got himself into disgrace at the opening of the pawn shop and we are all glad of it. It seems he made a speech and among other things said something about the "greetings of the American Republic to the Russian

Republic" and that made the Russians hot in a minute. Maslennikov jumped up and informed him that Russia was an Empire, *not* a Republic, and proposed the health of the Tsar, whereupon somebody else got mad and said it was *his* place to propose the toast, etc., etc., and it ended in their all going for Mr. Greener as the beginner of the fuss.[36]

20 September 1901 to Home
This noon Mr. Greener asked all the Americans in town to come to his office to arrange a message of condolence to Mrs. McKinley.[37] . . . Some resolutions were drawn up which Mr. Greener signed first, and Ted (at the motion of Mr. Clarkson because he had been here longer than the others) signed as secretary of the meeting, and then we all signed. Just as we were coming out we met Mr. Rodgers coming in to sign his name, and Merritt-san went over after *tiffin*.[38] Mr. Greener asked if we could think of any change or addition to what he had written, but no one suggested anything.

14 April 1904 to Home
[The Russo-Japanese War is in full swing.] About two weeks ago there came an inquiry for our safety from the State Department in Washington, and I am wondering who started it off—probably Mother, though I do not know how she managed it. I was feeling particularly blue when it came and it just warmed my heart for I felt that Uncle Sam was watching over his own. Greener at once telegraphed all our names with the information that we were well and safe, and I suppose it would be published in all the papers, so you and other anxious ones will see.

CHAPTER 5

Life at the Dacha

FROM THE SHORE OF AMUR BAY NEAR THE TRAIN STATIONS TODAY named Okeanskaia and Sadgorod, one can see the Peninsula of De Vries, with its stately avenue of trees leading north to a prominent hill. For more than three decades, this was the site of the Novogeorgievsk Estate, known simply as Goldenstedt's Farm. The place is beautiful, with breathtaking views over the sea, but it is difficult to imagine that today's village was once a bustling agricultural, commercial, and social center similar to some of the landed estates in western Russia.[1] After her first visit to Novogeorgievsk, Eleanor Pray exclaimed, "I had no idea there was anything like it in this part of the world" (27 July 1900 to Sarah). Like many country estates, Novogeorgievsk was vitally connected with its region's merchant and military circles, and the people who lived and died there helped make it a significant player in Vladivostok's economy. Owned from 1892 by Karl Goldenstedt, a Russian landscape architect of German extraction, and his Cossack wife Agafia,[2] Novogeorgievsk produced food for the city, proudly displayed its beauty and orderly management, and provided a rural escape from urban noise and dirt. Whereas some aspects of Novogeorgievsk's life were similar to those of other estates, its location in Asia—near China and Korea—also differentiated it from its cousins.[3]

EARLY VISITS, 1900–1907

Eleanor Pray became acquainted with Novogeorgievsk in 1900 through her friend Marie Dattan. Thanks to Karl Goldenstedt's business connections with Kunst and Albers, the Dattans were able to build their own *dacha* [summerhouse] on the estate, and they named it Villa Alwine, after Mrs. Dattan's mother. When she and the children left for Germany in 1904, Else and Paul Meyer (a nephew of Mr. Goldenstedt, also at Kunst and Albers) adopted the villa and continued the tradition of inviting friends out in the summer.

The Goldenstedts and the Dattans considered their summer houses to be *dacha*s without the sumptuous grandeur of more palace-like country homes, but contemporary photos show them nevertheless to have been splendid villas. On stone foundations topped with wood, their white walls and gracefully jutting gables were surrounded by pergolas and glassed-in porches; there were balconies, windows with screens, and elegant awnings. Situated on the "East Sea" (here, the Sea of Japan), the Goldenstedts' Big Dacha and the Dattans' Villa Alwine were well equipped for the local climate, supporting both comfortable vacations and spacious entertaining.

The journey from Vladivostok to De Vries was short enough for day trips, but arduous enough to make visits special treats. One would go either by train to 19th Verst (also known as "Platform"; today's Sanatornaia Station) and cross Amur Bay by motor or rowboat, hoping that all connections would match up, or by sea starting from a city pier. Although connected with Vladivostok, the estate was also, in Eleanor Pray's view, conveniently separated from it: "Our 'peninsular paradise' has its drawbacks in the way of communication, but to my mind the advantages and isolation more than make up" (22 June 1909 to Home). Mrs. Pray was not a happy sailor, often very seasick during crossings ("Why, why will people have country-places only to be reached by water?" 2 August 1901 to Home), but only in emergencies, such as on 20 August 1907, did the transport logistics cause real concerns.

27 July 1900 to Sarah
We had a most delightful time yesterday and I do hope our photos will be good. We left here on the *Pavel* a little after nine, Mesdames Hansen, Wohlfahrt, Langschwadt, Ivy, Bessie, Bertie and I; and reached Goldenstedt's farm a little before eleven. Mrs. Dattan and the children were waiting on the pier to meet us and took us straight to the house where we rested for a while. . . . Truly it is a lovely spot, and a big territory back of the house is laid out into a park, with paths, seats, swings and all sorts of things. . . . We took a walk through the park and then came back to luncheon, soon after which we started off again for a trip to the boundaries of the farm, three or four miles away. Mrs. Dattan and Mrs. Langschwadt went in the pony carriage, with Mr. Ringhardt (the boys' tutor) for a driver, and the rest of us went on a *dolgushka*

or in other words a "straddle cart." . . . The road was as smooth and level as possible, part of the way through vegetable fields, grain fields and then through the woods, sometimes within a few feet of the water, with only a few trees on the banks. It was lovelier than I can tell you and how we did enjoy it.

12 June 1901 to Home
Last year Mrs. Dattan had a part of the Goldenstedts' *dacha,* but this year she has a new one of her own built beside the other one and it is lovely. It is built in bungalow fashion with a veranda fifteen feet wide around the east and north side, and about six or seven feet around the other two sides, so there is territory enough in the veranda alone for a regiment. In case of bad weather, there are folding doors that shut out the force of the South East wind, and there are curtains all around to regulate the light and draughts, and here they live in fine weather. They use the North side for a dining-room, and as it is at least fifty feet long, it makes a fine one.

30 September 1906 to Aunt Anna
We have great fun here gathering mushrooms in the fields—I feel like a character out of Tolstoi's novels when I take my basket and start out.

16 August 1907 to Home
Life here is very quiet. . . . We have breakfast at eight . . . and then we sit around in the park and sew or read till about eleven, when we go down to the shore for a dip or a swim. The water by the bathhouse is too shallow to float me with any comfort, so I scarcely attempt to swim. By the time we get dressed and back to the house, it is time for *tiffin,* after which we go back to the park and rest and sleep in the lawn chairs and hammocks until three o'clock or so. Tea is at four, and after that we go for a walk or a drive. . . . Baby washing begins about half past six and as soon as the little ones are tucked up we have supper, and afterwards . . . we go for a walk, either along the West shore, or in the park. After that we come back here, have some fruit of some kind and go to bed about half past nine.

21 August 1907 to Sarah
We were all sitting yesterday on the veranda and were having great fun over a skit of Mrs. Wissing's, when [she] ran over to the quarters for a few moments and when she came back she asked Mrs. Meyer to come and look at Baby Schultz. He had been crying a lot in the night but they all thought it was his

teeth, but toward nine in the morning there was a great change in him and Mrs. Goldenstedt was called in. She said at once that there was no hope, but put hot water bottles all around the lower part of his body to draw the blood from the head. The baby died about half past twelve, and of course his poor little mother is heartbroken. Luckily it was a cold windy day, and by packing the baby's bath full of ice, the body kept all night till today. . . . I started for town, with barely time to catch the train, and a strong wind against us. But we flew, making the trip in twenty-five minutes from the anchorage here. I was drenched with salt water when we got there and will you imagine—I was not in the least seasick and hadn't an atom of a headache even. . . . It was very sad news to tell poor Mr. Schultz, but it had to be done and I got through it as best as I could—then . . . went back on the half past eight train with Mr. Schultz and Mr. Wissing. This morning, Mr. Wissing made a little coffin and covered it with a piece of brown cloth, and I made a lining of white gauze, ruffled so it looked soft, and then the *amah* laid her little charge into it and we filled in all around him with pink and white asters, and at the last moment the amah put in a little doll so baby should not "be *skuchno*."[4] It was too pitiful. When all was ready, Mr. and Mrs. Schultz and Mr. and Mrs. Wissing left for town on the *Paris* which had come up to meet them, taking with them the little box, all covered with flowers.

23 August 1907 to Sarah
Mr. and Mrs. Schultz and Mrs. Wissing came back yesterday afternoon, and for their sakes especially I am sorry it is such a horrible day [of pouring rain]. Before they came, Mrs. Meyer and I went over to their rooms and packed away everything that pertained to the baby—carriage, bath, basket, and all the little clothes, and changed things around as well as we could, but with all we could do, the rooms looked sad and empty.

THE NOVOGEORGIEVSK ESTATE

As Eleanor Pray noted during her first visits, Novogeorgievsk was a well-functioning small town unto itself. From about 1,620 acres of land in 1892, the holdings had increased to approximately 2,000 acres by 1911 (18 November 1911 to Aunt Anna), and from seventy-five seasonal workers at the end of the nineteenth century, to three hundred in 1908, mostly Korean tenants living in the nearby villages (9 July 1908 to Home). The herd of one hundred cattle that Mrs. Pray observed in 1906 grew to 280 by 1910, and there were also bulls, horses, pigs, chickens, guinea fowl, turkeys, and geese. The Gold-enstedts' farm provided the city of Vladivostok and its military with milk, butter, sour cream, and cottage cheese from the dairy; beef, pork, poultry, potatoes, and other vegetables from the agricultural operations; and oysters, crab, and fish from the sea, not to mention "the twenty thousand *poods* [one pood equals approximately thirty-six pounds] . . . of cabbage to salt down for the troops" (7 October 1909 to Home).

After the Prays and Sarah Smith rented their own *dacha* in 1908, Mrs. Pray settled into country life every summer for fifteen years, often moving to Novogeorgievsk already in April or May, and returning to Vladivostok in late October or early November. One of the estate's great misfortunes—a fire that destroyed the Big Dacha in October 1910—resulted in useful information on the estate map that she drew when describing the fire. In addition to the *dachas*, there were picturesque old-world stables with thatched roofs for the horses, ponies, and bullocks; a carriage house, a granary, and north and south cow stables; a home for the steward, several kitchens with servants' quarters, an ice cellar, a boathouse, and kennels for the Saint Bernards and dozens of guard dogs.

17 October 1909 to Aunt Anna
More and more I enjoy seeing the herds go home at sunset or a little before—I amuse myself studying the faces of the cows and there are so many different expressions on them: the intellectual cow, the woman's rights (or rather the cow's rights) cow, the peasant cow, the grand duchess cow, the lesser nobility and the cows who would be charwomen if they were humans. And most of them remind me of people I have met.

9 July 1910 to Aunt Anna
We had quite an excitement here yesterday. Buian, a young bull, nearly killed his herder and would have done so, had not Herzog, the old Holstein bull that came out from Germany, taken a hand in the row and given Buian such a lesson as he won't soon forget. The herder had his shoulder dislocated and was badly bruised generally. Now, Mr. Buian has a ring in his nose, a board over his head, and other less stylish gear which won't be at all to his taste.

9 October 1910 to Home
The cabbage harvest is going on now and all day long bullocks are passing here drawing carts loaded with cabbage. In the court of the stables eight or

ten Chinese sort it over, strip off the outer leaves, shred it on a sort of wheel, equipped with knives, and salt it down in hogsheads, as the Russians eat an immense quantity of that sort of thing. The outer leaves are fed to the cattle and we have such fun, gathering armfuls of them for our favorite animals. Even that wild Buian, who made so much scandal earlier in the season, will eat cabbage out of my hand, though, to be frank about it, there is a good strong fence between us. Herzog, the huge old German bull, is very amiable now when he sees us coming for he knows it means a delicious mouthful for him, and with Petka, who is very amiable for a bull, we have been cabbage acquaintances for more than one season.

30 September 1913 to Home
We had a very exciting time last night. Mrs. Goldenstedt sold five cows, a calf, and the bull "Ivan the Terrible" to some parties in Tsintau, and we went down to the pier to see them loaded on to the barge which was to take them to the steamer in Vladivostok. . . . It took all the herders and cattlemen on the place to get the cattle on board, and it was such fun to hear the Germans bellowing at the Koreans, who of course didn't understand a word and only got more confused. . . . I did pity the poor cows leaving this beautiful place. Tsintau, though in China, is more German than Germany, and the cows will probably have their teeth brushed every day. Their quarters will make them think they have strayed into Potsdam by mistake and one must walk very properly indeed.[5]

28 August 1917 to Sarah
When we came up from the shore yesterday morning there was the "Bremen Musician" in our inside corn patch, so Jan got a clothesline and tied him up in front of the house to the great delight of Jamie and John Rea, but presently he began to sing, which got on He Fa's nerves so that he untied him and chased him into the road.[6] Later on Dorothy . . . was riding [this donkey] up and down the road, when Mrs. G. sent Moitia over to say that as the donkey didn't belong here we mustn't ride him, otherwise, when the owner turned up (judging from past experience, especially with boats, this place is practically immune against owners turning up), he might hold us responsible for having worked the animal. . . . Nastia says there is a Russian law whereby the owner of a stray animal must pay a certain sum per day, unless he can prove that the animal has been used by the people who found him. Not being up in the ethics of stray asses, I didn't know of this, and . . . we have

no intention of charging the owner (whom we shall probably never see) for the corn.

2 June 1920 to Aunt Anna
This is Ted's birthday so I went out to the *dacha* yesterday to get all the special treats I could for my old man and came in this morning with a pail of oysters (probably the last till September), a pound of fresh butter, a bottle of cream and a pound of sour cream, so at least he will get some things we do not have every day. . . . I also brought in heaps of flowers, blue and white columbines and pansies from the garden and lilac, anemone, violets, etc., with sprays of larch for greenery.

THE HOUSE AND GARDEN

Although comparatively small, and far simpler than Mrs. Dattan's villa and those of the Goldenstedts, the Prays' and Sarah Smith's *dacha* also served multiple ends: the veranda became an all-purpose room for dining, sewing, conversing, playing cards, reading, writing, preparing vegetables, and even accommodating overnight guests. Living in the country was sometimes like camping ("The rain poured down by the bucketful, and Sarah and I were up at all times looking for new leaks on the veranda—before morning the place looked like a crockery and umbrella shop," 18 July 1914 to Aunt Anna), but the occasional discomfort was greatly offset by the beauty of the place and its healthy, down-to-earth life.

They named their summer home Dacha Seyuza, which, according to Eleanor Pray, was a "Chinese designation (North House)" (19 May 1909 to Aunt Anna). Transliterated *jie you zhai* from the words meaning "to liberate," "sorrow," and "house," the phrase evokes more than the location of this home in relation to Vladivostok, namely the rural imagery of the fifth-century Chinese poet T'ao Ch'ien (Yüan-ming),[7] who took refuge from urban turmoil at his quiet country dwelling, a house without sorrow or cares. This sentiment appealed to Mrs. Pray. She did not mention the poet, nor did she speak or read Chinese, but she had visited China in 1900 and 1902, and its legends and tales fascinated her. The name must have come from someone literate enough to have known Chinese poetry, and close enough to Eleanor Pray to have proposed it. Perhaps this was their faithful servant and friend He Fa. Always described with great respect and admiration, He Fa was responsible and hard-working, and was included in Mrs. Pray's birthday book, where he signed his name in both Chinese and Russian, Khan Khi Fa.[8] He may have told her the ancient phrase, and she, slightly misrepresenting the sounds, accepted its dream of quiet happiness.

For altogether fifteen years, Eleanor Pray was as regular a resident at Novogeorgievsk as its owners, and she rejoiced in this role: "I have concluded to be very good the remainder of my life in the hope that when I get to heaven, I'll have a fruit and vegetable farm and imps enough at my disposal to work it" (22 May 1917 to Sarah). With the Goldenstedts' permission, the Prays and He Fa prepared two large gardens with a tennis court between them and a simple golf course nearby, as well as sanded paths, hawthorn hedges, and flower beds. An excellent carpenter, Mr. Pray built cupboards and tables for the *dacha*, a jetty for the boats, and several pleasing surprises for Mrs. Pray. She, for her part, transformed their *dacha* and the land around it into a bucolic microcosm of the estate at large. Well attuned to the seasonal rhythms of rural life, in the spring they cleaned and made repairs, collected rain water in huge barrels, and planted all sorts of vegetables, berries, and flowers; in the summer they weeded, pruned, canned, and made jam; and in the fall they gathered walnuts and mushrooms, and transplanted trees from the woods. The provisions thus acquired had to last: "This season I have made about twenty bottles of peach jam, three raspberry, three black currant . . . two grape marmalade, three crabapple jam . . . six spiced crabapples, some tomato sweet pickle and some piccalilli" (10 October 1910 to Aunt Anna).

Neither capricious weather nor revolutions could keep Eleanor Pray away from Dacha Seyuza, but her greatest personal sorrow did. Forever after her husband's death on 2 April 1923 she found herself unable to return, but she appreciated old friends' reminiscences, such as this from Anna Wissing: "It seems to me like a fairy tale, especially the summer of 1907. Ma, do you think of it sometimes? Think of the walks, the 'talks,' the bath, the moon-lit evenings, and so on. I remember one night in the garden in front of Meyer's *dacha*! We had a little barrel there and up we jumped to the barrel and held the most gay, funny speeches, every one of us being in high gigs. Ma, all the memories! . . . I think we lived like in Paradise" (7 July 1922 to Eleanor).

16 May 1908 to Home
Our plans for the summer are settled at last and we have rented the new *dacha* at Novogeorgievsk. It was formerly [Mrs. Meyer's] kitchen . . . [which] has been made into a *dacha*, and a new building, containing two kitchens and four servants' rooms, has been put up half-way between. [Our] *dacha* has one large

room, three rather small ones, and a veranda, ten feet wide across the entire front, and glassed in at both ends, so this will be our dining-and-sitting-room till cold weather comes. A nice garden has been made around it, and Mr. Goldenstedt has promised me a small strip for lettuce and radishes.

5 June 1908 to Home
We are having awnings and screens made for the windows, and are constructing dressing tables and washstands out of packing cases, and I really think it will be very pretty. We have ordered two single bedsteads and two rattan couches, which will give us a place for seven people to sleep—as many as we shall probably be at any one time. . . . With the exception of the above-mentioned beds and couches, the only things we have had to buy are three pails, a dozen meat plates and a dozen soup plates.

7 October 1909 to Home
I wish I could lend you my eyes for a few moments. My table is in front of a Western window, and by raising my eyes I see the road, a corner of the park, and through the oaks, the blue water. If I look through the window at my right [to the east], I see the water over the tops of our garden shrubbery. In either direction it is less than five minutes' walk, and the depth of the blue these autumn days is something wonderful.

19 October 1910 to Aunt Anna
This afternoon I have been in the wood with Ted looking for trees to transplant and we found some very nice little oaks, elms and cork elms. There are grand old lindens all through the wood—trees two or three hundred years old, and often growing out of the stump of a still older one. Such a sight makes one feel very young indeed.

19 May 1913 to Aunt Anna
The extension to the garden is laid out and I have planted beans, peas, carrots, beets, turnips, celery, spinach, parsley, radishes, and lettuce. . . . Under glass I have planted corn and water and mush melons, as it is still too cold to put them into the ground.

13 July 1913 to Home
We couldn't find He Fa the whole afternoon, but at six he appeared with Ted and Dorothy, the latter bubbling over with delight at some "surprise" she and

Daddy had in store for us and which we were to see after supper. So, on their invitation, we strolled into the wood in spite of the wet, and there was, really, a very nice surprise in the shape of three nice strong benches, placed at some distance from each other, on the prettiest parts of the trail.

25 October 1914 to Home
This week He Fa has set out a hedge of hawthorns the whole south side of the gardens—seventy in all, and six oaks along the tennis court, which separates the two gardens, but three of them were already there. In two or three years the hawthorns will interlace so as to protect the garden from the typhoon winds very effectively.

21 May 1915 to Aunt Anna
When I got back from town Ted had the surprise of my life ready for me—it isn't a nice thing to write about, but I can't leave you curious. We had a detached W.C. so tall and so smart that one could see it for five miles in every direction, and no trees grew tall enough to hide it. Ted promised long ago to cut it down but of course didn't do it. Coming across [the bay] Wednesday, something in our landscape was wrong, and when I got here, there was the top off that thing and a new modest roof on it, which doesn't make it at all conspicuous, and which won't be seen at all as soon as the leaves are out. It improves the place from the bay a hundred percent.

13 October 1915 to Home
Kiku is having the final washer of the season this week, and lucky is the thing that escapes her eagle eye. I told Mrs. Goldenstedt she needn't be at all surprised, upon looking into the hedged-in clothes yard some fine morning, to see me and Sarah, hanging from the clothes line from the shoulders, victims of Kiku's mania for washing. She loves wash-day here because everything looks so nice and clean.

31 July 1921 to Home
Still no rain. He Fa and his partners have sixteen thousand tomato plants loaded with green fruit, and perishing of dry rot. Such a pity, for it means a tremendous lot of labor gone to waste. Our garden has never been so poor and it is sorrowful to see our pea vines, loaded with half-grown peas, shrivel up and turn yellow.[9]

As with all well-tended country places, one of Novogeorgievsk's main func-
tions was deeply psychological: to provide an "idyllic space" of languorous
relaxation, an atmosphere restorative of health and free from urban stresses.[10]
Great excitement therefore accompanied the official announcement in September 1907 that the regional governor-general, Pavel Unterberger, intended
to visit the estate. Exceedingly honored, the Goldenstedts prepared extensively: the gardens and park were spruced up in grand style, a welcoming
arch was built, and a "fatted calf" was slaughtered, along with a suckling pig
and several chickens (8 September 1907 to Sarah). Then, very bad weather
canceled all travel, causing bitter disappointment. Finally, with no advance
notice due to mixed-up telephone messages, the governor-general appeared
with his retinue early one morning when nobody expected them and all the
Goldenstedts were still in bed. What followed became a study in the knee-
slapping conventions of light theater:

> Mr. G. was still in his night shirt and, while he was getting into some-
> thing more respectable, somebody guided the party into the back
> veranda and Gen. Flug started in through the house, but to get to the
> sitting-room from that side of the house, one must pass the boys' bed-
> room, and there was Pasha, hastily sliding into his trousers, so Flug
> retreated, took the party back into the garden, where they walked
> around until Mr. Goldenstedt appeared on the front veranda and
> invited them into the room that way. In his excitement he had quite
> forgotten Tante Agatha [Mrs. Goldenstedt], and there she was, her
> exit cut off and her best capote in another room.[11] But, as usual, it did
> not take her long to get out of that. She put on her old capote, *climbed*
> out of the window (would it not have made a photograph?), went
> around to the back door, got in and got her capote, dressed herself
> and sailed into the drawing-room! (11 September 1907 to Sarah)

Despite the Goldenstedts' surprise at the early morning visit, and that of the
guests at these unconventional comings and goings, good manners soon
replaced farce, and a normal welcome was extended. General Unterberger's
visit became a priceless memory for everyone, and Mr. Goldenstedt himself
was "beaming all over" when he told Mrs. Pray (11 September 1907 to Sarah).
    Eleanor Pray, too, delighted in showing off the natural wonders of the

estate—its fresh-air activities and culinary treats—and both Ted, who came out for weekends and vacations, and their tired friends from Shanghai and Vladivostok benefitted from this medicine: "Mrs. Ramsay and her four-year-old son . . . came up Friday for two days, both of them pale as ghosts, but by Sunday they were looking so much better that I asked them to stay up a week" (23 August 1911 to Home). Rural life also offered a welcome relief from the social strictures of the city, allowing the lively spirits of Eleanor and her women friends relatively liberal rein. They could walk barefoot ("unless our husbands are here," 29 August 1907 to Home), scamper about "with our hair flying to get an airing" (15 August 1908 to Home), and eat in the kitchen with the servants ("a proceeding which would stand the hair on end of most of our acquaintances," 10 October 1912 to Home). All this made the hierarchical and regulated winter life in Vladivostok seem inhibiting, despite its entertaining social swirl. They all knew that returning to town meant "hats, gloves, and Reduso corsets" (21 September 1910 to Home).[12]

15 June 1908 to Home
Yesterday was Trinity Sunday and today is Whit Monday, and of course everything is decorated with green branches, even to the trains and boats, according to the German and Russian custom. Mr. Goldenstedt brought us a couple of young birches to put each side of the doorway as they always do in Germany on Trinity Sunday, and they looked very pretty until they began to wilt.

4 July 1909 to Aunt Anna
For the first time in ten years we had a real [Fourth of July] celebration and it was so jolly—we all feel quite young, but our bones feel old. The Kizhevi-ches came up yesterday afternoon and weren't we busy this morning: we went into the woods and park and gathered huge armfuls of . . . bracken and wild flowers, and began to decorate the veranda—banking them high up in the corners and in every convenient place. The stars and stripes were flying over the house—the first time over a private house in this part of the world, but we are too far from town for the police to make us take it down. . . . For dinner we had boiled salmon, beet salad, roast mutton with mint sauce, cauliflower and lettuce, ice cream, and lemonade, a whole water jug full which was a big surprise for everybody. At three o'clock, we packed up a cart with cups and saucers, tea, coffee, cakes, etc., and started for Irishain[13] . . . where we had tea, boiling the water over a gypsy fire. We invited all the Goldenstedts and

we were in all twenty-two people, so you can imagine what a good time we had. There were fire crackers galore, and big and little had a good time. Ted burned a hole both in his coat and in his vest, so he feels as if he had celebrated properly.

17 October 1909 to Aunt Anna
I don't like to think of going home a week from today, but at present that is the date set. Cosmos, phlox, pansies, sweet peas and nasturtiums are still blooming in the garden, likewise dahlias, but the zinnias are finished. One feels as if shut up in a box in town, after five months out at pasture.

29 May 1911 to Home
Dorothy has had a great and glorious time today—her beloved Kiku is here to help out . . . and she hasn't let her out of sight all day long. They have caught crabs for the Japanese supper, gathered wild flowers for Mother, hung out the clothes together, etc., etc.

24 July 1912 to Home
After *tiffin* Sunday I walked down to Irishain and it was so lovely I came back and told the others to come down. Ted, who was lying on his couch reading *The Man in Lower Ten*,[14] snorted and said it was going to rain, but Sarah, Mr. Engelbracht, Mrs. Stines and I started out with books, rubber blankets, pillows, etc., and made ourselves very comfortable under some big lindens near the shore . . . with the two long chairs He Fa brought down. I stretched out on a rubber sheet and went to sleep, just hugging myself to think I had thought of coming down there, and the next thing I knew Sarah was calling "Wake up, Roxy, the rain is coming." I awoke with a jump and there was a black cloud coming toward us at a good stiff pace. We grabbed our belongings and started on the run, but . . . we got caught and my word what a soaking we all had, straight to the skin. Of course when we got home, there lay Ted, cool and dry, making impolite remarks about people who didn't know enough to come in out of the wet. Catch me asking people to come down to the shore again.

11 September 1912 to Home
Today and tomorrow are big holidays so Ted is staying over, and he went out at half past four this morning for snipe. He walks four or five miles to the flats, waits around hours, comes home with twenty birds or so, half of them

the size of a flea, and the remainder the size of a walnut and thinks he has had a lovely time, in which I encourage him because the exercise is good for him. Then he and Dorothy and Sarah have snipe on toast for supper and think there is nothing so delicious.

27 June 1913 to Home
Wanda and her Mother came up Wednesday for a ten days' visit, and yesterday morning Mika Bryner came with her little Kiriusha, who is now five years old and big enough to play nicely with Wanda and Dorothy. The children had *tiffin* together at a little table on the lawn, which of course they enjoyed. Tea, however, was laid for them on the veranda and the two Goldenstedt children came also, and all the little people behaved so nicely that their respective mothers hardly recognized them. Cook spent hours over the decoration of the birthday cake and it was a work of art. Besides the usual elaborate frosting, initials, candles, etc., he made a tiny paper umbrella to stand up in the center with four paper birds dangling from it by threads as if they were flying and of course the kiddies found it beautiful.[15]

21 April 1914 to Home
In the whole year it seems to me the happiest morning of all is the first one we pass at the *dacha*—it is so good to wake up and hear only the birds—not that I am very keen on them, but it means country—no wheels and hoofs on the pavement, no clanging of trams, and no whistles (excepting in the far distance) from train or boat.

11 August 1914 to Home
Yesterday morning Sarah and I started out for the oaks to see if we could find some mushrooms. Just at the end of the park we espied a bullock cart en route for that part of the estate, and, by means of signs, got permission from an old Korean and two small boys seated therein to clamber aboard—which was easier said than done! Sarah sat at the back, her feet hanging off behind . . . and I squatted Turk fashion, next the old Korean, while the biggest boy drove. [Dorothy's dog] Tylo ran alongside first yelping, and then howling in desperation evidently thinking it a case of abduction. What would I not have given for a snapshot of that—Sarah's and my costumes certainly added to the picturesqueness of the load for she was dressed in a kitchen apron, I in a kimono night-gown, belted in and draped over a seersucker petticoat, with a grayish blue veil to cover deficiencies.

4 June 1917 to Sarah
[Ted turned fifty on 2 June 1917.] We had one of the big tables on the lawn with plates, knives, forks and serviettes in piles of six, and as soon as the bouillon (in cups) and *pirozhki* were finished, the *amahs* put on the *zakuska* and people helped themselves. We had cold salmon with mayonnaise, fish jelly, beef sausage, cold veal, eggs in mayonnaise, chup-chup, Danish salad, potato salad, hot boiled potatoes, gravy, horseradish sauce, cucumbers, lettuce, radishes, rhubarb jelly, ice cream and coffee—and maybe you think our summer picnic wasn't a success!

24 July 1921 to Home
After tea . . . to finish the day up, Dorothy asked me to go sailing with her—naturally, I wasn't very keen on it, but still went, having three varieties of nervous prostration before we got on board and got away from the anchorage. I know absolutely nothing about sailing and therefore paid no attention to what we were doing, and as for tack—the only kind I know anything about belongs in a carpet. We were beating up into the wind, when Captain Pray decided to tack, and her concise order to me was "Duck your beezer!" and while I was wondering which part of the boat a beezer was, the boom just missed the top of my head and she remarked, "I *told* you to duck." One more word added to my vocabulary! We tacked back and forth several times and then made a straight line for the pier, flying in good shape. Getting off the boat was another problem, but finally I found myself on all fours on the pier, with only one foot tangled in the rigging, so I felt that we had had quite a successful trip after all, but I felt quite tamed.

PHILOSOPHICAL MUSINGS

Another Novogeorgievsk joy that captivated Eleanor Pray was the perceived mystery of "the East." She liked the sight of the graceful Chinese junks hugging the waters around Vladivostok, and named a favorite spot at the estate Mandarin Hill, imagining that a mandarin's palace once stood there (17 May 1914 to Home). Some evenings, she watched the night fishing of the Chinese, as if in an old painting: "It was so pretty to see the lights out in the water—like big candles, but there wasn't a sound from the men excepting an occasional splash when a fish was speared" (20 July 1914 to Aunt Anna). The quiet contours and sparse light in shimmering reflection do recall the imagery of ancient Chinese hand scrolls.

Additionally, the most profound spiritual experience recorded anywhere in Eleanor Pray's letters occurred at Novogeorgievsk. As a rule, she preferred discussing politics to religion and seems to have found her spiritual sustenance mostly in communion with nature, in the company of friends, and in helping others. But in 1911, Eleanor had an out-of-body experience that filled her with such enormous peace, and such awe, that she could not tell her husband (who, she thought, "would have pooh-poohed" her account). She described the event to Sarah:

> The tide was very low, so I walked along the Western shore most
> of the way to the point, and finally, being rather tired, lay down on
> the dry warm sand. . . . I didn't fall asleep, but little by little, such
> a strange feeling came over me—it seemed to me that I was a part
> of nature and not a human being, with a human's hopes and fears,
> loves and hates. I was conscious that something lay on the sand,
> but it seemed to be in no way connected with me—if I could believe
> the soul could be temporarily disassociated from the body, I should
> think that was what happened. There was such a feeling of peace
> around me—and for a few moments perfect faith—it really seemed
> to me, Sarah, as if I had been with God himself and that he had filled
> my soul with calm. (15 October 1911 to Sarah)

This description perfectly captures the experience of unbounded, tranquil connectedness with all of nature that in Eastern philosophical traditions is known as Unity (or God) Consciousness, the highest state of human awareness.[16] Mrs. Pray was unaware that writers such as Hegel and Tennyson had described similar experiences; for her, the moments on that beach seemed to signify universal goodness concentrating at the Novogeorgievsk paradise. In stark contrast with public sentiments of the prewar period that stressed fear of Asian influences and the "yellow peril,"[17] Eleanor found the cultural crossroads of the estate to be infused with spirited life.

WAR

Soon after World War I began in late July 1914, the cosmopolitan backgrounds of many of Vladivostok's residents became a hazard: anyone connected with Germany was now an enemy. In early September—not six weeks after Russia joined the Allies—Eleanor Pray stood with friends on the platform at Okeanskaia to wave farewell when German friends bearing names such as Schultz, Tolle, and Lagerfeldt were sent into internal exile near Yakutsk.[18] She empathized especially with Marie Dattan, with whom she kept in touch by correspondence. Mr. Dattan himself, German-born but a naturalized Russian subject, was banished by "administrative exile" to the city of Tomsk.[19] Three Dattan sons, Alexander (Sasha, born in 1890), Georg (Gori, born in 1892), and Adolph (Adi, born in 1894) fought in the war; the latter was killed in 1915 in Lorraine, and Sasha in 1916 in Galicia.

For the residents of Novogeorgievsk, the war became horrifically tangible with the case of Pasha Mitt, one of the Goldenstedt grandsons.[20] His poignant story transformed the estate into a backdrop of inconsolable grief instead of the customary light-hearted fun. For many years, the four Mitt brothers had brightened the summers on the peninsula: "I am sorry they have gone [back to school], for they are nice boys and were all over the place with their ponies, boats, dogs, butterfly nets, etc., and are very sociable youngsters" (28 August 1908 to Aunt Anna). Mrs. Pray was especially fond of Pasha, who grew into an enterprising and caring young man. In mid-July 1914, home from his studies at the mining academy in Saint Petersburg, he organized a small charity bazaar at the estate, giving his guests "a royal good time." His idea to raise money for some Vladivostok classmates met with success: "He cleared over eighty rubles, which, as he says, will buy warm overcoats for three of his friends" (27 July 1914 to Aunt Anna).

Only days after this laudable event, Pasha joined Russia's military effort, "so enthusiastic over the whole thing that it made one's heart ache to see his bright happy face" (3 August 1914 to Home). He left behind the beautiful summers of his childhood: "We have just seen Pasha off and it was too dreadful. We took some group photographs, had tea with Mrs. Mitt and then went down to the pier.[21] Poor Mrs. Mitt did her best not to break down for Pasha's sake, as indeed did we all, and we gave him the best sendoff we could. Shall we ever see the dear boy again, I wonder" (5 August 1914 to Home). Yes, they would, but not as they had wished.

1 October 1914 from Pasha Mitt to Dorothy
Dear little Dorote [sic], Thank you very much for the grass with four leaves—I'll try to be happy. Now I am no longer a student, but an officer, and I shoot with guns at German aeroplanes. One aeroplane we already shot down, on 13 [13 OS/26 NS] September. If I am alive and return from the war, I'll bring a small piece of a blown-up German shell as a souvenir to kind Dorothy. Kiss

your Mama, Papa and Aunt Smith. If it is difficult to read my letter, ask Kolaika, he will be glad to tell everything. Pasha Mitt sends a cordial greeting to Dorothy. Pasha.[22]

25 October 1914 to Home
Dorothy had such a nice letter from Pasha from the acting army and she was proud of it. He wrote to thank her for a four-leaf clover she sent him, and I tell Dorothy she must always keep that letter, until by and by it may be an heirloom if she has children and grandchildren.

14 May 1916 to Home
The blow which has fallen on so many thousand homes during the last months, has at length fallen on Novogeorgievsk, and our bright, brave Pasha has gone—how we do not know, but probably by falling from an aeroplane, as he has been in the school of aviation for the past few months. He and Nina [Bryner] were married on the thirtieth, two weeks ago today, and five days later he died.[23] One can't bear to think of Nina, for she and Pasha were boy and girl sweethearts while they were still in school and only her own precarious state of health prevented their being married last autumn.[24] . . . I went to the mass in the Cathedral and an old priest, who, I afterwards learned, had taught Pasha for eight years, spoke so beautifully, his own voice almost breaking two or three times . . . that I was astonished, never dreaming then that he knew Pasha personally and probably loved him as everybody did. Friday I went to see Mrs. Mitt, and found her lying in a darkened room, fairly dazed with grief, but still with every nerve strained in the suspense of waiting for a telegram to know what really happened. The first telegram was four days en route and since then not a word.

6 June 1916 to Home
We have at last heard the details of Pasha's death, and, hard as they have tried to keep the real truth from Mrs. Mitt, it was impossible. They told her all the time that he died of heart failure, fearing the shock of the awful truth on her weak system. He was alone in his aeroplane and some peasants who were watching saw the machine turn over (as it does when it strikes a vacuum), then right itself, and then turn again. The second time, Pasha fell out and came down head first with the result one can imagine. The machine came down safely. Poor Nina—a bride one Sunday and a broken-hearted widow of two days the next. She came, with her father and sister last Friday, and spends

most of her time beside Mrs. Mitt's bed. Her one prayer now is that she may have a child.[25]

17 July 1916 to Home
Yesterday was Pasha's funeral, and at last all that is left of him rests in [his native] soil. The body reached here Saturday, escorted by his body servant, a soldier who was attached to his personal service all through the war, first in the artillery and then in the aviation corps, and it was such a comfort to them all to hear what this Gralko had to tell, for of necessity, Pasha's letters had been brief, although he wrote his mother often. The *dolgusha* made a fairly good hearse and catafalque, and for twenty-four hours, the coffin rested on it under the shade of the huge old lindens in the park, and there the funeral service was held, the same old priest officiating as at the mass in the cathedral. The people came out from town by the ten twenty [train] and the service was at noon. The wealth of flowers on the estate went to cover the coffin, and the temporary hearse and some of the wreaths were beautiful—there were also garlands of oak leaves, and the road from the park to the turfed avenue leading to the cemetery was carpeted with oak leaves. Besides the roses, stocks and pansies of the gardens, the wild purple iris, white briars and meadow sweet are in bloom, and we made some beautiful things from them. The same flags, which waved so gaily when Pasha went off to war, waved at half mast yesterday from both *dachas*—for his homecoming. His three uncles, his soldier and two other friends were the bearers, and Kolia (the only brother at home) and some of his school friends shoveled the earth into the grave.[26] The old general, under whom Pasha served out here four years ago, came, with an escort of ten artillerists from Pasha's old regiment. The service at the grave was a long one, and again the old priest spoke so nicely. One's heart aches to bursting for Mrs. Mitt and Nina—the two on whom the blow falls hardest—and worst of all is to think that their grief is only a drop in the ocean of suffering caused by this war. Nina isn't yet twenty-one and her sweet sad face brings tears to one's eyes—remembering as we all do how she looked before. Pasha had received four decorations for brilliant service, and Gralko told Mrs. Mitt that he gave them all to the fund for the starving in Poland, only keeping the documents for himself. They were of gold and he said he could buy for himself when the war was over. . . . Gralko said that Pasha was always talking to him about the estate and had promised to find him a place here if he cared to come to the East when the war was over.

Mr. & Mrs. Pray   Mrs. Smith   Dr. Ivy   Bertie   Mr. Smith

The Smiths and the Prays with their English friends who are visiting from Shanghai, summer 1894: *Seated, from left*: Frederick and Eleanor Pray, Sarah Smith, Robert (Robin) Ivy with son Herbert (Bertie), and Charles Smith. Mrs. Pray is wearing the yellow dress with stripes of black velvet ribbon that was made for her in Yokohama during the journey to Vladivostok. The handwritten identifications are by Mrs. Pray. Photograph by Anne E. Ivy.

The Prays in Dom Smith's "veranda room," so named because it was located under the second-floor open veranda; mid-1890s. This room was used as a library and sitting-room, and was pleasantly furnished with rattan armchairs, warm rugs, and one of the desks where Mrs. Pray wrote her letters. Note the two heavy tomes next to the framed photos: Eleanor's dictionaries, marked R[ussian] and E[nglish] on the respective spines.

The Prays and friends elegantly ready for a game of tennis at the Danish House, 9 September 1900. *Left to right*: Bessie Ivy, David Clarkson, John Walsham, Leon Merritt, Eleanor and Frederick Pray, Bertie Ivy, Harold Newhard, and Dr. and Mrs. Ivy. Note Ted Pray's cummerbund, and all the "summer-white" clothing, including "Jack" Walsham's shoes. Courtesy of the Arseniev Museum.

A photograph of Dorothy Pray, sent to Anna Guptill, Eleanor's maternal aunt, in late 1912 with the following greeting (in Mrs. Pray's hand): "Wishing Grand Aunt and Uncle A Merry Christmas! Dorothy. P.S. I hope you notice my pockets!"

Two views of the walkway along the wing of Dom Smith to the two-story main part of the home, featuring Mr. Pray with Dou Kee in the lower photo, and an *amah* and two coolies, one of them probably Dou Kee, in the upper photo. The winter view was taken after the big snowstorm of January 1910, and the summer view probably in 1905. Dom Smith's main entrance is in the distance, next to one of the windows of the veranda room, with the veranda itself, above, surrounded by its wrought-iron railing. The second-floor window is in the east bedroom, used as Dorothy's nursery after she was born in 1906.

O Hiro-san, Cook, and O Tsuki-san in the veranda room, probably late 1890s. The Japanese man serving as Dom Smith's cook was known (in the English manner) simply as "Cook." He and O Tsuki-san were married. O Hiro-san, of an old Samurai family, married David Clarkson in Yokohama in 1908. Courtesy of the Arseniev Museum.

"A Vladivostok Crab" in the hands of Cook by the front door of Dom Smith. Eleanor Pray received her camera in March 1899, and this was one of her very first photos that spring. Courtesy of the Arseniev Museum.

Close friends, 1901. *Left to right*: Minni Langschwadt, Marie Dattan, her sister Anna Cornehls, Sophie Wohlfahrt, Sarah Smith, Eleanor Pray, and Eleonora Hansen. Tina Behn, also a member of Mrs. Dattan's tea party, was in Europe and could not be included. Photograph probably by T. Mori, a professional photographer in Vladivostok.

Svetlanskaia Street, looking east, with "the old Kunst & Albers building" that reminded Eleanor Pray of a palace when she first arrived in Vladivostok. The city is decorated for the coronation of Nikolai II and Alexandra Fedorovna, Russia's last tsar and tsarina, in May 1896. Dom Smith is visible to the top right of K&A, featuring a large garland on the veranda. To the extreme right is the tower of the Admiral's House with its St. Andrew's flag, the ensign of the Imperial Russian Navy, 1712–1918. Photographer unknown. Courtesy of the Arseniev Museum.

"SROOTCH"   BKT. "JOHN BAIZLEY"

Part of a panorama view of the center of Vladivostok, looking south, focusing here on the western side of the Bay of the Golden Horn. The railway station, where the Trans-Siberian Railway began, is visible near the shore just above and slightly to the right of the group of sailboats. The *John Baizley*, an American bark, visited Vladivostok in July 1895, when Anne E. Ivy took the photograph from the premises of Dom Smith.

Ted received his bicycle in early October 1894 and liked to take it out for practice during the still warm and pleasant "Velvet Season" (Indian summer). This is a picnic with the Ivys, probably 1894 or 1895. Photograph by Anne E. Ivy.

The Tsesarevich Nikolai Arch decorated for Coronation Week, May 1896. This north side of the Arch (looking south to the Bay of the Golden Horn) shows Vladivostok's coat of arms with the inscription "28 April 1880," the date (OS) when the naval post was declared a city. Photographer unknown. Courtesy of the Arseniev Museum.

Three families in the Lindholms' garden, summer 1894. *Left to right, seated*: Bertie Ivy, Sarah Smith, Aina Lindholm, Nathalie and Otto Lindholm, and Charles Smith. *Left to right, standing*: Frederick Pray, Lolla and Tullie Lindholm, Eleanor Pray, and Dr. Ivy. Photograph by Anne E. Ivy.

"Buried in Dostoevsky." Aina Lindholm at the family's *dacha* in Nakhodka, on the Sea of Japan, about seventy-five miles east of Vladivostok, probably July 1901. This photo by Eleanor Pray was part of the large banner gracing the Arseniev Museum for the presentation of the book *Pisma iz Vladivostoka* (Letters from Vladivostok; in Russian) and the opening of the exhibit based on it, in October 2008. Courtesy of the Arseniev Museum.

Anne Ivy's Vladivostok panorama looking east from Tiger Hill over the city center and the Bay of the Golden Horn, 1894. The two green areas are (*middle left*) the public park, with the Kunst and Albers department store on Svetlanskaia just beyond it, and (*center*) the Admiral's Garden (with the Cathedral of the Assumption in the far distance). The prominent two-story mansion on the hill (*left center*) is K&A's Fernsicht, with Dom Smith immediately to the right (note the veranda). This photograph by Anne E. Ivy was included as an image of "Wladivostok" in Isabella Bird Bishop's *Korea and Her Neighbors*.

Dr. Richard T. Greener, United States commercial agent to Vladivostok, at a picnic in Sedanka, 1901. *From left to right*: Dr. Greener, William Davidson, Frederick Pray, Eleanor Pray (facing away from the camera), probably Dr. Ivy, Eleonora Hansen, and Sarah Smith.

Mrs. Dattan's tea party visiting her at Novogeorgievsk, probably 1901. *From left to right*: Eleanor Pray, Anna Cornehls, Sophie Wohlfahrt, Marie Dattan, Sarah Smith, Eleonora Hansen, and Minni Langschwadt.

At the Novogeorgievsk Estate: "Mrs. Dattan's Summer House" (Villa Alwine) and the Goldenstedts' "Big Dacha," 1901. Photograph by Eleanor Pray.

Using the north side of Villa Alwine's veranda as a summer dining-room, probably summer 1901. *Seated, clockwise from front*: Marie Dattan (on the high chair), Adi and Sasha Dattan, Eleonora Hansen, an unidentified man, Frederick Pray, Marie Dattan, Eleanor Pray, Sarah Smith, Bessie Ivy, Sophie Wohlfahrt, and Pasha and Gori Dattan. *Standing in back*: two servants and Dr. Ivy. Photograph by Anne E. Ivy.

Dacha Seyuza, seen from the dirt road that went through the estate park and the woods to the southernmost cape on the peninsula.

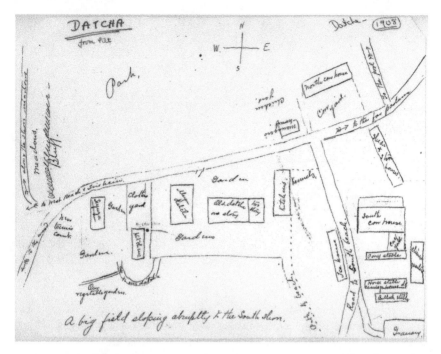

The map of the Novogeorgievsk Estate that Eleanor Pray drew after fire destroyed the Goldenstedts' Big Dacha, October 1910. The year noted on the top (not in Eleanor Pray's hand) is incorrect.

"The Ruins, 23 Oct. 1910." This photograph was taken from a corner of Villa Alwine, looking east. Note the water barrel, visible also in "Mrs. Dattan's Summer House," p. 117.

Harbor of Vladivostok, 9–10 September O.S. 1903.

Panoramic view of the "Harbor of Vladivostok, 9–10 September OS 1903," looking southwest over the prominent "L" of the Golden Horn. This was the last Vladivostok gathering of the majestic Pacific squadrons. Within two years, most of these ships had been destroyed or captured in the Russo-Japanese War. Photograph by Eleanor Pray.

Dr. and Mrs. Alexander Stein on vacation by the Black Sea, 11 August 1928. On the back of this photo Alexander Konstantinovich wrote a poem comparing the majestic Crimean scenery with faithful old friendship. Photograph by a professional photographer in the Crimea (whose business stamp is not legible).

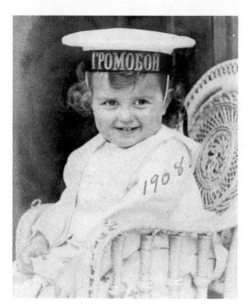

Two-year-old Dorothy in a *Gromoboi* officer's hat, 1908. Both Mrs. Pray and Dorothy loved and mentioned their memories of the *Gromoboi* for the rest of their lives.

The staff of the "American Consulate/Amerikanskoe Konsulstvo" in Vladivostok, located in the Sinkevich House on Pushkin Street, 1920. Vice-Consul Pray stands in the middle at the back.

"The Sewing Circle at the Admiral's, 1914–17." Mrs. Borisova, Admiral Schultz's sister who led the circle, sits in the center foreground; Mrs. Pray is to the extreme right by the wall. The women sewed shirts, socks, bandages, and other necessities for those wounded in the First World War, as well as organized fund-raising events to buy the necessary materials.

At the US consulate, June 1922. Consul David Macgowan sits at the front table; vice-consul Frederick Pray stands in the back room. The woman in the dark blouse, seated slightly to the left of center, is secretary Elizaveta Gustavovna Pestrikova, university-trained (in Saint Petersburg and London) and fluent in Russian, German, and English. The office was closed in May 1923. (Information about Mrs. Pestrikova gratefully received from her grandson, Robert Hunter.)

Part III
The History

CHAPTER 6

The Russo-Japanese War, 1904–1905

THE RUSSO-JAPANESE WAR, CAUSED BY THE TERRITORIAL AMBITIONS of several world powers, raged in Manchuria and on the seas between Korea, Japan, and China for a year and a half. The surprise attacks at Port Arthur and Chemulpo (today Incheon, the port of Seoul) on 8–9 February 1904; the battle of Mukden in early 1905; and the annihilation of Russia's Baltic Fleet[1] at Tsushima on 27–28 May 1905 are some of the events recognized as among the most horrendous of modern warfare. Russia was not well prepared for this conflict.[2] Supremely disciplined and motivated Japanese forces fought disillusioned Russian troops led by frequently lackadaisical officers, and the final outcome included not only Russian losses of land such as southern Sakhalin and parts of Manchuria but also hundreds of thousands of casualties (more than 30,000 killed and 100,000 wounded just at Mukden).

Although telegraphic communications were well developed by this time, news stories in Russia and Japan were regularly censored by being delayed, exaggerated, or not printed at all, and in her letters Eleanor Pray often mentions the blackened-out telegrams in the local papers.[3] Victories were magnified, and speculation about both the military advances and the retreats thrived, as one observer put it, "rather to conceal the truth than to disclose it," adding, but "that is fair in war, and no one can object to it."[4] From her friends on the Vladivostok squadron, Mrs. Pray learned the details of some of the battles, and (despite most Americans' and Europeans' pro-Japanese stance) she came to empathize deeply with the Russian people in the increasing difficulties. Remaining on the periphery of the military activities, "our dear Vladivostok" (27 December 1903 to Aunt Anna) was not badly damaged in terms of its buildings and streets, but the residents' psychological scars were deep. Despite as a child having "long[ed] to live in war times" (19 September 1905 to Home), Eleanor Pray turned against all wars due to their inordinate human cost: "It is too bad that the people who make these wars could not be obliged to fight it out man to man, instead of embroiling so many thousands of others in it" (10 February 1904 to Home).

Usually cheerful and comforting, Eleanor continued to send regular letters to her family in New England and to Sarah in Shanghai,[5] and also instituted a regimen of weekly, open-faced postcards, more than twenty of which still exist. In a peculiarly compelling mixture, this correspondence reflects not only the violence of the war but also the peaceful everyday moments that permeated Eleanor's home front. On the one hand, a gallery of war-related portraits illuminates the letters: there is Lieutenant Diachkov of the *Gromoboi,* who asks her to alert his fiancée in Australia when war breaks out; midshipman Blok of the *Russia,* who is supremely honorable in all of his dealings with her; and chief engineer Ivan Vasilievich Ivanov, who dies a hero on the *Rurik.* Did Lieutenant Kogan, who seemed so youthfully invincible, really commit suicide because of gambling debts, or because of the war's unbearable pressure on Russia's thinking population? On the other hand, the survivors of the military actions would come ashore and again engage in life's ordinary activities: taking walks, dropping in for tea, and resuming their English lessons. Thus, Eleanor Pray's calendar-like vignettes from these years flash by like slide images, intensity filling each message, yet soon replaced by new views. That is how humans survive the horror of war.

WAITING FOR WAR

Already in the fall of 1903, war with Japan was anticipated. Eleanor Pray followed the political developments with both interest and dread, and, on 22 and 23 September, took two remarkable photos of the Bay of the Golden Horn from a popular vantage point high on the hill over Pushkin Street. These haunting images show the harbor dotted with almost a dozen great ships of the Vladivostok and Port Arthur squadrons, splendid in their lines and strong in their reassurance of safety and protection. It was unimaginable that after this war, most of them would not return. Still, despite the troubling possibilities ahead, life at Dom Smith proceeded almost cheerily. Mrs. Pray enjoyed seeing her friends, and the amateur theatricals on the *Gromoboi* in December were a welcome winter diversion.

For the Prays and Sarah Smith, some of the best moments of these years were spent with Alexander Konstantinovich Stein, the well-known physician on the *Gromoboi*. He became Eleanor Pray's intrepid walking companion, and as they tramped around Vladivostok's hills, they argued about politics, literature, and life itself. He studied English with her, and in exchange taught her advanced constructions in his own language. When the *Gromoboi* was ordered away from Vladivostok after the war, Eleanor Pray was distraught: "I shall miss him very much indeed. I have never had a friend or a comrade in the least like him and shall probably never have such another one for I do not make friends easily. It has been a liberal education in many ways to be with him so much, and while he is occasionally as dry as bones in the subject of his conversation, it is always solid and always worth remembering" (29 September 1905 to Aunt Anna). A widower when Mrs. Pray met him, Dr. Stein eventually remarried and settled into a medical career in Saint Petersburg. He and his wife continued corresponding with Mrs. Pray well into the 1920s.

17 October 1903 to Aunt Anna
The squadron went the twenty-third of September, leaving absolutely nothing bigger than a saucepan to defend Vladivostok. Last Sunday, to our delight, back came the cruisers which we consider particularly our own—i.e., those that stand here all winter, the *Gromoboi*, *Russia* and *Bogatyr* and with them the *Rurik*. . . . The junior doctor [Stein] on the *Gromoboi* . . . came to see me yesterday and we had a long walk over the hills. He had hoped for war because he wants to get killed (his wife is dead), but I told him even if there was war, he had no business to be killed for his place was to help the wounded.

28 October 1903 to Home
A most horrible thing has happened. . . . I think I have often mentioned Lieut. Blok in my letters—a midshipman off the *Russia* who has been having English lessons with me. Just before the time when he should have come for my lesson yesterday, Mrs. Lindholm came in and said—"They are just burying Lieut. Blok who has killed himself." I could not believe it, so I wrote at once to Dr. Stein and he confirmed it.

29 October 1903 to Home
The cause of Mr. Blok's suicide is said to be a reproof or a challenge for a duel given him by one of the older officers on account of a flirtation with his wife,

who has been running after the boy all summer long, and they say the officer, [Sergei A.] Ivanov, is almost off his head about it.[6] . . . Mr. Blok thought he had disgraced himself forever, rushed on board ship (he was at the Ivanovs'), his comrade after him, probably fearing something of the kind, but just as his comrade got his hand on the doorknob of his cabin, he heard the shot on the other side of the door. Mr. Blok was so much liked by everybody that of course there is a great indignation felt over the whole affair—that he was in love with Liza Ivanova is nonsense and yet she has been the cause of his death. . . . They say that [though] he could have no honors paid to him, the coffin was literally buried in white flowers showing the love and devotion of his comrades and superior officers. Only a week ago today he was here for his lesson, well and strong, and telling me in his frank, boyish way of his plans for the future.

16 November 1903 to Home
When Liza came into the room at a dinner at the Brandts' last week, Lieut. Diachkov . . . looked straight at her and said, "Murderess."

11 December 1903 to Home
The affair on the *Gromoboi* came off night before last and I enjoyed myself very much indeed. . . . Dr. Stein, whose guests we were, was of course waiting for us, and presently we went to the little theater that had been arranged between decks. The sailors had done everything themselves and it was so nicely arranged. The drop curtain had a seascape with the *Gromoboi* and *Retvizan* in the foreground, done in oils, also by a sailor, and really well done for a thing of the sort. The play was a farce called *The Marriage* by Gogol and of the ten sailors who took part, four very successfully represented women. . . . [Later] we sat around and talked. There were various cozy lights in flower shades fitted up between decks and there were so many palms, camellias, and smaller flowers that one could hardly believe it was a ship. It was rather borne upon us, though, that it was a ship and between decks at that, for as we sat there chatting, the biggest rat I ever saw in my life ran across one of the iron beams. Luckily only Mr. Bryner, Lieut. Diachkov, and I saw it, so nobody had the opportunity to faint and we said nothing. . . . At midnight, supper was served and it was so jolly. Mr. Bryner, Ted, Sarah, Lieut. Manturov, Dr. Stein, and I had a small table to ourselves, in a corner of the enormous wardroom, from where we could see everything and everybody. There was a band just outside each end of the room—just far enough away for the music to be a bit

softened, and when one finished playing, the other one began. We were about a hundred people—the officers and their guests—just enough for a very nice evening, but not at all a crush. . . . The Russian men-of-war each have their own special holiday, just as the people have their name-days, and the twenty-sixth of November [OS] (our Dec. 9) belongs to the *Gromoboi*.

27 December 1903 to Aunt Anna
My favorite pupil is, as always, Dr. Stein from the *Gromoboi*. . . . Next is Lieut. Diachkov and also a Lieut. Vilken, both from the *Gromoboi*. The former is engaged to an Australian girl and the way he talks about her is a caution. He is rather shy but to save his life he can't keep his Georgie out of the conversation, and I have all I can do to keep a straight face. Lieut. Vilken only began yesterday so I haven't got him fairly sized up yet, but he draws very long breaths over his dictations, which amuses me.

7 January 1904 to Home, Russian Christmas
Today the weather is simply superb and I have been for a long, long walk with Dr. Stein. Sarah has a sore toe and could not go, and Ted has gone skating. I was so glad Alexander Konstantinovich could come today because I am sure such holidays are very lonely for him, and he does so enjoy walking.

3 February 1904 to Home
The tension increases every day until now it seems that something *must* snap before long. It was bad in October,[7] and bad the first of January but nothing to be compared to this. Last night the Japanese in town held a mass meeting and as a result hundreds of them are leaving by the boat this afternoon.

7 February 1904 to Home
Lieut. Kogan, one of my two military pupils, is to be stationed in the Tiger Battery and I am very glad because it is nice to have a friend one can go to in time of need, and if we are obliged to leave town, we shall ask him to live in the house. I have another artillery officer among my pupils—Capt. Iuzbashev—but I do not know him very well yet. Lieut. Kogan says that as Capt. Iu. comes for his lesson at eleven o'clock, I ought to make him help get *tiffin*, and that he (K.) comes at six o'clock so he will help get dinner! Lieut. Diachkov says he will bring his sailor and help me clean the rooms, so you see, we are not without offers of help!

8 February 1904 to Home

Yesterday noon Mr. Schwabe, the British consular representative, was here and privately informed us that war would be declared last night or today,[8] so we might make plans accordingly. [Our] servants are all leaving tomorrow morning and I shall send this letter on that boat.

THE ATTACK ON PORT ARTHUR, THE *PETROPAVLOVSK*

In late January 1904, Eleanor Pray took another remarkable photo of the Bay of the Golden Horn, this time from high on Tiger Hill. As portrayed from west to east, there lies the squadron frozen in mid-winter ice: closest to Tiger Hill, near the skating-rink by the Admiral's House, was the *Russia*, then the other cruisers—the *Bogatyr*, the *Rurik*, and the *Gromoboi*—and at the farther end of the Bay the supply ship *Lena*. Icebreakers kept a lane open for their regular exits into the Sea of Japan. If war came, their military objective would be, among others, to offer "panic deflection," by diverting Japan's attention from the activities in the Yellow Sea.[9]

Under the guise of darkness, Japanese boats attacked the Russian fleet at Port Arthur at midnight on 8–9 February 1904. This harbor, within its intriguingly shaped spit of land, and located in China about 1,200 miles by sea from Vladivostok, had served as a Russian naval base since 1898, but was not well developed. The passage into the inner roadstead was narrow and easily blocked, and large ships could get through only at high tide. Although repeatedly attempting to escape, the Russian ships became trapped within Port Arthur, and the Japanese attacks continued. On 13 April 1904, they sank the *Petropavlovsk*, the flagship of the commander of Russia's Pacific Fleet, vice admiral Stepan Makarov. On board were not only Makarov and rear admiral Mikhail Molas (who both died), and grand duke Kirill Vladimirovich (who survived), but also the well-known Russian artist Vasilii Vereshchagin, many of whose paintings reflect strong antiwar sentiments. He, too, perished with the ship amidst the "gruesome spectacle" of the volcano-like explosions.[10]

Port Arthur was under siege until 2 January 1905, when its commander, general Anatolii Stoessel, surrendered to his Japanese counterpart, general Nogi Maresuke. Whether he based his decision on facts or not, Stoessel cited the epidemic of scurvy among his troops as the cause for surrender, and begged the tsar's forgiveness: "Eleven months of ceaseless fighting have exhausted our strength. . . . The men are reduced to shadows."[11] Despite having capitulated, Stoessel was admired for his lengthy stand at Port Arthur.

10 February 1904 to Home, Wednesday

[10.00 AM] It has come at last and in the past twenty-four hours it seems as if we had lived and suffered a lifetime. Monday . . . Alexander Konstantino-vich was here for his lesson and then he gave me mine, and set a long translation for me to have ready today, and then we had tea together and he only went away from here at six o'clock. An hour later Pavel Pavlovich [Diachkov] came for his lesson and he was so happy with plans for going to Sydney to see his English fiancée next autumn. Yesterday morning I was printing some photographs when I heard a gun. My heart almost stood still and it seemed an hour before the other two came and then I knew it was the signal of war from the *Russia* which is the Admiral's ship. Soon after I got a hasty note from Pavel Pavlovich enclosing his fiancée's address and asking me to write to her that *Gromoboi* had been ordered out to sea and as he was on duty, he had no time to write. . . . I wished them victory and gave Dr. Stein my blessing (a Russian custom). . . . And then the ships went out, one by one—first the *Russia*, about two o'clock, then the *Bogatyr*, then the *Rurik*, and last of all, about four, the *Gromoboi*, and I prayed over her till she was out of sight. It was bad enough for all who had friends on board, but God only knows what it must have been for the wives of the officers. I did not go down on the ice to wave them farewell for I could not stand it. Some of the ladies fainted and they say it was so pitiful. At noon it began to leak through the town that a Japanese torpedo boat had disabled three of the Russian battleships [the *Tsesarevich*, *Retvizan*, and *Pallada*] off Port Arthur in the night.

[5.45 PM] As if we did not already feel dismal enough, a howling snow-storm has started in, the first since early in December—and we can only think of those four cruisers somewhere out in this.

11 February 1904 to Home

The news from Port Arthur is very bad. . . . The Jappies hit below the water line almost in every case. *Poltava*, *Retvizan*, *Askold*, *Novik*, *Diana*, *Pallada* have all been more or less injured—the first two are of the strongest battleships and the second two are supposed to be first-class cruisers, especially the *Novik*. . . . As soon as lunch was over Sarah, Mrs. Merritt and I took our two *amahs* down to the steamer. We would not let them go alone for, although there are policemen about every ten *rods*, one can never tell what will happen. Ted could not leave the office as his clerk has been drafted to war. No one said anything but one man leaned over toward O Tsumo-san, glaring, and called her a very bad name. I returned the compliment by calling him "a cursed

Turk" in my best Russian and he passed on. . . . The streets are in a fearful condition with such a quantity of snow and, although the coolies are working as fast as possible, it will be days before they get it away, and to make matters worse it has begun to snow again.

14 February 1904 to Home
The ships have come back safe but for what or for how long we do not know. It is enough to see them here. I was at the first of the course of Red Cross lectures which are to be given in the hall of the museum and suddenly I saw Mrs. Stemman, the wife of the captain of the *Bogatyr*, make a dash, and after her Baroness Grevenits, and I felt sure the ships had come.

16 February 1904 to Home
The bad news still continues to come from the South for there has been a battle in Chemulpo and the *Koreets* and *Variag* have been destroyed. The commander of the latter, when he found he could not save his ship, sent all the men ashore, blew up the ship and went down with it to prevent it falling into the hands of the Japanese, a grand and heroic deed.[12]

22 February 1904 to Home
Today we heard for the first time the details of the torpedo attack on the first night and one can but laugh, for a cheekier thing I never heard of in my life. The Russian ships were in three rows, three abreast, and the Japanese torpedo boats steamed past the first two rows, shouting in Russian through the semaphore, and went straight to the two best ships which were farthest in of all, and tried to sink them. . . . The impudence of the Japanese in talking Russian through the semaphore, and using Russian signals, was really too funny and there the Russians were watching them and complaining that the men at the semaphore did not speak plainly enough![13]

16 April 1904 to Home
We are simply filled with horror at the terrible catastrophe which happened to the *Petropavlovsk*, news of which reached here yesterday morning. . . . The whole world will mourn Admiral Makarov for he was a clever, upright, progressive man and was supposed to be Russia's leading admiral. . . . We knew [Rear Admiral Molas] slightly for when we first came out here he was the commander of the *Admiral Kornilov*, and, [he] being a great friend of the Lindholms, we often met him there.

29 April 1904 to Clara
Last Saturday three ships of the squadron left and returned only Wednesday night and we were so mad with anxiety for them that I can't tell you what a relief it was when we saw them enter the harbor—their lights looked like the lamps of paradise. They had had rather an eventful voyage for they had sunk two merchant ships and a transport and brought in over two hundred Japanese prisoners, among the number eight officers.[14] Most of the others were non-combatants and a motley-looking crowd they were. At five in the afternoon they were paraded through the streets under a strong convoy of soldiers, with a mounted detachment as advance and rear guards, on their way to the station for they are to be sent up into the country somewhere.

THE BOMBARDMENT OF VLADIVOSTOK

Several times in the spring of 1904, Japanese ships under the command of admiral Kamimura Hikonojo approached Vladivostok, but bombed the city only once, on 6 March, a Sunday. The shelling began about 1.20 PM and lasted for less than an hour, causing more excitement than fear. Masses of people gathered on the Eagle's Nest, the city's highest hill, to watch the unfolding drama. It appeared that Kamimura was reconnoitering to ascertain if the Vladivostok squadron was in port.[15]

16 February 1904 to Home
I prefer to stay in Vladivostok and do not feel the least fear. It is not as if we were strangers in a strange place.

6 March 1904 to Clara
At two o'clock this afternoon the town was bombarded from the eastern side by seven Japanese cruisers, the action lasting about an hour. I sat here writing and Ted sat beside me. Of course we heard the guns but we thought it was only battery practice and paid no attention to it. Ted noticed that the sounds were coming nearer and said, "It's the Japs this time," but neither of us really thought it was. Then we saw the [Russian] ships pulling up anchor and we knew that something sudden must have happened because the ships did not have half steam up, and a lot of the sailors were ashore. Then Dou Kee came and said that someone had been killed at the other end of the town. Upon this, Ted grabbed his field glasses and ran as fast as he could go to the top of the hill, and from there he could plainly see seven Japanese cruisers going

away and saw several places at the other end of the town where shells had fallen, three of them on the ice not far from the Lindholms' house, and not over a mile and a half from here. He saw our squadron going out, hugging the shore so as to keep under the batteries because they, being cruisers, have no very heavy guns. . . . Our squadron came back just at dusk and wasn't I glad to see it.

7 March 1904 to Clara
The Japanese have appeared again—or at least, so they say—seven cruisers, two battle ships, a coast defense . . . and some torpedo boats and they expect the bombardment to begin again. Ted has gone to the top of the hill (which is already black with people) to see if there is any truth in the report.

8 March 1904 to Clara
Nothing at all happened yesterday—Ted . . . saw the Japanese ships moving off to the south, so the town drew a breath of relief because the ice protects us there. This morning there is a fog so we are wondering if they will steal back under the cover of it and begin again.

10 March 1904 to Clara, Thursday
Everything was quiet all day Tuesday, and . . . that night there was a great uproar in the town—cheering, etc. . . . We supposed it to be simply the arrival of a new regiment, a little noisier than usual. Mlle. Marcel has a sister of mercy in her quarters and when the uproar began the sister came rushing to her, screaming that the Japanese had landed in the town and were marching down Svetlanskaia. They both rushed to a window, threw it open, and, as Mademoiselle expressed it, "stood on their stomachs" to see what was up. Sure enough a crowd was coming up the street, and the sister grabbed her icon and held it out in defiance to purge the town of the enemy. Then they heard a band and at length distinguished the strains of "God Save the Tsar," whereupon they decided that the Japanese had landed somewhere and that the soldiers were marching out to battle, whereupon defiance faded from the sister's face, and she leaned out of the window, waving her icon as a blessing over the soldiers, singing solemnly as she did so with the band. Suddenly they heard from the crowd in the street the words "100,000" and they saw a carriage in which were two men, and one of them stood up and read something and the soldiers cheered again. "It is a victory—we have killed 100,000 Japa-

nese," screamed the sister, and again she waved her icon, this time in triumph, singing "God Save the Tsar" at the top of her voice. They could not understand what the man had read so they went on the street to find out—and what do you suppose it was? Nothing more or less than a telegram from the Tsar, congratulating Vladivostok on its baptism by fire. They were sold, and spent the next hour laughing over all the emotions they had passed through—fear and defiance—then pity—and lastly triumph! The best thing was M. Plarr, the French Agent who . . . lives opposite the Governor's House, and when the people stopped there to read the telegram, he took it as a compliment to himself like the egoist he is and screamed down from his balcony, "Thanks to the Sovereign Emperor—vive la France!" which naturally amused the people immensely.

12 March 1904 to Home
Fancy a shell, thrown from a ship at least ten miles off, entering the upper corner of a room where were sitting two women and three children . . . cutting one woman's body in two, smashing a table en route, then out through the wall and exploding in the yard, and the other people were not even scratched. . . . Over a hundred and fifty shells were thrown into the town, and each shell costs no less than five hundred gold dollars—so the battle must have cost nearly a hundred thousand,[16] and all for the life of that one poor woman.

23 April 1904 to Home
Day before yesterday, to my great surprise and pleasure, Lieut. Kogan came to see me for the first time in two months. It was his birthday and he was in town. He is stationed at Fort Linevich which is several versts [old Russian measure of distance equaling 3,500 feet] out of town, and is where four of the shells exploded during the bombardment, doing no damage excepting to the roof of one house. He sent me a piece of one of them and I was so pleased for Ted has done his level best to get a piece and could not.

24 May 1904 to Home
[Mrs. Pray recalls 29 April.] From three o'clock in the morning till about an hour before sunset, the Japanese squadron was in sight of the town and of course we wondered which side of the town would catch it first. Tullie came here in the morning for her husband was out on his torpedo boat and she

spent a terribly anxious day. Her face was almost glorified when Ted came in at half past six or so and told her that the signal flag on Tigrovaia had come down, signifying that the enemy had retreated from sight.

SUMMER AND FALL 1904

For several months after the fierce beginning of the war, its din—although continuing—remained mostly beyond Vladivostok's everyday life. Then, two bloody sea battles in five days—in the Yellow Sea on 10 August, and in the Korea Strait on 14 August—resulted in major losses: numerous Russian ships were damaged; rear admiral Vilgelm Vitgeft, commander of the Port Arthur squadron, was killed; and the proud member of the Vladivostok squadron, the *Rurik* (under the command of rear admiral Nikolai Skrydlov), was sunk. Eleanor Pray comments: "Until this week we here have scarcely realized that there was a war after that first terrible week when our squadron went to sea, but this week . . . I cannot tell you what it was to see our beautiful *Gromoboi* and *Russia* come in, raked by shot and shell, and to see with an awful sinking of the heart that *Rurik* was not with them" (20 August 1904 to Aunt Anna). Then, from 24 August to 3 September, the fiercest land battle, heretofore, raged at Liao-yang in Manchuria. The Japanese were victorious in each instance, and Mrs. Pray shared the bitter mood, fantasizing about the reaction in Vladivostok when Admiral Skrydlov would reappear: "I hope . . . the crowd will yell at him, 'What did you do with our *Rurik*?'" (7 January 1905 to Clara).

22 June 1904 to Aunt Anna, Wednesday
Vladivostok is just now in a very happy frame of mind, because our squadron has been out and sunk three Japanese transports, and about five thousand people perished.[17] . . . Our *Gromoboi* took the leading part and did all the work. They came back here Monday morning bringing with them many prisoners whom they had rescued from the water. That afternoon Lieut. Diachkov came to have tea with me and told me all about it. He is the ordnance officer and it had been a trying cruise for him. On the day of the action, he was obliged to be in his position, kneeling down in a turret from half past four in the morning till one in the afternoon and when he stood up for the first time, he reeled like a drunken man. The next day, yesterday, Dr. Stein came and he also told me about it, but he said it was terrible—so terrible that he hoped no sight approaching it would ever come to my eyes—to see hundreds of human beings, some of them torn by shot and splinters, strug-

gling in the sea, and shrieking with despair as they sank. Of course he was very busy with the wounded that were brought on board, and has been ever since. Even if they were the enemies of his country, they appealed to him as fellow beings and that is where the horror of it came in.

17 August 1904 from Dr. Stein to Eleanor
Very dear Eleonora Georgievna, I managed to get out of the battle completely well, because two shells could not break the defense of our firing post. Forgive me, there is no time; if I can get away tomorrow, I'll try to drop by, because I very much want to see and speak with you. With great respect, A. Shtein.[18]

21 August 1904 to Home
A week ago Friday, at daylight, the squadron went out very unexpectedly, probably with the intention to join what would be left of the Port Arthur squadron [after the Battle of the Yellow Sea] and escort it up here. Monday [15 August] there was a Japanese telegram in the papers, saying that a battle was on near Tsushima,[19] and of course the anxiety here became intense. . . . Tuesday afternoon I saw *Gromoboi* and *Russia* coming in through the straits and as glad as I was to see them, my heart went down in a lump of ice, for *Rurik* was not with them, and when they got nearer to our horror we saw that they had been banged and battered in every direction, a sick sight indeed. The town went wild and people by hundreds rushed down to the shore to see what had happened, and the suspense was something dreadful. . . . Ted went out alongside in a *sampan* at once, but, being a foreigner, did not like to ask any questions or to ask to see anybody on board because then they were all busy taking off the wounded, so he came back. . . . The following morning I went with Newhardsan in a *sampan* around the ships and a sick-looking sight they were with holes in every direction, but luckily the holes, while bad, are all above or at the water line and the machinery and boilers are intact. . . . While going around the ship I saw Diachkov walking on deck so I knew that he was all right, but saw nothing of Alexander Konstantinovich and I still felt uneasy. At noon however, I received a short hastily written note from him and then I felt satisfied. . . . Wednesday afternoon Pavel Pavlovich came to see me and told me all about the battle, and he had a good chance to see it all for, as chief ordnance officer, his position is necessarily where he can see the effect of every shot on the enemy. With the exception of the engineers and doctors, whose stations are in strongly protected places, every officer but one, Khalkevich, was killed or wounded, and he, though in an exposed position, was not scratched. Pavel

Pavlovich has three wounds, on the abdomen, shoulder and face, but they are mere pin scratches. Gusevich, a very nice boy, was burned to death by a powder explosion and Tatarinov, who was working the range finder, was blown into inch bits so he never knew what happened to him. I detested him when he was alive, but I am sorry he died in such a dreadful way. Vilken has a bad wound close to the jugular vein, but day before yesterday they did an operation and removed the largest piece of shell, but there has to be another and perhaps a more dangerous operation for the smaller pieces. . . . Thursday afternoon late, A. K. succeeded in getting away from the ship for a few hours, so he came here and spent the evening. His account of the battle was also very interesting and like Pavel P., he too showed in his face what he had been through. He was so pale and worn and his big dark eyes burned like coals.

[Later] Alekseev has been here since last Monday and I saw him on Tuesday when he came from the mass for Admiral Vitgeft. He was in a carriage with Cossacks in front carrying a standard, a Circassian body servant on the box beside the coachman, and a mounted guard of the Vladivostok volunteers. Yesterday morning while five of us ladies were sewing at the Club, Admiral Skrydlov, with a couple of his adjutants, dropped in for a moment to pay their respects to us. I was the only one whom he did not know but he came along and shook hands with me without giving anybody a chance to introduce him.

25 August 1904 to Clara
Bad news still continues to pour in though most of it is carefully suppressed from publication. The *Novik*, the fastest cruiser in the world,[20] got separated from the Port Arthur squadron during the battle two weeks ago and made a dash for Vladivostok by going out around Japan. She put into the harbor of Korsakovsk on Sakhalin for coal and there the Japanese treed her.

5 September 1904 to Clara
At last we have heard of the fate of the *Rurik* officers—a telegram came from the priest who had ended up in Shanghai, for of course the Japs would not keep a priest in captivity. I am very sorry to hear that Capt. Trusov was killed, and Engineer [I. V.] Ivanov drowned, but the other two husbands, Dr. Solukha and Lieut. Salov, are both in captivity and but slightly wounded. . . . I know all four of the wives and I have been so sorry for them during these three weeks of suspense. Mrs. Ivanova is very young and can perhaps recover from such a blow, but with Mrs. Trusova it is different—she is not far from fifty and was devoted to her husband. Poor, poor woman, she and her daughter will have a

sad journey home to Petersburg. Her only son is in Port Arthur and of course no one knows what may happen to him. These things make one realize war in all its hellishness, and it is always the innocent who suffer the most, like the wives and mothers. On top of this comes the official news late this afternoon that Kuropatkin has been obliged to evacuate Liao-yang after a desperate battle.[21] Wednesday afternoon they were telling all over town that news had been received of the utter rout of Kuroki's army, and that scarcely a thousand men were left alive. The officers drank champagne all the afternoon and the sailors were given a half holiday and the town prepared for an illumination as soon as the news should be officially confirmed. And this is the confirmation!

6 September 1904 to Clara
Our papers seem to admire Skrydlov immensely, but I cannot say that I do. It is all very well to send the squadron to sea to get banged up, and if he went with it, one might find room for praise, but it does not take an exceedingly brave man to sit on shore while other people go out to be shot at. Skrydlov's record during the Turkish war proves him to be a brave man beyond doubt— there can be no question of that, but as far as this business is concerned the others seem to have borne the brunt of it and no one hears a yip about them. Of all the leaders, I admire Kuropatkin the most, for he is making a brave fight against terrible odds. It is not only the Japanese that he has to contend with, but the inefficiency of many of his officers.

MUKDEN

Although fighting raged in the area for several months, the Battle of Mukden started seriously around 20 February 1905, and ended with the fall of the city to the Japanese on 10 March. The fortunes of the battle changed many times, and, when the slaughter was finally over, the world gradually learned of the vast burying grounds that foreshadowed those of eastern France in the world war. The massacred troops were movingly honored in the widely popular, lilting waltz "On the Hills of Manchuria," composed by Ilia Shatrov (who participated in the battle) and Oskar Knaub, and first played in 1907.[22]

6 February 1905 to Home
Skrydlov has gone back to Petersburg and the ladies are inconsolable. I heard a military officer say he hoped [Skrydlov] would get a bullet through his hair when he got there. I told him I did not believe in bullets, but I thought he

would probably get his wife in his hair if she heard of his doings out here and that would be worse than ten bullets.

22 February 1905 to Sarah
[Mr. Meares] said that between Shinwantau and Mukden you could have easily made your way by walking from the top of one carload of champagne to another, there was such a traffic in that and other drinkables, and he also said that the main street of Mukden, as far as the shops were concerned, was almost a solid phalanx of bottles, containing champagne and cognac.

2 March 1905 to Sarah
Last week it was reported that a flotilla of Japanese torpedo boats were on the horizon and the officers flew to their stations—six trains stood here in readiness to take the women and children to Nikolsk in case of a bombardment—all this being arranged by the commandant. And in the end it was not torpedo boats, but cakes of ice with seals on them!

8 March 1905 to Home
I do not recognize myself these days—I never sing, and am in rather doubtful humor most of the time—the strain of the war is telling on me more and more. . . . At last, the account of our work has been published and I will translate it for you. Beginning from the twenty-third of March last year till the first of January this year, our [Red Cross] society made the following: 670 shirts, 670 pairs of drawers, 661 pairs linen socks, 123 pairs foot clothes (something the soldiers wrap around their feet in place of stockings), 70 sheets, 612 pillowcases, 85 pillows, 3 quilts, 60 dressing-gowns, 95 dark curtains, 70 operating aprons, 353 towels, 365 neck cloths, 24 doctor's dressing-gowns, 280 bread bags.

14 March 1905 to Sarah
If today's news is true, poor Russia is in a bad way and Kuropatkin's army nearly annihilated. It makes one ill to hear all the reports of killed and wounded.

17 March 1905 to Sarah
Well, who do you suppose came to light this morning—my nice Lieut. Kogan and wasn't I glad to see him! He came here last week and expects to go to Manchuria soon, but was feeling very blue indeed over affairs generally.

20 March 1905 to Sarah

We are thunderstruck at the way Kuropatkin has been dismissed—the telegram was worded most offensively, I thought.[23]

15 April 1905 to Sarah

Not long ago Ted came up to tell me a very bad piece of news—the death of my nice Mr. Kogan, which was announced in the paper this morning. It did not say of what. It was only a month ago that I saw him and he looked well enough then.

21 April 1905 to Sarah

Lieut. Kogan would have been thirty-five today, and last year he came to see me on his birthday. I should really like to know the truth about his death—he shot himself, they say, on account of some money scandal, but nobody seems to know just what. He was so unlike anything of that sort that I cannot help feeling that he did it to shield somebody else.

THE BALTIC FLEET AND THE BATTLE OF TSUSHIMA

Setting out in October 1904 from Libau, the Baltic Fleet of more than thirty ships under admiral Zinovii Rozhestvenskii (1848–1909) and rear admiral Dmitrii Felkerzam (1846–1905) approached the Far East very slowly, but with the hopeful objective of assisting the Port Arthur squadron in what they assumed would be a successfully decisive sea battle against Japan. After a widely publicized incident on Dogger's Bank in the North Sea, where an English fishing fleet was mistaken for Japanese torpedo boats and attacked, the Baltic ships continued to Vigo on Spain's Atlantic coast. Rozhestvenskii then meandered around Africa, and Felkerzam passed through the Mediterranean Sea and the Suez Canal, reuniting on Madagascar. They met the Japanese on 27 May 1905, and the Battle of Tsushima took place at once. Virtually the whole Baltic squadron was destroyed. This indeed decided the outcome of the war.

7 May 1905 to Home

This has been Russian Easter week and everything has been very gay in spite of the war.

28 May 1905 to Sarah
People seem to think there has been a battle down South but whether it is anything more important than the harassing of the Russian squadron by the Japanese cruisers, no one seems to know.

29 May 1905 to Sarah, Monday
[7.30 PM] About an hour ago the [*Almaz*] came in and you can imagine how the whole town turned out to meet her, and all the cheering and music—how champagne, even our sour kind, will flow in the town tonight. They say that *Izumrud* [is] also in sight and they say that there is a big Japanese squadron in sight and they say many other things besides their prayers. They say that there was a big battle Saturday in which seven Japanese cruisers and three battleships were sunk. I went to have tea with Mrs. Kizhevich in her new rooms [at the Grand Hotel, overlooking the harbor] this afternoon but I was too nervous with excitement to enjoy myself and we spent a good part of the time on the balcony . . . watching for the ships.

30 May 1905 to Sarah
Dr. Birk was here this morning and says the report is that *Navarin* and *Suvorov* and four transports are sunk, and that Felkerzam has gone down with his ship.[24]

2 June 1905 to Sarah
The official report of the commander of the *Almaz* states that the *Kniaz Suvorov, Borodino, Osliabia,* and *Ural* sank and that the *Alexander III* and the transport *Kamchatka* were seriously damaged in the afternoon battle. Telegrams from Tokio seem to point to a Japanese victory, but at what cost, or with what details, nothing as yet has been published here. . . . I am truly sorry for [Dr. Stein], and for Kostia [Tyrtov], for Mr. Kizhevich, and what other Russians take these losses to heart.

3 June 1905 to Clara
[The day after the *Almaz* returned, a hole in her side, brought much worse news.] Two destroyers [*Bravyi* and *Groznyi*] came in, one crowded in every available space with the sailors who were picked up from the *Osliabia,* and still we waited, and then the dreadful news began to creep into the papers that these were all we should ever see of that magnificent squadron. . . . Since

the very beginning everyone has thought that when the Baltic Squadron reached here, the Russians would command the sea and thus be able to starve the Japanese out of Manchuria.

PEACE

Eleanor Pray was shaken by the long wait for peace and the violence that continued in the meantime, including the mutiny on the battleship *Kniaz Potemkin* in Odessa in June 1905: "One horror follows another—with the memory of that terrible battle at Tsushima fresh in our minds, comes the news of that horrible affair in Odessa, of which as yet we know only the barest details. The first officer killed was Lieut. Giliarovskii, the former chief officer on *Gromoboi*, whom I knew slightly last year. On account of a serious lung trouble he was transferred to the Black Sea squadron a little over a year ago" (11 July 1905 to Home).

In the Far East, Russia's military energies were depleted, and the warring sides agreed to meet for negotiations in the United States on the invitation of president Theodore Roosevelt. The main negotiators were Komura Jutaro, the foreign minister of Japan, and Sergei Witte, Russia's former minister of finance. The peace treaty was announced on 31 August, and signed on 5 September by emperors Nikolai II and Mutsuhito.

23 June 1905 to Sarah
Tullie says if peace comes by means of Roosevelt that she will send him a bouquet, a letter, and the biggest box of Russian sweets she can afford.

30 June 1905 to Aunt Anna
When I get to be an old woman it will seem like a dream that I have known and talked with so many people prominent in this war, and whose names we see mentioned so continually in the newspapers.

8 July 1905 to Sarah
Mr. Cornehls thinks peace is coming—I only hope he and Mrs. Lindholm are true prophets. Mrs. Lindholm says when stupid people in high places redouble their screams for war, and wise men in high places keep their mouths shut, it is always a good sign.

1 September 1905 to Sarah
Yesterday . . . on the way home I saw everybody reading a small one-column telegram and as soon as I got here, Ted sent out for one and sure enough there was Witte's sugar-coated announcement to the Emperor. In two minutes, Ted had a bottle of champagne packed [with ice] and at supper he, Mr. Clarkson and I drank about every toast we could think of. The first one Mr. Clarkson gave and it was to you and your speedy return, and then we drank to your glorious twin Teddy and his front teeth—long may they wave! Then to O Tsui-san, Roli-Poli-san, O Tsumo-san, O Wasa-san and all the "sans" in general (Mr. C. fervently emptied his glass on this),[25] and then I don't remember what we drank to, but we finished the bottle. . . . When Elisabeth [Cornehls] said her prayers, her father told her to thank the lieber Gott for having made peace. "Aber es war nicht der lieber Gott, Papa, es war Linevich!" was [five-year-old] Elisabeth's response which amused her father immensely, and us too.[26]

18 September 1905 to Home
Friday *Russia* and *Bogatyr* and the two destroyers went down toward Genzan to meet one of the Japanese admirals, also with two cruisers and two destroyers, in order to exchange friendly greetings and congratulate each other on peace! The last time Admiral Iessen met a Japanese admiral, they exchanged explosives,[27] and this theatrical performance strikes me as rather funny.

23 September 1905 to Sarah
Two years ago today that the squadron left here for Port Arthur the last time and how pretty they looked in their white paint. Now of them all, only these three here [the *Bogatyr*, *Gromoboi*, and *Russia*] remain and the others are either in the hands of the Japanese or at the bottom of the sea—it is really too dreadful when one thinks about it.

29 September 1905 to Aunt Anna
It is so nice to see the ships putting on the white garment of peace again— *Bogatyr* is painted a light gray, and *Gromoboi* and *Russia* are being painted white. The war color, dark gray, makes a ship look as grim and terrible as possible.

5 April 1916 to Home
Day before yesterday I stood in the window and watched a sight that simply made me boil and I cried in spite of myself though it is not my own Country

that is concerned—the shame of the thing was too much for even a resident to bear—about ten o'clock there was a cannonade and in came five Japanese men-of-war, three of them being the *Poltava, Peresvet* and *Variag,* captured by the Japs in the late war and, now that they are fit only for junk, sold back to the Russians. Were I the latter I would take them out in the Japan Sea and send them to the bottom, rather than disgrace the St. Andrew's cross by letting it fly where a Japanese flag has flown. . . . [The *Variag*] has never been here before, but I thought of that beautiful September day, now almost thirteen years ago, when *Poltava, Peresvet* and the rest of that magnificent Port Arthur Squadron sailed out of here for the last time—and this is the way they came back![28]

CHAPTER 7

The Riots of 1905–1906

AFTER PEACE WAS ANNOUNCED IN AUGUST 1905, THE PRAYS HOPED FOR Sarah's speedy return and for a resurrection of their home's remembered splendor. Sarah dreamed of refreshing both Dom Smith and the American Store, repainting surfaces, replacing household goods and wallpaper, and adding new furniture. Dom Smith was in bad shape, especially the veranda and the dining-room, where leaks had caused major damage, and where a wholehearted effort to make extensive repairs had seemed futile during the war: "[W]e could not tell from day to day whether the next week would find us here, in Heaven, or in Tokio" (3 September 1905 to Sarah). Now, the Prays began to trust that their faithful Japanese servants could be invited to Vladivostok again, and that jolly guests would spend cozy evenings. Steamer passenger service revived, allowing people to meet returning friends, "instead of going to say goodbye as we have been doing now for almost two years" (23 October 1905 to Home), and Dom Smith would be made pretty: "I finished arranging the veranda and drawing-room and with the exception of its glaring need of paint, it begins to look 'like befo' de wah'" (21 October 1905 to Home).

But the revolutionary spirit enveloping Russia was also reaching Vladivostok. When Sarah came home, in December, her joy was mitigated by the stark realization of what the war and the riots had cost: "Sarah is quite shocked at us all up here—she left kind-hearted people and she finds us all turned blood-thirsty, even to Mr. Szentgali, who, up to now, never wished anybody any harm in his life, but he can't get over the loss of his violin which he had had for twenty years, and which he treated like a human being" (26 December 1905 to Home).

Vladivostok's distance from the mutiny in Odessa and the July demonstrations in Saint Petersburg allowed Eleanor Pray initially to feel safe in her city: "I am more than glad that we are inhabitants of Vladivostok and not of any of the big towns in [western] Russia, for I am sure there will be some dreadful riots" (21 August 1905 to Sarah). But signs of unrest were increasing in Vladivostok, too, particularly between the sailors and soldiers, on the one hand, and their commanders, on the other; they argued about hierarchy, about decision-making authority, and about professional respect and demeanor. Eleanor faithfully kept Sarah informed, often making light of it: "It is rumored that both naval and military officers are to be allowed to wear civilian's clothes when off duty. If that is true, I fear our Svetlanskaia will look more like a misfit shop than ever" (11 July 1905 to Sarah). But mere disobedience turned to stark violence, and, by early August, before any news about the peace agreement, Eleanor noted, "About ten days ago a sailor nearly killed a drunken military officer who hauled him up for not saluting, and every week there is some scandal or other of that nature. Night before last another sailor, also reprimanded by an officer for not saluting, picked up a heavy rock and banged it down on the officer's shoulder" (9 August 1905 to Sarah). As the strikes and uprisings moved eastward across Russia, the security offered by Vladivostok's distance from the capitals was about to be removed. From 30 October, telegraphic communications with the rest of the country were broken, yet the Prays still felt no fear: "Thank goodness we are in Vladivostok" (30 October 1905 to Home).

12 November 1905 to Home
[3 PM] Many thanks indeed, but I prefer a war to a revolution and we seem to be in for a little taste of the latter at the present moment. The trouble began this afternoon in the Bazaar—the soldiers and sailors wrecked all the stalls there, beat an officer who remonstrated with them and two shots were fired— Ted, at work here in our yard, heard the bullets whiz. One of our coolies was down to the Bazaar on an errand but when he heard the shooting he concluded there was no place like home and ambled for here as fast as he could go. Ted says there is a big crowd gathered up on the hill back of our premises, watching the proceedings in the Bazaar from a safe distance. I just gave our house servants orders not to stick their noses outside the gate, an order which they were only too glad to obey. There was a crowd of soldiers gathered at the

corner of our *magazin* where the lane that comes up to the house joins the Svetlanskaia,[1] and an officer came along and began to talk with them. They were respectful but not inclined to obey and then the [fortress] commandant, Gen. Kazbek himself, came alone with exactly the same result, but as he drove off Ted distinctly heard a very opprobrious epithet applied to him. Ted was standing on our wall a matter of a hundred and fifty feet from them so they did not speak in either a low or a humble tone. I am sorry they have begun in the Bazaar for it is only the Chinese who will suffer there, innocent men who are in no way to blame for the wrongs of the people.

There was a huge mass meeting in the circus last Wednesday,[2] at which about two thousand five hundred people were present, among them many soldiers and sailors and everything was orderly and quiet. There is to be another one tonight but an order has been issued by the Governor that the soldiers and sailors are not to go, which of course, has made trouble. Then some of the prisoners from Japan are expected today and they are to be kept under guard until they leave town as the authorities do not want their comrades here to talk with them. That made the soldiers and sailors here furious, and that is another cause of the trouble.

[6 PM] The last few hours while interesting have been anything but agreeable and we begin to wonder what will happen before morning. It has been a lowery day so it got dark very early which made things worse. About half past three some officers rode up [Svetlanskaia] for dear life, hugging as closely as possible to the necks of their horses, and the crowd on each side of the street throwing stones at them as they ran. Then two companies of soldiers were marched down the street to quell the disturbance and ever since there has been more or less shooting, mostly, we think, with blank cartridges. Just at dark we heard an awful crashing of glass, and the rioters were running up the other side of the street smashing every window they passed. We heard some stones go bang against the iron shutters in the Piankov block where our *magazin* is, but whether it was ours or not we do not know. Ted must not show his face for he would certainly be recognized and forced to open our store and let the crowd help themselves. I begged him to let me run to the commandant and ask for some troops to protect our store but he wouldn't hear of it. I am sure I could have gone safely and no one would have recognized me. The coolie, after things quieted down a little, made a reconnaissance and was stopped by a soldier. The coolie said he only wanted to see if our store was all right, and the soldier said, "Yes, we are on guard here." It is a lucky thing we are next to the Post Office for there is now a whole company on guard there. . . . We dare not have a lamp in the windows that face the street, so I am writing here in the dining-room, which is not so visible and which has heavy draperies, completely concealing the presence of a lamp.

[8 PM] There are big fires burning in three different places, some of them not far from us but we do not know where. . . . Our servants are frightened nearly out of their lives and have pinned blankets over the kitchen windows so the light will not show through. I have given them permission to sleep in the school room tonight where there are iron shutters. . . . With seventy thousand troops here, we ought to be safe but how many of that number are among the rioters?

[8.30 PM] The fires are increasing in every direction and one never knows where the next one will break out. . . . I have all my trinkets on my neck and am prepared to pack my albums, etc., at a moment's notice if this part of the town is threatened. We have neither water supply nor any adequate fire department. This will be a night of terror such as we read about, but do not care to experience personally.

[10 PM] It is dreadful, and only ten o'clock now—God knows what it will be before morning. A large section [of the city] about a quarter of a mile from us is on fire and they seem to have no power whatever to check it, and the fire at the other end of the town still rages but we can only guess what is burning, not being able to see more than the glare and smoke. Occasionally we hear shots and the last ones have been rather near.

[11 PM] The row down here in front continued for about half an hour, yells and pounding, etc., evidently against the Admiral's fence, but is quiet now. We are slowly gathering our things together in as safe places as possible, in case we are homeless before morning as so many people will be. Who could have dreamed of this last night? That there would be trouble everybody thought, but few expected that it could or would assume these proportions.

13 November 1905 to Home
[7 AM] Thank God the night is over and so far we are safe but the danger may not be over yet. You cannot imagine a more awful sound than that of human beings over whom reason and justice have lost control and who only seek to destroy. . . . There is not much rest sleeping more than fully dressed, with a pair of golf boots on, my valuables on my neck, and Wang's chain around my waist. Ted had all the keys on him and at the foot of the bed, on the shoe box, lay our coats and hats ready.

[9 AM] Mr. Nielsen was here just now and we told him to bring Mrs.

Nielsen, the *amah* and baby here at once. They had an awful time last night at the Moscow [Hotel]—soldiers broke in and even crawled under beds to look for the officers who live in that hotel, and they say the officers got into any kind of disguise to keep away from them, some even dressing themselves in woman's clothes. They also say that *Slobodka* (the East end of the town out beyond the Lindholms) is in ashes and there was one fire on Missionerskaia (the next street beyond Prudovaia), where the Moscow is. Kunst and Albers' immense store was smashed open and not a vestige of the goods remain, and you can imagine the size of it when I tell you they employ about a hundred clerks.[3] There was a fire in their oil department, which they were still fighting when Ted was down there an hour ago. Even in the big house where Mrs. Cornehls lives, many windows were smashed. Egorov's (the confectioner's) and Jankowski's (the bookseller's), both in the Startsev block, were wrecked and more or less damage was done to Churin's.[4] Of course all that saved our store was its position, beside the Post Office and opposite the Admiral's, but the rioters may be too much for the soldiers if they renew operations again tonight. We feel very anxious for our clerk, Mr. Molchanov, and his family as they live in a bad part of the town, so Ted has sent for them to come here, bag and baggage, if they survived the last night. We shall have a regular hotel here tonight and I am glad I have the places to offer people. The Chinese are horribly frightened and no wonder. The Bazaar is a pile of ashes this morning, as is most of the square formed by Svetlanskaia, Pekinskaia, Kitaiskaia and Aleutskaia, below the railway crossing. The big hotel, Golden Horn, where is our only remaining theater, and the headquarters of the biggest club in town, is still burning and we are wondering what else has gone.

[10.10 AM] Mr. Clarkson has just been here to know if we wanted to go to [his dacha at] the mine, or to go on board any of the ships in the harbor, and Mr. Nielsen thinks he will send his family on board ship and they both wanted me to go, but I won't move a step unless Ted goes, and of course he must stay here and do what he can to guard the property. All the German ladies and children went on board last night.

[8.30 PM, on the Norwegian SS *Mandal*, "lying in mid-stream."] When Ted came back this morning, he insisted that I pack up at once and come out here with Mrs. Nielsen and her baby. I protested with all my might, but everybody had been at Ted to send me so it was of no use. . . . We threw a few things into a trunk and some bags and Ted took me down to the shore—such a sight as it was, whole families crowding down there with only one thought—to get on board some craft, no matter what or how. The *sampans* would not go and there they were—poor people, many of them without homes. Ted put me on board [Mr. Clarkson's] *Samson* and they brought me out here, where this kind Norwegian captain and his wife received me with every thoughtful attention possible—I can never forget their kindness to an absolute stranger and I can never repay it. Mrs. Nielsen and her baby were already here, and with me came a Russian lady, whose husband is in Mr. Clarkson's [firm], and her baby—they were wandering around last night three hours because everything around them was burning and they dared not stay in their house. The poor baby is suffering for it today, and is very ill—the husband did not come out tonight and the poor woman is nearly frantic.

14 November 1905 to Home
Another day and they say the outlook tonight is worse than ever. Yesterday afternoon the soldiers demanded the presence of the commandant and the leading officers of both fortress and port in the church, and presented their requests. Gen. Kazbek talked with them and promised them what he could, and they marched down street playing "God Save the Tsar," and we thought everything was lovely but in the night they got into another champagne cellar and the shooting began again. . . . Today five hundred Cossacks arrived in the town and are patrolling the streets, with their long, double-headed lances, and that is even worse than letting loose our Indians—they are perfect devils and absolutely without mercy. Seven sailors defied two or three of them somewhere this morning and they made mincemeat of them as coolly as if they were handling beef instead of human beings. The town is a terrible-looking sight—the Lindholms' house with all its lovely things has gone and Tullie is a refugee on board some ship here in the harbor. Poor girl—I do hope Kostia is all right, but can hear nothing. . . . It will be such a blow to them all, for half the house is old and all three of the children were born there. Every one of the big houses where there are quarters for the naval officers and their families is burned, and the people are crowded on board the ships like rats. . . . This trouble could not have happened at a worse time for cargoes of drinks were rushed in here as soon as the [peace] treaty was ratified because everybody knows what sells best here. There are no facilities here for handling such an immense amount of cargo so a great deal of it is still stacked on the beach. Sailors are on guard there and when we passed yesterday morning, the guard at one pile was lying there so dead drunk that people kicked him as they passed and still could not rouse him. . . . One of the best things I have heard happened at Yun Ho Zan's

magazin—there were iron gratings across the windows and two Chinese with axes behind each window. When the rioters broke the glass and stuck their hands in to steal, the Chinese, probably with the greatest pleasure, chopped off the hands or the fingers according to the celerity with which they were withdrawn and they said the shop was strewn with hands and fingers the next morning.

15 November 1905 to Home
This morning I went ashore, but first went on board the *Erna* and there I found Mrs. Cornehls and poor Tullie. Their house was burned at four o'clock Monday morning by eight sailors, three of them men who knew what valuable things there were in the house. Tullie and Kostia escaped with just what they stood in and Tullie's jewels, and were very glad to get out with their lives. The sailors broke into the strong room and stole everything—all the silver that Mrs. Lindholm has collected in thirty years and all Tullie's wedding silver. There were three pianos in the house and such a quantity of nice furniture and pictures, mirrors, bric-à-brac, etc., to say nothing of Mr. Lindholm's library. Tullie said the loss was at least five hundred thousand rubles . . . it was something dreadful coming through the streets with dead sailors lying around in every direction, and the streets full of broken bottles and all sorts of things.

16 November 1905 to Home
I have such a frightful cold in my head that I could not go ashore today, but Ted, Mr. Nielsen and Mr. Greene came out to tiffin and have just gone back. Mr. Greene is our new consul here, a very nice young man from Cambridge who has lived in Japan some years. He landed up here last Wednesday [8 November], and Sunday night, when the Golden Horn was burned, he lost everything excepting what he stood in, and there were lots of others in the same plight. He came up to call on us Friday afternoon, bringing a letter of introduction to Sarah from Mrs. Atkinson of Kobe and we had such a pleasant hour before the fire in our drawing-room . . . and it was so nice—who could have thought of this then? Admiral Terentiev's house, where Mrs. and Miss Iessen lived, was burned and they are refugees on board some steamer that is leaving tomorrow. Many of their things were saved but Mr. Szentgali's violin and music, which he usually kept there, were lost. Langelütje's, Keller's, Toong Lee's and Kunst and Albers' hardware shop, as well as their *godowns* . . . were intact. The rabble began looting Korean town, and the police told the

Chinese and Koreans to kill every soldier and sailor who molested them, a request with which they complied with great alacrity, as the soldiers and sailors behave abominably to the Chinese always and rob them every time they get a chance. . . . The other day some Cossacks came across a party of sailors with a huge bag of money which they were dividing. The Cossacks chopped them every one to bits, and took the loot to headquarters. Wirt's jewelry store was one of the first places attacked, and they looted from that goods to the value of a hundred and thirty-five thousand. It is still impossible to buy anything to eat in town but you can steal as much as ever you like from the supplies on the wharves. Today Churin's *magazin* opened up their back door and in two hours they sold preserved things and clothing to the amount of eleven thousand rubles.

17 November 1905 to Sarah

Yesterday [Chinese] Consul Lee met Smirnov, the acting governor, in front of Toong Lee's—grabbed his most high excellency the lord *populorum* by the front of his coat and shook him as a dog shakes a rat, saying, "You call us barbarians and savages, but never in the history of China has anything like this happened excepting once and that was the Boxer rebellion, which you Russians yourselves stirred up. You are the savages and not we"—there was a lot more to it and quite a crowd heard the affair. A Mr. Christansen told Ted about it, he having heard it, and then Col. Koch, a relative of Kostia's who also saw the performance, told me.

Tullie's cousin, Tonia Nordman, went back to the house after they left it, and in spite of the sailors, hunted around till he found [their dog] Mignon and brought him to Tullie. Won't Mrs. Lindholm be proud of that? That shows the blood of the old admiral, her father. He did all sorts of things in the town that night, picking up wounded and bringing them out to the ships. He is a very quiet, bookish-looking young man, but just the kind that one would expect to quietly rise to an emergency when occasion demanded. . . . Mrs. Bushueva is all right, and has stayed at home all the time, with some soldiers and sailors to guard her. It was a dreadful sight to see the streets today and the bazaar. I have not been down there before.

Poor old Liza Foo came to say goodbye to Tullie yesterday, and at the last moment he cried like a baby and taking hold of Tullie's sleeve, he said, "Tell the *barin*[5] to come back and build it all up again, and we can be happy once more." . . . One baker in town is selling bread, a loaf at a time, which he passes out through a small round hole in his barricade.

20 November 1905 to Sarah

Really I think we are as safe ashore as in the harbor. Last night about nine o'clock, a torpedo boat came blundering along and struck the *Resolute*, the steamer lying close beside us, denting one of her plates badly and springing several rivets. As the ship had four lights out, it seems to me an absolute piece of carelessness. . . . A temporary bazaar has been arranged between Mrs. Cornehls' house and Iadzhoglu's [grocery] and there one can buy anything. Meat has dropped to thirty and thirty-five kopeks a pound as the *Lady Mitchell* came up loaded with cattle and has now gone back after another load.

21 November 1905 to Sarah

[2 PM] Yesterday noon, quite close to the *Mandal*, a torpedo boat ran into a launch, they say Capt. Egermann's, and sunk [sic] it at once. The *Argun*, after running down the *Suez*, steamed out to sea without so much as offering assistance or asking if they needed any. The bows of the *Suez* are ashore, but the afterdeck is quite submerged.

[8.30 PM] Dr. Birk came this afternoon and . . . he says everything beyond his house is burned flat and his house was set on fire three times, but each time he talked with the rioters till they themselves put the fire out. Dr. Birk thinks that the trouble is over now, because they have begun to send the reserves home and only the young soldiers will remain here.

11 December 1905 to Home

The town is beginning to look a little bit like itself—that is, what is left of it, but of course there are ruins sticking up in every direction.

VLADIVOSTOK'S BLOODY SUNDAY

The November riots were barely over when telegraph, mail, and railway strikes cut off communication with the outside world, essentially paralyzing Vladivostok: "We know absolutely nothing of what is going on in Russia, and of course the outside world knows nothing of what is going on here. It is fully three weeks since the beginning of the telegraph strike" (23 December 1905 to Home). All of 1905 was full of disturbances, caused not only by the suffering connected directly with the war but also by burning issues of workers' rights, legal questions awaiting the tsar's decisions, and a general feeling of societal malaise. In Saint Petersburg on 22 January, Russia's "Bloody Sunday"—a peaceful demonstration meant to inform the tsar of the participants' poverty and request his help to alleviate it—turned into a massacre of hundreds of innocents.

A year and a day later—23 January 1906—something similar took place in Vladivostok. To commemorate the previous year's event, railway workers, sailors, troops, and other concerned residents gathered at Station Square. They listened to speeches and approved a plan immediately to march on the headquarters of Lieutenant General Selivanov, the commandant of the Vladivostok Fortress, with their specific political demands. Despite Selivanov's opposition, the demonstrators persisted. When "sharpshooters and Cossacks opened fire with machine guns," about thirty people were killed.[6]

11 January 1906 to Home
We have a new commandant now who seems to have a backbone and he has refused even to receive the deputations of the soldiers. There was a big open-air mass meeting three days ago at the other end of the town and trouble was anticipated. Whole companies of Cossacks patrolled the Svetlanskaia all day long, and they had orders to let the soldiers and sailors yell all they wanted to, but if they smashed even one pane of glass to kill at least five men for every pane. As a result nothing happened. . . . Kazbek, the old commandant, with his staff left very quietly. . . . amusing [us] because there is usually such a send-off when a commandant leaves.

20 January 1906 to Home
Here in Siberia matters are still settling and there is a big mass meeting here every day. Yesterday the soldiers decided to send notice to the Cossacks that if they interfered with them any more, the whole garrison would fall on the Cossacks and kill them. As there are only about six hundred Cossacks to between fifty and sixty thousand troops, it ought not to be a very difficult matter. . . . Monday some soldiers in the Bazaar stabbed a Chinese through the heart and robbed him. Down came the Cossacks and killed four or five soldiers to teach them manners and that is probably what occasioned the threats yesterday.

23 January 1906 to Home
Everything is very uncertain now as it has been ever since the riots, for we never know when the beasts may break out again. Today they threaten to take the Post Office by storm and the superintendent [Korn] came up here to ask for shelter for his wife and children in case they really attempt anything. . . .

There is a meeting this afternoon at one o'clock and the trouble is expected after that. The new commandant, [Lieutenant] General Selivanov, is not inclined to knuckle to the disaffected and I hope he will continue to be firm.

24 January 1906 to Home

These are lively times in which we live and sometimes they are a jolly bit too lively for people of quiet tastes, and yesterday was one of those occasions. As soon as *tiffin* I went down to the wharves with Mrs. Hansen to help her about some things that had been detained in the customs house. On our way back, just before we got up to the Svetlanskaia we saw everybody looking up street, and all the stores were hurriedly putting on their outside shutters. We got across the road to Kunst and Albers and just in time, for there came a procession of sixteen hundred sailors, armed with guns and bayonets and headed by a band of music, marching to the meeting, all looking immensely satisfied with themselves. Of course we got home as quickly as possible, and we found here Mrs. Korn and her little daughter. . . . Mr. Korn himself came shortly after. The sailors had marched to guard the mass meeting and to enforce their demands on the commandant if any resistance were shown. The meeting was to demand (1) the immediate release of Dr. Lankovskii, who was imprisoned some time ago, [and] (2) . . . the settlement of the telegraph difficulties according to the wishes of the Union of Unions. Dr. Lankovskii is very well known here and is the head doctor in the railway, and he was imprisoned for asserting that Col. von Kremer's brain was affected and that he was more or less crazy, and therefore not responsible for his actions. That all may be true as far as I know—it is never surprising when an officer turns out to be crazy or a fool either, but I can't see from what I have heard that von Kremer did anything but his duty. He is the superintendent of the railroad and in the beginning of the disorders he promptly kicked out every disaffected official which I would consider a very virtuous act indeed. . . . In case the commandant refused to be intimidated, the sailors were to use the persuasive elements of their guns, storm the commandant's house and then the Post Office. Of course, as the Post Office is directly in front of us—under our very nose, in fact—this did not make us feel particularly happy. There were soldiers stationed all around, even up the lane, but could they be trusted in? I doubt it. When the sailors marched past the Post Office going down, Ted saw some of them shake their fists at the soldiers and call out: "Don't you dare fire at us." . . . A little after four we saw people running up the street and looking behind as they ran, and the soldiers of the Post Office guard quickly crowded up onto the second terrace (we are on the third) and began to examine their rifles to see if everything was in order. Then the rapid-fire guns began to pop, not far away, and after some minutes we saw a company of Cossacks coming past at full speed, and some of them dashed up our lane. I fairly shouted with delight when I saw those devils incarnate (that is just what they are) for I knew by the way they urged their horses that they were out for business. Our middle terrace was full of soldiers, and on the lower terrace were Ted, Mr. Hansen, Mr. Berner and some of the other Danes, where they could see a lot. That is the advantage of being a man—Ted of course insisted on our staying in the house as "it was too dangerous for women" so we could only see what passed in the space of perhaps a hundred feet wide on the Svetlanskaia. Ted saw a detachment of seven or eight Cossacks come up the lane on the other side of the main street, brandishing their sabers in the air, and, flying for dear life in front of them, a few members of the sailors' band that had marched down the street so gaily a couple of hours before. The sailors of course disappeared into every available rat hole where a Cossack on horseback could not go, but they caught one, tied him to a saddle and made him keep up with the horse, a Cossack on the other side plying the whip over the sailor to keep him moving. One Cossack rode by, holding in triumph a big trombone that he had captured. I should like to send him a blue ribbon to tie on it. There was a lot of shooting and some of it so near here that the smoke blew into our yard but by dark all was quiet. . . . We had twelve Winchester repeaters in the house—five of them hung in our bedroom, and each loaded with seven bullets, and then of course everyone had a revolver and plenty of ammunition.

25 January 1906 to Home
Yesterday we here passed a very quiet day until four o'clock when we heard that the commandant, Gen. Selivanov, while inspecting one of the batteries in the morning had been shot at and seriously, perhaps fatally, wounded in the stomach. All yesterday afternoon there was a battle raging between the soldiers and the Cossacks up beyond the cemetery (about half a mile from here, but behind the hills), but what was the result we do not know. Night before last the Cossacks raided the whole [Navy] Equipage and drove every sailor out and now the trouble from that quarter is over. From the meeting

[23 January] a delegate was sent to the commandant, but the latter refused to receive him, so he went back—then the whole force turned out—the band in front, then a crowd of civilians among which were women and even children, and, bringing up the rear, sixteen hundred armed sailors, and down they went to the commandant's house. They say he gave them ten minutes to disperse, but some deny that. Out in front was a small rapid-fire gun with fifty soldiers and it was turned loose on the crowd; and simply mowed them down. They say the soldiers refused to fire and that the military officers themselves worked the gun, but I do not know if it is true. The band was the first to get the bullets and few of them escaped alive, and then it was the turn of the civilians. The sailors, like the cowards they are, fled in every direction, flinging their guns as they went. There were other rapid firers nearer to the circus where the meeting was held and they also let loose on the fugitives and then the Cossacks swooped down. It was altogether a dreadful thing and between three and four hundred were killed and wounded. The celebrated Mrs. Volkenstein was killed—poor woman—I am sorry for that, because she had cause to hate the government if ever anybody had. She was thrown into prison when she was twenty-one and was confined in that awful Petropavlovsk fortress thirteen years and was then sent out here to Sakhalin where she finished her time.[7] Her husband, who had been told that she was dead, had married again, but when he found she was alive and was here in Vladivostok, he threw up everything in Petersburg and came to her at once. They are very clever people and do such a lot of work for the poor but very quietly. The second wife came out here with her son a year or two ago, and spent some months with them.

[Later] We have just heard from trustworthy sources what happened to the commandant—the men in one of the big forts sent word to him that if he did not send the Cossacks out of town, they would bombard the town. Gen. Selivanov himself with a small party went directly then to take the fort, but as he approached it, they opened fire on him, wounding him in four places, killing the officer next in command and eight of the Cossack escort. I must say Selivanov proved himself a hero—he went ahead himself, straight into the danger, instead of sending someone else.

1 February 1906 to Home

On Monday there was a funeral for twenty-two of the victims, chiefly soldiers and sailors. Twelve of the bodies were carried past here and I never in all my life saw such a crowd of people. The open coffins were borne aloft, each on the shoulders of four men and in front were men carrying the covers. The crowd carried red flags and banners with various inscriptions. One was "Republic," another—"To the battlers for freedom" and the largest of all "Eternal remembrance of the murdered—eternal curses on the murderers." The bodies were all buried in one huge grave in a small public garden close to where they fell—near the railway station—and these banners and the red flags were all left there.

CHAPTER 8

Wars, Revolutions, and Foreign Intervention

IF THE RUSSO-JAPANESE WAR SEEMED TO ELEANOR PRAY A SERIES OF haunting still pictures, the cataclysms of 1914–22 increasingly recalled an engrossing movie at full speed: "Life is more or less like a cinema with its quick changes" (22 March 1916 to Aunt Anna). Millions dying in war-related misery, ordinary life disintegrating, Russian society turned upside-down— such were the early results of the "Great War" (1914–18), the revolutions of 1917, and the Russian Civil War (1918–22). While the massive destruction distressed and exhausted Russia's population, Eleanor was also profoundly, albeit oddly, inspired by the fast-moving events. She was close to the making of history, not only as an observer of the calamities but also as an eager participant in the relief efforts. In 1918, amid tumultuous sorrow, she summed up her life in Russia as a splendid gift: "Twenty-four years ago today we came ashore in Vladivostok—has anyone, take it all in all, had a better time of it than we, in all those years? I doubt it" (23 June 1918 to Sarah).

Materially, the Prays were initially quite safe and comfortable. Keeping the American Store open until January 1918, Fredrick Pray then accepted a position as clerk at the US consulate in Vladivostok, eventually attaining the post of senior vice-consul. This reliable connection with official America pleased the Prays on several levels: It afforded them rare access to news, goods, and highly placed military leaders, especially during the presence of the American Expeditionary Force (AEF) in 1918–20; it gave them a steady income and a new status in Vladivostok's foreign circles; and Eleanor Pray could volunteer more directly among the destitute and injured than before. She plunged into extensive assignments for the Young Men's Christian Association

(YMCA) and the American Red Cross, both active in Vladivostok; and, after April 1923, when Frederick Pray unexpectedly died and Eleanor Pray's own safety and comfort were no longer assured, this spiritual mission of caring for others helped assuage her grief.

THE WAR AFAR, 1914–1916

Eleanor Pray was at Dacha Seyuza in July 1914 when Ted arrived from Vladivostok with an extra news sheet announcing the declaration of war between Austria-Hungary and Serbia (29 July 1914 to Aunt Anna). A member of the Central Powers (with Austria-Hungary), Germany declared war against Russia on 1 August and against France on 3 August, both members of the Allied Powers, the Entente. Great Britain, also a member, joined against Germany on 5 August. Mrs. Pray's first reaction was one of horror, coupled with a sense of isolation. Soon she writes, "If Ted doesn't come out this afternoon, . . . I shall go to town tomorrow—I am longing to be in the thick of things and to see what is going on" (4 August 1914 to Clara).

While the United States joined the war only in March 1917, Mrs. Pray's sentiments mirrored those of her close mentor, her maternal Aunt Anna Guptill, who expressed strong opinions with unflinching candor: "I could write a book about this dreadful war. But it wouldn't do any good and I am afraid it wouldn't be neutral and we have been told we must be neutral, and I am so neutral I don't care who licks Germany as long as she gets licked; is that neutrality? I haven't any grudge against the Germans as individuals but as a Nation I think they ought to be wiped off the map for their treatment of Belgium" (19 May 1915 from Aunt Anna to Eleanor).[1]

2 August 1914 to Home
Bang!! and here we are with war and rumors of war, racial feeling at fever heat, troops mobilizing in European Russia and newsboys yelling extras on the street.

3 August 1914 to Home
There was a demonstration in Vladivostok yesterday and they smashed the German eagle over the consulate. . . . This evening I was talking about the war with Grigorievna,[2] and she said in her homey peasant patois—"It is not for nothing that there are so many mushrooms this year—when that comes, war comes too."

8 September 1914 to Home

What is going [on] inside me would boil a samovar—we have just come back [to the dacha] from Okeanskaia where we went to say goodbye to our friends who are being sent into captivity. We took flowers for Mrs. Schultz and Mrs. Tolle, and Mrs. Kästner took for Mrs. Hansen. Mrs. Tolle did not come out, and we were not sure she was on the train until it was too late to look her up. I was so sorry because she is the oldest of my friends in that party and is the daughter of a Russian officer. We saw Mrs. Schultz and Mrs. Hansen, and then, through the window of the third class wagon almost at the end of the long train, Messrs. Schultz, Ebert, Ollandt, Kogan, Jänich and several others. We talked with them a little and then one of the guards rather roughly told us we must speak in Russian. Some woman spoke up and said, "These people are not speaking German but English." "No matter—they must speak Russian," was all she got to that—and as far as I remember we kept on in English, at least we said goodbye to them in that. Behind this wagon was a common convict wagon with barred windows and there Messrs. Tolle, Lagerfeldt, Wübbens and one other were confined, several soldiers being on guard. Our friends did not come to the window, so we did not see them. Common thieves, murderers, etc., travel in those wagons, and these were four perfectly respectable men, whose only crime is that they are German.

25 October 1914 to Home

Going out on the train Saturday was a soldier's wife with a tiny baby in her arms and an undersized boy of eleven with her. The baby was crying and the mother crying too, so I asked her what the matter was. She told me her husband's regiment was leaving for the front and she was hunting for him to say goodbye, but couldn't find him at First River, so she was going on to Second River on the chance of finding him there, but her terrible fear was that the regiment had already gone and she would never see him again. She had two other children between these in age, and the poor woman sat there and cried—and I cried with her, though I had never seen her before in my life—I couldn't help it.

24 December 1914 to Home

Christmas Eve at home—the eve of Christ's birth and more than half of the Christians in the world at each other's throats, more like wolves than like human beings—how terrible it all is. And all over Germany tonight they will sing "Stille Nacht, heilige Nacht"—even in the trenches, and the night will be anything but still with the thunder of cannon and the rattling of the smaller guns.[3]

3 January 1916 to Home
The washwoman, Iustinia, came this morning with a face like sunshine as she had had a postcard from her boy who is a prisoner in Germany. . . . He is at Schneidemühl and writes to ask his mother for a little money.[4] She brought five rubles to get me to have it transferred for her. . . . The card was written in September.

31 January 1916 to Home
There is a report in town that an aeroplane was seen here the other day, and the searchlights spend the nights waiting for its reappearance. They say it was seen early one morning off Russian Island, but I don't believe it—I think someone saw a sea gull through the edge of a champagne glass, for it seems an impossibility that the Germans could find a base for a descent of that kind on Vladivostok, but nevertheless some people are assured that it is true.

8 October 1916 to Home
I had luncheon with Ida Fedorovna [Borisova] Friday, and she read me five letters from the regiment to which we sent the five balalaiki two months ago—they were so pleased to get them. . . . [They had written] asking us for one, as they were so near the German lines that they were not allowed to sing, and it was very hard to be without music.[5]

THE YEAR OF TWO REVOLUTIONS, 1917

After the "February Revolution" on 8–12 March 1917,[6] Tsar Nikolai II abdicated on 15 March and the Russian Empire became a republic. Vladivostok soon heard the news: the tsar signed his letter in Pskov, southwest of Petrograd, at 3 PM (late evening on the Pacific coast), and the announcement was published on 16 March.[7] Momentous as that event was, the most far-reaching of this year's political, economic, and cultural upheavals was the October Revolution on 7 November, when Vladimir Lenin and the Bolshevik party took power, declaring the country a new, Soviet, Russia. "A fine outlook, if it is true," noted Mrs. Pray, not without irony, "but perhaps for the best" (9 November 1917 to Sarah).

Eleanor Pray's reaction to the constantly shifting news was a complex combination of compassion for her adopted country and deep American patriotism. She empathized with Russia and rejoiced in the promise of political change that might involve democratic equality. But she also recognized that the result of indiscriminate "freedom" might bring more ignorance and brutality. She noted with grievous disgust the scurrilous writings, now uncensored, about members of the imperial family and the Church, and felt comforted by the presence of an American cruiser in Vladivostok that fall: "To our surprise *Brooklyn* appeared yesterday soon after *tiffin*, so we have something to depend on in case of trouble, which, however, we don't anticipate" (24 November 1917 to Sarah).[8] This was not yet an official move by the United States to intervene in Russia's internal affairs, but the American shadow was resented by many and was considered part of the "Entente's intervention in the Far East."[9] Facing what historian John Stephan has since characterized as that year's "uncoordinated scramble in a fluid domestic and internal environment,"[10] Eleanor Pray determinedly continued to fulfill her hostess duties as a consular wife and a friend of the American consuls John Caldwell, and, from September 1920, David Macgowan.

Although not yet a theater of war, the gateway of Vladivostok was becoming crowded with people moving both into and out of Russia. Former émigrés were returning home, political agitators hoped to excite the masses, and war refugees arrived from across Siberia looking for safe passage out. Everyday commodities—food, housing, transport—were deteriorating so absurdly that luxuries were sometimes more available than necessities. Mrs. Pray used caviar on bread instead of butter: "This afternoon we went shopping—got some porridge, a pound of candles, two packets of matches, some red caviar and bacon. No dried fruits in town, no cocoa, few sweets of any kind, no smoked fish, very little salt fish" (21 November 1917 to Sarah). Most disturbing was the enormous stock of war matériel collected in the city: "The whole place is so congested with cargo that [I] wonder they can ever find anything. There is cargo piled all the way from the Admiral's Pier to the Svetlanskaia, and that end of Suifunskaia which runs past Mrs. Albers' house is piled solid full, not even a place for carts to pass being left" (2 March 1917 to Sarah).

11 March 1917 to Aunt Anna
The way they talk of the Empress is shameful and I don't for one minute believe in any immoral relations between her and that swine Rasputin.

17 March 1917 to Sarah

[The Tsar has just abdicated.] Well! It is rather upsetting to awake this morning to the new state of affairs and we all feel as if we were standing on our heads. For several days now everyone has been uneasy because no telegrams came through from Petersburg, so this, to many, came like a shot out of a cannon. . . . The telegram was published late yesterday afternoon, and Aleutskaia, around the office of [the newspaper] *Dalekaia Okraina*, was packed with people waiting for it to be given out. I was so tired when I came home that I undressed and lay down for a couple of hours, and while I slept Ted came in and stuck the huge telegram on to the mirror, though with my usual cleverness I got up without seeing it, until he came and called my attention to it. It all sounds beautiful and if the people who are doing it can make good their words, a new era will dawn for Russia—instead of imprisoning the ministers they ought to hang the most of them, but it wrings one's heart to think of the Emperor and Empress and of what they must be suffering with all the people turning against them. That the Emperor is weak, everyone knows, but that is his misfortune rather than his fault.

20 March 1917 to Sarah

The house of Romanov began with a Michael and ended with one, though the reign of the last one seems to have been only the length of time it took him to get a pen into his hands and refuse the throne. Everybody now is "Grazhdanin" and "Grazhdanka" which in itself has a most gruesome sound—it reminds one too much of the "citoyen" and "citoyenne" of the French Revolution.[11]

21 March 1917 to Sarah

Yesterday Gen. Shinkarenko was arrested, also Baron Taube and two other officers. Shinkarenko is the head of the military court[12] and a strict disciplinarian of the old regime to whom the salute or non-saluting of a soldier is one of the big things in life, and the soldiers have always hated him for the way he reprimands them on the street. He simply refused to recognize the new regime—said he was too old to change so quickly. Of course, he is and always was a pig-headed old chap, but one likes to see a bit of backbone, however mistaken the cause. Baron Taube, on the contrary, has always severely criticized the old regime and has worked like a Trojan these war times to bring order out of chaos as far as his department was concerned, but a man named Taube has simply no right to live—he should long ago have let someone with a more stylish-sounding name mess things up—that is a clear duty. . . . We hear nothing else [than about the revolution] and there are meetings from morning till night. There was a women's meeting Monday and everybody was yelling at once, they say. The women were yelling "Out with Taube" and somebody asked one of the huskiest ones why she wanted Taube out and she said she didn't know. They also yelled "Out with the Chinese," "Let everybody have Russian servants." What a hash it all is. These people don't know what they want, so they yell anything because yelling and meetings have never been allowed before.

23 March 1917 to Sarah
At the Narodnyi Dom [the People's House, a community center] the other day, some woman got up and denounced Mrs. Meyer—think of that! Said she was unjust to her servants! Think of that, too! She has been away from here eight years, and as I lived with her [at the *dacha*] in all three months and know a little about her family life, I should like to wring the neck of that ranting liar, whoever she was. Mrs. Meyer always scandalized some of the other German ladies by her happy-go-lucky household and the way her servants did what they pleased.

25 March 1917 to Sarah
This is revolutionary Sunday and they are proceeding to paint the town red, so far only with cockades, badges, flags, etc.[13] . . . The garrison, the militia (who have replaced the police), and all sorts of delegations are marching up to the rendez-vous at the cathedral, each accompanied by one or more red flags—sometimes with, sometimes without inscriptions. Most people have red flags flying from their flag staffs, and those who have the old red white and blue flag have either cut off the white or are flying it upside down, with the red on top.

29 March 1917 to Sarah
The other night, Ted went to the theater to see a play called *Black Crows*—a piece which has never before been allowed and such a horrid thing, showing up the monks and nuns—it may be true, but it seems to me extremely unwise to exhibit such things to an ignorant populace in times like these. One doesn't doubt such things take place, but there must also be good monks and nuns. They have given it three or four times already to crowded houses.

3 May 1917 to Sarah, Thursday
There was a tremendous parade Tuesday—about fifty thousand people out, but extremely quiet and orderly. . . . It was a sort of Labor Day and is to become a permanent thing on the calendar.

6 June 1917 to Aunt Anna
Representatives of the IWW are spreading over Russia like cockroaches . . . and making all kinds of inflammatory speeches, and as we have freedom now, there is no one to stop them.[14] For two Sundays they have been making these speeches at mass meetings in town, telling the people that the money in the bank, the goods in the shops, and private property belong as much to them as to the nominal owners, and advising them to help themselves, beginning with the banks. . . . One speaker had on a very nice overcoat and a tramp said to him "In accordance with those principles, please give me your overcoat—I have none," whereupon the speaker peeled it off and handed it to him, which of course, as was probably intended, made a big impression on the crowd, but one is willing to bet that the scene had been rehearsed beforehand and that the coat was back with its owner before night.

9 July 1917 to Aunt Anna
The boat [bringing Dorothy home for summer] was crowded with emigrants returning from Australia, and everything was dirty and in confusion. . . . I thought there might be something touching in seeing these people return to their native land after in many cases years of forced exile, but they looked for the most part so smug and "free" that one longed to biff them—one could see to look at them that they had only come to make trouble. But there was one sickly-looking man with great, sad eyes, who felt what one should feel at such a time—one could see it in his looks, and the tears came into my own eyes as I looked at him, for he has surely only come back to die.

5 November 1917 to Sarah
The *Simbirsk* was over twenty-four hours late in leaving owing to the fact that one of the stokers called the chief engineer a *durak* [fool] and a *bolvan* [blockhead] and, when the chief officer was called in to settle the dispute, passed the compliments on to him. Then it was reported to the *T[ovarishchi]*, and there was all sorts of a mess.

25 November 1917 to Sarah

It is getting very dangerous on the street at night now and there are robberies all over town. Friday evening the assistant bookkeeper of the Imperial Bank, who was escorting a lady home, was murdered near the corner of Poltavskaia and Nagornaia [Streets], quite near the Newhards'. Two men attacked them and while [the bookkeeper was] defending the lady from her assaulter, the other ruffian drew off and shot at the man till he fell, wounded mortally. He died in the hospital an hour or so later. The murderers, of course, disappeared without trace.

28 November 1917 to Sarah

Yesterday the Admiral asked Mrs. Caldwell to bring some "nice girls" out for tea [to the *Brooklyn*] and the first name he mentioned was mine.[15] We went out at half-past three and I never felt more like a feather (perhaps ostrich plume would express my meaning better) than when I stood on the deck and patted one of the great steel monsters, aft. There are moments in life beyond words and that was one of them. This is only the second time in my life I have had the privilege of visiting one of our own men-of-war, and life has produced much deeper feelings in me than I had when we visited the *Olympia*.

ALLIED INTERVENTION, JANUARY 1918–APRIL 1920

The foreign intervention in Siberia was a muddled affair. Military representatives of numerous nations eventually participated—including Canada, China, France, Great Britain, Italy, Japan, Lettland (Latvia), Poland, Serbia, and the United States—and, although united against the threat of continuing German war actions, they saw their presence in Siberia in often conflicting ways. Some argued that their troops were merely protecting their own country's residents, others that they were securing the safety of the Trans-Siberian Railway, but all were alarmed by the spread of communism. Their disparate official instructions prevented steady cooperation, and the Russians themselves were far from unified in their approach to Soviet power in Siberia, a "confusing array of petty political centers working at cross-purposes."[16] Soon after the first Japanese ship, the *Iwami*, arrived in the Bay of the Golden Horn, Eleanor Pray expressed her fears about the divisive struggle: "No one wants to see the Japanese take Vladivostok, but then, no one wants to see Vladivostok as it is now, in the hands of people to whom individual rights is nothing at all—that is, outside the individual rights of the powers that be" (17 January 1918 to Sarah).

The United States' official stand was particularly ambiguous, putting its military leaders in a position of visible strength without an actionable mandate. President Woodrow Wilson's instructions in his famous Aide-Mémoire (17 July 1918) to the American Expeditionary Forces about to be dispatched to Russia ring eloquent but impractical: "The controlling purpose of the Government of the United States is to do everything that is necessary and effective to win [the war]. It wishes to cooperate in every practicable way with the allied governments, and to cooperate ungrudgingly." Further, "military intervention" would not be useful, for it "would add to the present sad confusion in Russia rather than cure it," and so the US troops should only "guard military stores," help "the Russians" in "their own self-defense," and "safeguar[d] the rear of the Czecho-Slovaks [arriving across Siberia and] operating from Vladivostok."[17] These words seem oblivious to the multifaceted reality of Russia's chaos.[18] Questions such as "Which governments and which Russians? Self-defense from whom?" hover around the Aide-Mémoire, but were not addressed.

Watching the allied landings from her windows, Eleanor Pray immediately chafed under the yoke of "non-interference"—troops being sent into a war without the right to fight—whereas major general William Graves, commander of the AEF in Siberia, tried to follow orders, often against his better judgment. Admiring his integrity, Eleanor explained to her impatient Aunt Anna Guptill, "Don't think ... that anyone is really hoodwinking Gen. Graves, any more than they were able to hoodwink Admiral Knight, for Gen. Graves is a clever man; but he is a soldier and has to do what he is told" (2 May 1919 to Aunt Anna). In the end, he left his own revealing summary of a thankless task: "I was in command of the United States troops sent to Siberia and, I must admit, I do not know what the United States was trying to accomplish by military intervention."[19]

While disagreeing with her country's official policy of only nonmilitary assistance, Eleanor Pray eagerly participated in both American and other foreign circles during these years. She and her husband's new acquaintances included Admiral Kato and Commander Lin (China), general Josip Broz (Czech high commissioner), and Mr. Girsa (Czech civilian representative), as well as the feared General Rozanov (Russia), and they were frequent guests at lavish dinners and receptions. A letter to their daughter from Frederick Pray describes Admiral Knight's farewell supper on board the *Brooklyn*: "The table at which Mother and I sat was in hollow, square shape, the center of which was full of plants with a fountain playing in their midst. I sat second to the left of Admiral Knight, with Mrs. C. H. Smith between us, and at the other end was the [US] Ambassador [to Japan, Roland Morris] and General Graves and then Mother. So you see we were both up with 'the upper ten'" (10 October 1918 from Dad to Dorothy).[20] Vladivostok's pivotal position also allowed its residents to meet famous revolutionary figures. Mrs. Pray regretted not having tried to see Ekaterina Breshko-Breshkovskaia, when she "passed through here last week" (6 December 1918 to Clara),[21] but she offered only disdain for Albert Rhys-Williams, the American socialist, who visited in July.[22] Later in life, Mrs. Pray was convinced that the Josip Broz she knew in 1919–20 was the man who in 1945 became Yugoslavia's president, Tito. Although intriguing questions remain about Tito's years in Russia as a young man, any connection with Vladivostok must, probably, be discounted.[23]

Many of the personages connected with the intervention are of captivating interest, but the better part of Eleanor Pray's life during this time was spent with "our boys," as she called the American soldiers and sailors who frequented the "Hut" of the YMCA. This was a café and reading room where Mrs. Pray regularly, and joyously, volunteered as a hostess: "You can't think how interesting it is to serve tea there. In the early afternoon the guests are chiefly our boys but later on the Czechs, British, French, and Italians begin to drop in, and there is a confusion of tongues" (3 November 1918 to Clara). The YMCA has been rightfully praised for its down-to-earth assistance to the soldiers and seamen gathering in Vladivostok,[24] and Mrs. Pray became near-expert on the mind-boggling complexities of work at the cash desk: "Money matters here are getting worse and worse, though the rate [of currency exchanges] hasn't moved much for a week or two. The Omsk bills are so badly printed in many cases that the counterfeits are better than the originals, and it causes endless confusion" (21 December 1919 to Aunt Anna). As remuneration for her translations of newspaper articles for the AEF,[25] Mrs. Pray suggested an old-fashioned barter system: "I was asked what I should like to have from the *Brooklyn* for my trouble and I promptly said 'flour.' It would be delightful to have a loaf of bread that didn't taste musty" (30 March 1918 to Sarah). The Prays still had the money, but often not the opportunity, to find even basic food stuffs in the stores.

Hand in hand with the economic changes went Russia's bewildering political experiments. A diarist in Moscow wrote, "As before, it is impossible to get any kind of understanding about what is going on around us."[26] Vladivostok's *zemstvo* (locally elected assembly), the *uprava* (city council), and the "Sovdep" (Council of Workers' Deputies) usually represented different angles of a perplexing spectrum of views and activities, but sometimes they worked together—and then the political winds turned. When, in August 1918, General Horvath, the manager of the Chinese Eastern Railway, attempted to form a government in Vladivostok, Mrs. Pray commented, with humorous aplomb, that "things [have begun] to get more interesting. You see, we are to that degree spoiled by excitement that we consider the day which passes without some new national or international episode as a sort of rainy Saturday" (26 August 1918 to Aunt Anna).

12 January 1918 to Sarah
Just now, upon looking out of the window, I saw a big Japanese cruiser lying down here in front, with a flag at the stern the size of a tablecloth.[27]

14 January 1918 to Sarah
Russian New Year and a cruiser flying the Union Jack has just come in. Thank God the outside world hasn't forgotten us—but the shame of it—the shame for Russia, to have sunk to this level where foreign cruisers have to be sent to protect their subjects.

17 January 1918 to Sarah
Yesterday on a crowded tram a soldier kicked up a row with the conductor, an elderly, pitiful-looking woman, about the fares—he told her what would happen to her, and that there were soldiers enough here to do what they did in Petersburg and a lot more of the same kind. The tram was crowded and I was standing close to them. The poor woman shrank back toward the window, quite dazed with all this tirade, and not finding any words after the first two or three rounds. It was none of my business, but I simply couldn't stand it, so I sailed into the soldier and asked him if he weren't ashamed of himself to bully a poor woman who had to work for her living like that. He started to argue with me, but attempted no rough language, though as there were four or five soldiers together, I thought he might knock me down for a *bourgeoise*. Of course my Russian words left me, but I played variations on the original phrase till he shut up and left the woman alone. I looked him straight in the eye till he finally turned his head away, for I wouldn't turn mine.

18 January 1918 to Sarah
This morning there is a new Japanese ironclad here, anchored very near the old bazaar, a little in front of the one that came in the other day.

21 January 1918 to Sarah

I've been out this morning to pay for some sweets I bought Friday which came to three rubles. They couldn't change my twenty so I left it there . . . and took a credit slip from them. Meanwhile I managed in two days to rake up three rubles in postage stamps and one, two, and three-kopek bills, which I took down there and redeemed my twenty-ruble bill!

26 January 1918 to Sarah

Mrs. Reuben [Smith] typed some sharply worded posters and went out with Tetia Sasha to fasten them to the billboards, but they got so excited that when they turned to go away they found that Tetia Sasha in her haste had stuck one of the thumbtacks through her glove, too. They were well written and let us hope someone reads them.

14 February 1918 to Sarah (1 February, OS)

This is a great day in Russia—the day they begin to reckon time as we do, instead of thirteen days behind. We are all laughing at Mrs. Smith . . . and telling her she has no birthday this year—it is the second of February [OS], which ought to be tomorrow, but the Russians have dropped the first thirteen days in February in order to catch up, and there is consequently a mess.

21 February 1918 to Sarah

Yesterday I went after our sugar cards—they are given out in Mrs. Crompton's old flat, and the last time I was there was to congratulate her after Stephen was born—much water has flowed since then. She and Stephen are in the deep sea (*Lusitania*)—and her pretty rooms in charge of the other part of the saying.[28]

24 February 1918 to Sarah

I pulled myself together enough to go to Mrs. Sanford's tea, for in times like these one hates to miss a gathering of acquaintances. This occasion proved to be quite an exciting one, for just as we had settled down to a game of bridge, someone came in waving a telegram and calling out "Russia is finished." The telegram was about the German peace terms which had been agreed to, and of course we were all talking at once, so you can imagine what kind of bridge we had.[29]

11 April 1918 to Sarah

Mr. Hodgson has fifty British marines and an ambulance to look out for him.[30] The ambulance is really a most artistic and business-like touch and has made a great impression.

30 April 1918 to Sarah

Yesterday there was a fine scandal in front of the governor's house when they began potting three thieves who were trying to get away in a droshky—not the least of the treat being to see the ladies in Kokin's [café] dive under the tables. They killed a horse, also two of the thieves, wounded a third one and winged a peaceful old woman going along the street. It is a wonder there were not more casualties as at that time, three o'clock, the streets are pretty full.

3 May 1918 to Sarah

The latest is that the *bolsheviki* have chased out the *Uprava* and put their own men there. They also published an address to foreigners telling them that the reins were in bolshevik hands now and that foreigners were on a level with the Russians and that they should "requisition" from them anything they found necessary. . . . Kostia Sukhanov, who probably never did an hour's real work in his life, is the leader of the working people and the master here at present.[31]

2 July 1918 [from Eleanor's diary]

What a day! I wound my legs in putties in case I had to do the trek to town on foot, and left on the milk boat [from the *dacha*] early this morning. At Okeanskaia, however, a train was being made up and I saw Gen. Tolmachev, who gave me a few of the details—the Czechs had taken the city, and there had been quite severe fighting at the station, no foreigners concerned, which reassured me a little. . . . In an hour or so our train was off and we got to town. Never in all the years I have lived in V. have I seen [it] looking so happy—the vicious circle which the red guards had been slowly drawing around it had been broken. At the corner of Suifunskaia I saw one of our Marines on duty and another one farther up the hill toward the Consulate. When I got past Dom Monakhov I looked up at our house—and there, for the first time since the house was built, was our own dear Flag flying from the pole on the roof. . . . Saturday morning [29 June] as Ted and Mr. Kravtsov were driving up to the State Bank they saw the Czechs lining up in front of the Governor's House—now a soviet nest, and they gave the soviet just one half hour in which to get out. This was at ten. At twenty past ten the Czechs fixed bayonets and out came the soviets pretty nearly on their dirty knees. . . . Of course there was a crowd and, seeing this, Ted's *izvozchik* (they were then on the way back) refused to go farther, asked them to get out, whipped up his horses and went tearing up one of the side streets. . . . The Czechs spent the day cleaning out bolshevik nests but the only real fighting was at the barracks opposite the station, their last stronghold, and there about a hundred and eighty bolshies and five Czechs were killed. The Czechs had their machine guns on the steps of the station and did a good job. [Reuben] Smith was walking in the Western part of the town and saw them clean out a nest of anarchists who had shut themselves into a small wooden house and refused to surrender. A Czech simply went back a few steps, hurled a bomb and not only did all the anarchists come out, but they were preceded by the whole front of the house. When the fighting at the station began, Admiral Knight gave the order for our Marines to land and guard the Consulate—the longed-for order after almost three months, and they fairly leaped ashore lest he change his mind and recall it.

9 August 1918 to Home
In town again . . . for I wouldn't have missed the landing of the French troops for anything. The transport [*Kersaint*] came in early this morning and at five this afternoon there was a parade, and we were fortunate enough to be asked to Mr. Fenton's flat, which is just opposite the Admiral's House which is now the Czech Headquarters. All the high officials were grouped there and the house was beautifully decorated with flags—the Chinese, ours, the Czech, the Russian, the British, and the Japanese, with a detachment of marines, of [each] respective nationality in front—lined up along the sidewalk.

19 August 1918 to Home
The Albers' big nice house has been commandeered for our [AEF] headquarters and everything looks so busy as one passes the big open doors. This afternoon the parade took place and it seemed as if my heart would burst with pride to see our splendid boys marching up the Svetlanskaia. . . . Sarah and I watched the parade from the window of the Czech Headquarters . . . and Dorothy and Wanda, preferring to be higher up, were on Mr. Fenton's balcony opposite, from where they threw flowers down into the street, and cheered and waved small flags.

26 August 1918 to Aunt Anna
I had a little tea for Sarah, but it was at such short notice that we couldn't get hold of many people. Admiral Knight and Lieut. Patterson [of the *Brooklyn*] came of which I was very glad for I wanted them to meet Sarah. The admiral was so pleased to see a strip of turf that in spite of my order to keep off the grass, he insisted on walking the whole length of the garden and back on the lawn.

9 November 1918 to Aunt Anna
With the exception of Paris, Vladivostok is probably the most interesting place in the world just at present, and to my mind, the Hut is the most interesting thing here, as that is where one sees all kinds—our tall splendid boys in khaki, the Britishers, Canadians, Czechs, Italians, French, etc. I love them all and do my best to get them to talk to me. The French sailors off the *Kersaint* drop in, with their sailor uniforms and the cap topped by a huge red silk pompom, and I make conversation with them in my best Great Falls High School French—and their innate French politeness is extremely evident else they would roar with laughter at the mess I make of it, and I'd laugh with them. Then, through the open door of the Hut we often see German, Austrian, and Turkish prisoners taken along in gangs to work with an escort of our boys to keep them moving. Such luck for us here in Vladivostok to have all these interesting things about us.

8 December 1918 to Home
I was on duty at the Hut Friday afternoon, and . . . some of the Russian soldiers who were leaving the next morning for the front asked permission to sing, and what glorious music it was. There were about twenty of them standing there in front of the big fireplace and I did enjoy it. All that is beautiful in a Russian soul goes into his song.

9 February 1919 to Aunt Anna
I have been at the Hut three whole afternoons this week. . . . My place is nearly always at the cash drawers as only a fair expert can be trusted to take in cash in these days of countless kinds of paper money and counterfeit bills as well. The varieties we have to handle are one, three, and five-kopek paper scraps; ten, fifteen and twenty-kopek reinforced postage stamps, often so dirty that were it not for the color, one couldn't distinguish them at all; one-ruble bills of the old regime, patched up with paper in every direction; three,

five, and ten-ruble bills of the same regime but usually not so much the worse for wear as the ones; twenty- and forty-ruble notes of the Kerensky money, which are nasty little bills about 2 × 2 1/2 inches;[32] fifty-kopek scraps; and then begin the endless variety of coupons—fifty-kopek, one ruble, 1.25, 1.37 1/2, 2.50, 2.75, 3.00, 5.00, 6.56 1/4, 10.00, 12.50, 13.75, 25.00 and 27.50, and one must verify the date on each one. . . . There hasn't been a coin in circulation for nearly a year and a half.[33]

1 November 1919 to Aunt Anna
There was a spicy scandal [at the YMCA Hut] which I didn't witness, but which did my soul good. Our officers are not at all careful about the sort of women they invite to the dances. . . . Well, it happened that Gen. Graves himself was in the *salle* when three screamingly loud specimens of the Vladivostok—well—demi-monde is a little too high up—we might allude to them as quarter-monde—appeared. Something popped at once—the women were ordered out and the officer responsible for inviting them, a navy man, was called down in front of everybody, even the soldiers, which delighted my soul as the soldiers are not allowed to ask such women to the Hut dances and have always complained that the officers asked whom they pleased to the big evenings.

17 November 1919 to Aunt Anna
Here I sit and every minute or two one hears the tra-ta-ta of the machine guns and the cracks of the single rifles—dealing death. We don't quite know what this revolution is about, but from the direction of the firing, it would seem that [the ataman] Kalmykov and the Czech general Gaida had come to blows. Their trains (armored) are facing each other down beyond the station, about three quarters of a mile from here, but as it is raining we can't see anything even through the [field] glasses. . . . Gaida is fighting in his quality of a colonel in the Russian army and the Czechs are not mixed up in this, it being Russian against Russian.

18 November 1919 to Clara
For a long time here, we have felt as if we were sitting on the lid and matters came to a head yesterday. We knew it was coming as all the stores closed up in the morning. . . . By the people on the street one could tell that something was wrong and even the rain, which at times fell quite heavily, did not prevent them from gathering at corners and watching the course of events;

motor trucks and cars were flying up and down the street, and after I had seen two truckloads of our boys go down armed for trouble, I simply had to go down to the street . . . and while I stood there two more truck loads went down looking as unconcerned as if they were off to school. . . . From eleven till three there was more intensive firing, and as we learned afterwards, the cadets went so bravely into an attack on the station, where many of them lost their lives, but their sacrifice was not in vain as they dislodged Gaida's men and chased them on board the *Pechenga*, a big old Volunteer boat lying at the wharf. I slept a little between half past three and five, waking up shortly before the latter hour. A few minutes later there was a crash from a big gun followed by several more, and the battle was on again, and this time there was no letup for over an hour—it was crash, bang, crash, bang from big guns, machine guns and rifles until the uprising was quelled and Gaida and his staff captured.[34]

[Later] Bodies are lying about everywhere down in that neighborhood of the station and the wharves, and the wet snow which fell yesterday made everything more gruesome. . . . I am so sorry for the cadets who fell taking the station—so many many young lives have been sacrificed since these awful times began, till one wonders that any of the braver ones are left. I know many of these boys by sight, as one sees them at the Hut, and these two afternoons I have been looking and looking to see if those I know best are still alive. One navy boy turned up yesterday and one cadet this afternoon. Mr. Mattesen, from his office on Aleutskaia, saw seven people shot, five of them civilians. . . . One of these men, shot badly in the leg, was saved by a Russian Red Cross nurse, who flew out from somewhere, and regardless of the hail of bullets, snatched off her own garter, made a tourniquet of it and got the wounded man into a house. Mr. Mattesen saw this and said for cool bravery he had never heard anything like it. The same woman, when volunteers were called for in the station square, came forward, but the British general (I believe) didn't want to let a woman go there. However, she insisted, went, and helped the wounded again at the risk of her own life, and again came back unscathed.

7 December 1919 to Aunt Anna
Friday afternoon, just as a matter of curiosity, I counted the tea, cocoa and coffee checks at the Hut and found we had served thirteen hundred and sixty-two cups, and Friday is usually the smallest day of the week. Saturday we served more, and Thursday we must have served nearly two thousand as

it was a holiday and there was a big crowd. . . . Ted came home with invitations to a Czech concert and . . . I have never heard—and never dreamed of—such wonderful music. The orchestra was made of more than eighty pieces, the leader being the composer Karel.[35] . . . We came out of that dirty old theater to find the world white with the softest, shiniest kind of snow, as beautiful as the music, and a pale moon just showing through the clouds. . . . This is the fifth or sixth concert the Czechs have given during the past year and a half, as one orchestra after another happens to be here with their regiments, for they are all soldiers. It is a treat Vladivostok had no right even to dream of, for many of these men are artists from the Grand Opera in Vienna, Budapest and Prague. Tickets are not sold, but issued with the invitations, so there is no question of money at all—this is the beautiful way the Czechs have taken to show their gratitude for what the Allies have done to help them. . . . We, as of the smaller fry, didn't have a box, but had very good seats in the main part of the house, just far enough from the stage to be pleasant. Major Broz, the Czech High Commissioner, and Gen. Cechek (I think it was) received the guests as they came in, and all the ushers were soldiers.

26 December 1919 to Clara
Yesterday I had charge at the tea counter and there was a perfect mob of people in the Hut. Miss Breck was hobbling around on her crutch and we came just as near an international rumpus as I want to get. I must explain that there is a great deal of tension between the Czechs and Allies on the one hand and the Russians on the other. The Russian feelings are very near the surface in these days of uncertainty of which way the cat is going to jump, and many of them are very sore over the defection of the Allies. The Czechs are also sore for they did what they could here, and seeing everything which promised so well go to pieces means that the blood they shed here was in vain and that it is a thankless task. Miss Breck was sitting behind the line of men who were coming along for tea and cakes, and a Caucasian [a man from the Caucasus], in the Russian uniform, kept pushing in behind though repeatedly ordered not to do so by an old man stationed there for that particular purpose. That time he began to make a row, whereupon Miss Breck jumped up, holding up her hand and saying in English "Get out of here." Like a flash the man whipped out his *poignard* [dagger] and raised it at her—I was standing beside her and it seemed ten minutes before I was sure he would not stab her with it, though of course it was less than a second in reality. Miss Breck never flinched but looked him squarely in the eye till he lowered the weapon

and then she called for someone to arrest him. It happened that just then there were only Russians in the line though there were plenty of Czechs in the hall and sitting at the tea tables. Thirty lined up downstairs like a flash to prevent any attempt to escape, and the Russians shouldered the man across the balcony to the other side where he sat down and refused to move and dared any one to arrest him, as he was a Russian soldier. . . . I can tell you that it was a most uncomfortable place to be in for a few minutes—most men were probably armed and the tiniest spark would have started a shooting affair. . . . The man certainly was not drunk though some of the Russians contended that he should have been left free as he was said to be a little off.

23 January 1920 to Aunt Anna
For the first time in weeks Miss Breck came to spend a day with me. She came up from the Hut at one o'clock and had *tiffin* and tea. I sent a note down to Gen. Graves and he and Col. Eichelberger came up to have tea with us, which was very cozy and nice—the luxury of a grate fire and the tea table laid with the Danish china. There was no cake but the General enjoyed hot scones and jam very much. He seldom takes anything at tea and I was therefore delighted to have something he couldn't refuse.

2 February 1920 to Home
Oh, by the way, I'm forgetting that we had had a little revolution [on Monday 26 January] but it didn't last long. The Jäger Regiment [rather, battalion] had mutinied and arrested their officers Sunday afternoon. . . . The trouble was right here in our block but as it practically went on from seven to nine in the morning I heard little of it and saw nothing excepting the disarmed Jägers marching down the Svetlanskaia to be shipped to Russian Island. A rattle of hand grenades aroused me from my peaceful slumbers at half past four but after twelve or fifteen explosions, nothing more was heard until seven when they began shooting on the Commercial School, almost over our heads but around the NE shoulder of the hill from us. . . . The Commercial School, one of the finest buildings in town, looked slightly sick afterward.[36]

25 March 1920 to Home
While Admiral Gleaves was here, his wife and daughter came in one of the transports and spent a few days in town. Mrs. Macgowan gave a dinner and dance for them and we were asked to both, so we met the daughter and a Mrs. Poe, the mother of an *S. D.* [*South Dakota*] officer, but did not see Mrs. Gleaves

as the admiral took them out for a drive in one of the Headquarters motors, and they rolled down a five-hundred-foot bank, which rather shook them up. The car was luckily of steel, else they might have been killed. As it was, it turned over once and a half and hauled up against a stump, badly shaking up the occupants but not breaking any bones. The daughter, Evelina (an awfully pretty girl), and Mrs. Poe had to walk the eight miles back as the car sent for them missed the road, so they came to the dinner just as they were, already an hour late, Miss Gleaves' tailored skirt badly torn. Mrs. Gleaves excused herself and remained on board. The dance which followed the dinner was very nice, about a hundred and fifty people present. General Oi, the Commander-in-Chief of the Allied Forces in Siberia, shed the effulgent glow of his presence on the assembly, and he is a treat to look at. Along in the evening it occurred to Mrs. Macgowan that he was not getting the attention his rank would lead him to expect, so she put me down beside him to talk and the only foreign language he speaks is German. The mere fact that I cannot speak German didn't, as usual, bother me in the least and I sailed in with the admirable result that inside three minutes, His Excellency took to the tall timber, made his adieus and left, so anyone who wants to get rid of him can send for me to talk to him in German, and that will do the business.

JAPANESE OCCUPATION, 4–5 APRIL 1920 TO 25 OCTOBER 1922

After most of the interventionists left Vladivostok in early April 1920, the Japanese occupied the city: "What we have so long spoken of, dreaded, and yet, these last days, looked upon as the last hope for the town has come to pass—the Japanese flag is flying over Tiger Hill and all the more prominent buildings in Vladivostok.... Nastia, good Russian patriot that she is, is heartbroken" (5 April 1920 to Aunt Anna). Keeping track of the constantly shifting local powers remained complicated—Were the Merkulov brothers, the Kappelites, General Diterikhs, or yet someone else in charge?—but every group trying to govern Vladivostok had to consider the occupation: "Japanese policies and actions cast a shadow over the political and economic life of the territory they dominated, and no political force could make a move without first considering the potential Japanese reaction."[37] In other words, an overlordship.

For everyone remaining in Vladivostok, the relationship with the ostensible and the real authorities required balancing the skills of tact and ingenuity, as well as the aptitude to read between the lines in all official pronouncements. Eleanor Pray continued participating in Vladivostok's multinational world of military and diplomatic glitter: "[At Mrs. Caldwell's] tea table I had the Polish consul and the Chinese consul on my left, Gen. Lavergne (French commander in chief) and Major Broz on my right, and we were obliged to speak Russian! Gen. Oi himself came but refrained from getting too near me, evidently remembering his last experience when Mrs. Macgowan made me speak German" (4 May 1920 to Home). Inwardly, however, Mrs. Pray was no friend of the Japanese. She considered the occupation deeply humiliating and the occupiers deceitful, commenting, for example, when two Russian factions vied for power in June 1922, "Trouble is brewing and two governments are preparing to go for each other, the Japanese doubtless backing both of them" (6 June 1922 to Home). Mrs. Pray was also unable to contain her anger about the Japanese role in the brutal murder of Warren Langdon (1888–1921), chief engineer on the USS *Albany*.

Eleanor Pray first mentions Lieutenant Langdon in March 1920, when he attended one of the official dinners. Because he was honest and responsible, Consuls Caldwell and Macgowan included the lieutenant in sailing trips, and the Prays liked to invite him home for afternoon tea or dinner. On 15 July 1919, Langdon had written to a friend about his by then almost four months' stay in Vladivostok as a member of the AEF. Although the Russian girls were attractive and liked to dance, he had found the city itself unimpressive: "When it rains, the mud is knee deep, and when it dries off, the dust is like a cloud all the time." He noted that the *Albany* would be "cruising around China and Japan" for several months during the fall, and, matter-of-factly, that one or two murders occurred in Vladivostok every night, and that he had seen one even the day before writing.[38] Little could he know that in a year and a half he himself would become such a nocturnal victim. His death caused an international incident, and Admiral Gleaves returned on the *New Orleans* to bring his body home.

The intensifying poverty and suffering all around Vladivostok also offered Eleanor Pray an inspiring challenge. She renewed and expanded her volunteer work with the Red Cross, opening up a distribution center next to the old storehouse at Dom Smith, and venturing out into the villages, including Kiparisovo, along the railway north of the city with clothes, food, and other necessities. This enterprise became so absorbing that no time was left for other activities: "I often think of asking for a pass to attend a meeting of the [political] Assembly, but never get around to it as my work is far too engrossing for me to take a live interest in anything else" (11 June 1922 to Sarah). Mrs. Pray was forced into close personal contact with the anarchy, corruption, and unimaginable cruelty of the times, but also with the strong survival spirit of Russians whom she had never known before: "I feel that I have missed a lot in all these years in not getting to know more of the real Russian people, this being my first real experience with the villagers—and townspeople are never so nice" (27 September 1920 to Home).

5 April 1920 to Aunt Anna
It is lucky I have a typewriter, such as it is, for after this night and especially the strain of the past half hour, I simply cannot hold a pen for trembling, though as long as the strain was on, I didn't realize it. . . . We were tired last night and went to bed early. Ever since these unsettled times, Ted sleeps on a couch downstairs so as to know what is going on in this part of the house, and I sleep in my bedroom as usual with the window open, protected by a screen on the top of which are always three empty tin cans ready to fall down should the screen be touched ever so slightly. I was sitting up in bed reading *The League of the Scarlet Pimpernel,*[39] *faute de mieux,* when a shot rang out not far away—but that is too common an occurrence for one to take much notice. This one, however, was followed after a short interval by four others, then by three, and then by fifteen or twenty scattering ones which sounded like an automatic rifle. All was then quiet for about half an hour and then it began again, more guns taking part, then machine guns, and finally field or fortress guns of heavy caliber. . . . When we got up we saw the Jap flag every-where.[40] About nine this morning, M. Chartran, a French acquaintance, came in to tell me the Japs were preparing to take the Post Office . . . and he advised us to keep away from the front of the house. I . . . of course couldn't keep away from the window to save my life, though forbidding the servants to go near one. I could see the crowd in the street and presently spied some Jap soldiers creeping along the middle terrace just under our windows and expected nothing but that some Russian would begin sniping at them from the street, but after twenty minutes or so the crowd dispersed, all was quiet, and the P. O. had evidently changed hands without bloodshed.

28 April 1920 to Home
Feeling runs very high here among the foreigners at present, some of them going the Russians one better in indignation against the Japanese, and others

seeing clearly that the Japanese are all that stands between the country and anarchy.

30 October 1920 to Aunt Anna
After we finished doing up parcels in the evening [at Kiparisovo], Nastia and I went out and walked across the garden . . . as far as a little wood, and the night was perfect, not very cold and a bright full moon, . . . and the village looked like one in a fairy tale. Two stout horses, tied to a fence, were munching their supper and that is a sound I have always loved but seldom heard of late years. . . . When I awoke, about seven, there was a peculiar light in the room and what do you think? It was snowing hard and the ground was already thickly covered. The whole place looked like a Christmas card—one of the kind with frosting on the highlights, and I could have spent the morning just enjoying it, had there been nothing else to do, but the people were beginning to come and we had to get our breakfast and get to work.

9 January 1921 to Home, Sunday
Such a terrible thing has happened that we can think of nothing else. Saturday morning, about two o'clock, as Chief Engineer Langdon of the *Albany* was coming home from a Christmas party, near the Nikolai Arch, he was challenged by a Japanese sentry who asked him if he were an American to which Langdon replied "*Da*" [Yes] and passed along; without warning the Japanese shot him from the back, the bullet just missing the top of the heart and going clean through the left lung, coming out and tearing the front of his coat all to pieces. He was alone and the place where it happened is at the least four hundred yards from where the *Albany* stands, but Langdon turned and shot twice at the sentry, then walked on board the ship, saluted the officer on duty, reported himself, and only then called for the doctor and told what had happened. . . . [Yesterday] about half past four two sailors from the *Albany* came up here bringing to me the brass hob which Langdon had promised to make for me and which he had been intending to bring himself. Just think of his remembering to do that when every breath may be his last. I had said to him that I had wanted a hob for twenty years but never succeeded in getting one, and Langdon said that if I could describe it to him, he thought he could make one, so he and Ted and I sat there and planned and measured and the last thing he said was that twenty years was quite long enough to wait and that he would answer for my getting the hob at last.

14 January 1921 to Home
The Japanese publicity bureau here have published a statement that the murder of Lieut. Langdon was due to a "regrettable misunderstanding"—very
regrettable indeed!

17 January 1921 to Home
We hear that when the Japanese were questioned, they answered that the
sentry thought it was a Russian—which strikes one as a most naïve excuse.
Even the Japanese were nonplussed when the next question came: "And what
if it had been?"

18 February 1921 to Home
This afternoon Mrs. Findlay got the loan of an automobile and . . . we drove
out to Second River and went to the Old Folks' Home, a trip I have been planning for a long time as I had some bags for the old people. Each bag had a
little coffee, tea, sugar, hard candies, cookies, tinned milk, thread, needles,
handkerchief, safety pins, tape, etc., and I also took out a tin of lard for them
to divide, and a warm dressing gown each, also a pair of socks. I have never
seen children any happier with gifts than these twenty-one old people were.
Some of them laughed with delight but more of them cried. One old lady
insisted on presenting me with some twigs of pussy willow which she had
been forcing in a bottle of water.

1 March 1921 to 14th Division, American Red Cross
Many of our supplies are being diverted from their normal function in life
and quite successfully. Operating leggings are gratefully received and worn
in lieu of drawers and socks; splint straps, of which we have hundreds, serve
as suspenders and belts; the better variety of pot-holders, when there are five
or six of a kind, will make a pair of knickers for a little boy and the variegated
collections are sewn into bed quilts; khaki property bags also make good,
strong knickers. From absorbent pads people make warm linings for winter
coats, and shot-bags are useful as patches. Scraps go to the orphanage for
patch-work, and hospital slippers, have, on occasions (odd ones!) been made
into quite presentable caps.

26 May 1921 to Home
[11.30 AM] The [anti-Bolshevik] revolution has begun and from the shots
[one can hear that] they are taking the Navy Staff, and I am watching the

tower to see when the good old red-blue-and-white is run up—people are carrying them on the streets and there is of course a lot of excitement.[41]

[Noon] The revolution caught me right in the middle of a chocolate frosting and I had to go back to it, but it is on top of the cake now, and I can stand at the gate with Nastia and watch the people scurry along the street, the Chinese carters turning down toward Beregovaia to get out of the range of bullets. The militia have surrendered and everywhere one sees the new militia with the tricolor on their arms instead of that loathsome red.

3 June 1921 to Home
So far the town has been quiet but things are seething underneath and we can expect anything. Instead of the Kappelites being in power, it seems to be the Semenovs and their name is not exactly one to conjure by, as, aside from their anti-bolshevik principles, they are almost as bad as the *bolsheviki*.[42] . . . Semenov himself is said to be on a Jap transport in the harbor and unable as yet to come ashore. That may be, but if I did not see him in a car on Aleutskaia, then it was someone uncommonly like his pictures.

2 February 1922 to Dorothy
All sorts of funny things happen in Red Cross work—today I got a letter from the Manila chapter, practically asking me to look up and propose to a girl one of our soldiers wanted to marry! And then I had a letter from a Russian in jail here asking for clothing and enclosing documents to prove that he was in jail only for stealing!

5 March 1922 to Sarah
This week I have passed out ten *poods* of buckwheat, a pood of lard, a pood of sugar, half a case of milk, lots of scolding and a lot of good advice. One wonders which will do the most good. . . . The latest news is that Spiridon Merkulov has been forced to resign. This promises nothing good as, as far as one could judge from the outside, he is a patriot and a pretty good uphill fighter. The government is of course in a very critical position for lack of money but in the nine months they have been in power, there has been passably decent order in the city, good light and tram service and no reprisals.

12 July 1922 to Sarah
Last Thursday Miss Talko's commanding officer asked me over to their car to have tea and I enjoyed myself very much. . . . They sent a carriage for me,

drawn by a horse belonging to the officer who came for me, a man from the Urals who, through "thick and thin" has hung to this horse because it was bred on his home place. It is scarcely more than a Mongolian pony, but stood all the hardships of the retreat from Omsk and is still in good condition. These people belong to the Railway Brigade, and live in a train which stands on a siding beyond the volunteer wharf—half a mile or so. The commanding officer's car stands on the very edge of the bay, with a clear view over Egersheld, Churkin, Russian Island and the entrance, and it was very pleasant having tea with them. There were four or five officers and the wives of three of them. They had coffee and buns and I was the only one who really took anything besides coffee. . . . I sat there with them two hours and a half and enjoyed myself thoroughly.

30 July 1922 to Home

Yesterday to my amazement, I was asked to come to the Cathedral at eleven o'clock to hear a prayer of thanksgiving or rather of gratitude to the American people for the help that had been given [to the Russian people]. . . . On the floor in front of the altar on a small stand was a loaf of black bread with a cellar full of salt set into the top of it, a small bouquet of flowers and a long Russian tea towel. These objects the priest sprinkled with holy water and blessed, after which the women presented them to me. The towel was made of a strip of cotton, done in cross stitch with odds and ends of cotton, and the inscription was as follows: "From the pure Russian heart/City of Vladivostok/To kind/ Eleonora Georgievna Pray. 1922/Maria Bezuslavina/Maria Cheruimisina/ Domna Ivanovna Gavrilova/Maria Suterina." There was a three-inch border across each end edged with crocheting, the whole being about twelve inches wide and three yards long. . . . After the blessing the women brought the things to me with very touching expressions of gratitude.

A RED CROSS SAMPLER

Eleanor Pray's written reports to the American Red Cross vividly highlight both her pithy narrative style and the little Vladivostok chapter's difficult yet far-reaching work. With a few bold strokes in a report to the Philippines chapter, for example, she made Primorie's sharp winter winds come alive: "Thank you so much for all [your help]; we are candidates for anything you can spare which is too warm for Manila. When the quicksilver is prancing around twenty below and the North wind is howling its prettiest, NOTHING is too warm here" (26 June 1922 to Knowlton Mixer). And in a letter to the Japan chapter, her imagery is so immediate that those described seem to step off of the page and touch us: "One would enjoy introducing you to some of our clientele—to little, bright-eyed Anna Korukhina, whose fireman husband was killed last year and who lost her baby in January—she looks like a robin beating against a storm and has a hard struggle to keep herself and her little girl alive" (26 June 1922 to J. A. Welbourn). The endeavor itself—identifying the neediest cases, then distributing the meager means as fairly as possible—was profoundly interesting to Mrs. Pray, but working with the staff and those receiving the aid was even more so.

The following letter, included almost in full, gives a comprehensive overview of the American Red Cross work in Vladivostok at this time, with bright human portraits and poignant glimpses of Vladivostok life toward the end of the Japanese occupation.

27 June 1922 to Charles H. Forster, Assistant Executive Secretary in charge of Insular and Foreign Chapters, American Red Cross, Washington, DC:
First let me thank you for your kind letters of the tenth and eighteenth of May—you will understand that we are very glad to know that you approve of our work and, with the aim of putting you a little more in touch with it, we are writing this frank, personal letter, describing as well as possible the joys and sorrows of the Vladivostok Chapter. It will not be the sort of thing for the Red Cross archives but we hope that, as a man, you will [be] interested in the very human side of our work which does not, as a rule, appear in our quarterly reports. . . . The spice of life is not lacking in our work and . . . a broad field of studies in human nature is thus opened up to us. . . .

We rent a part of a warehouse and a room where the sewing is given out, received and stored and distributed, for which we pay sixty-six yen monthly. It is centrally located, just up a short lane from the Post Office and in the compound where we live. Our office and reception room consists of the yard in front of the storehouse, tastefully furnished with Red Cross packing cases, made to do yeoman's duty as desks and counters, by the aid of a few skillfully driven nails—and our background is a glorious one, Our Flag. The canopy, which keeps the rain from dripping on the distribution books as we write, is fashioned of four gunny sacks (ex-receptacles for buckwheat), four long splint straps, and some staples. This is not a shining success but when the rain, as sometimes happens, begins to penetrate it, the "office" "beats it" to the storehouse and finishes up from there. The weather has been rotten all the spring, cold and rainy, though it has improved a bit lately. In this impromptu office we receive the petitioners and here, four days a week, we issue to them flour, buckwheat, lard, sugar, tea, milk, steero [bouillon cubes], and occasionally soap. The line begins to form as early as six in the morning and by nine, when operations begin, there are often a hundred persons of all kinds of descriptions in line, many of whom have walked anywhere from five to ten miles. There are Russians from all parts of what was once Russia, there are Poles, Ests [Estonians], Letts [Latvians], Lithuanians, Finns, Tatars, Gruzians—in fact almost anyone that could be asked for from Eastern Europe.[43]

Now let me introduce our Russian personnel. The right-hand man in the distribution is Peter Sakharov, a young student, the son of a priest, who supports his widowed mother, a young brother and [a] sister. He gets fifteen yen weekly to do all the Russian writing, typing, etc. In the storehouse Mrs. Alexandra Pershina, a lone capable widow whom I have known for years, superintends the weighing and measuring and also devotes a part of her time to investigations, receiving weekly eight yen. Then comes Tania Savkina, an eighteen-year-old girl, who is the second of a family of seven, six of them girls. The only son and Tania have, up to this week, been the only wage earners. She receives five yen a week and a ration for her family. The mother has a little cottage but is in constant danger of losing it as they are badly in debt owing to the long illness which preceded the father's death last summer. Tania has had one year in the trades' school and is an excellent assistant in any kind of work. Maria Pastukhova, also eighteen, is a refugee from Chita— a girl who has finished the high school, and is quite alone here. She gets three yen for three days' work weekly which, with a small ration, enables her to live among decent people. We do not really need her but one is sorry for a young girl so stranded, who can find no employment, and it is wiser to let her earn a little money than to assist her financially. Far too many girls of her age take to the streets and, when driven by hunger, as is now so often the case, who can blame?

Our warehouse man, Mikhail Voronko, is rather nondescript, but is all right for what we require of him. He comes at eight in the morning and stands at the gate, giving out turns, and trying—albeit usually in vain—to keep out the people who have no cards. The *babas* have no trouble in getting the best of him as he is quite ready to climb the nearest tree when they begin to argue with him. Standing in the path of a determined Russian *baba* is no mere joke and the average one who appears is bound and determined to have a word with some of the "Amerikanskys" before leaving. A mere *muzhik* standing in the way is of little more account than a fly. Voronko is too reticent and retiring for investigations, but he can handle cases, sacks, measure portions and do what little carpentering is necessary for which we pay him a yen and a half a day and a ration, as he has a wife and three children. He is so very quiet that aside from the fact that he was a man with a family, out of work, and a trench comrade of our last warehouse man (who recommended him), I knew nothing about him until the other day when I offered him some little thing for his boy. The man broke down, and with tears running down his face, told me his troubles, his bitter intensity in the relation of them being all the more effective and impressive coming from such a quiet, unobtrusive man. By trade he is a joiner and had got along so well that he had left the firm he was working for and set up a small shop for himself in one of the places up the [railway] line where he had ten men working for him. Then came the revolution, his shop and all his tools were destroyed, his home burned, and there he was. The firm he had worked for here had also been ruined and there was almost no demand for fine joiner work, and dozens of other joiners in the same position. He told me that more than once in the last two years he had gone down onto the Svetlanskaia, intending to stand on the corner and beg, but could never bring himself to it, and that more than half the time his family had gone both hungry and cold. They live in a basement, the rent of which he has been unable to pay for months, and last winter the eldest children had to stay at home from school because they had no warm coats. Be sure we promised him that that should not happen this winter.

Miss Maria Vladislavovna Talko, a Russian sister-of-mercy both in the Russo-Japanese and in the Great War, well known to those of our people who were stationed at our hospital on Russian Island, works for us all her spare time, sometimes in the storehouse, sometimes investigating—this amounts to about ten days a month for which she is paid ten yen. The rest of the time she is on duty at the dispensary of the Railway Battalion, for which she gets nothing but a small ration. With her clear humorous blue eyes, impertinently tilted nose, pock-marked face and thoroughly human outlook on life, she is one of the biggest treats I know of—having a heart like the ocean and a tongue like a razor. She knows dozens of people in all parts of the town and it is always to her we apply when we want to know just how to get at the truth in disputed or obscure cases.

Outside our paid helpers, we have various sources of information, chiefly through doctors, teachers, Parents' Committees (these exist in connection with all the schools), consuls, city supervisors of the poor, and occasionally the Russian Red Cross. To know who are the deserving and needy and who are not is by far the most difficult part of the work and . . . in many cases, indeed in most, it is hard to get at the truth, for poverty is comparative and the woman who cannot have sugar in her tea considers herself every whit as poor as the woman who has no tea to put it in. . . .

The Russians are artists at expressing themselves—a never-ending source of wonder to us of the more reticent natures and awkward tongues, who have never been accustomed to turning our souls inside out to any who will listen. At vivid description, the average one can outdo Dickens. It so often happens that an artistically worded tale of woe wrings tears out of my hardened old eyes when I have every reason to believe that the person telling it is lying with such fervor and art that for the moment she forgets quite that she is not telling the truth—gets carried away with her subject, as it were. . . .

The life of a person known to be an investigator is not a bed of roses for he is besieged day and night—even threatened, so we have no regular investigator but send first one and then another. There was a case last spring in which our man came out second best having had to beat an ignominious retreat before the onslaught of thirteen angry *babas* to whom he refused recommendations. One *feldsher* [medical assistant] on Russian Island, who is a very trustworthy man and in a position to know who the poor in his locality really are, has got in so bad by refusing people who should have been ashamed to ask at all, that he simply has to refuse all investigation. One *baba*, who had calmly asked him to give her a certificate to the effect that she was a widow with five small children and had just come out of the hospital after a two months' illness (note the artistic touch), was deeply offended when Mr. Novitskii reminded her that she had only three children and that, as far as he knew, had never been ill a day in her life. . . .

The best investigators we have had are a former warehouse man named Chadyi and Mrs. Krasikova, a volunteer worker, occasionally quite invaluable. They are both common Russians with very little education but very keen minds and their methods are as a rule very successful. They gossip all through a neighborhood, and strike a general average between the tales of the neighbors and the tale of the person who is applying for assistance. The tales they bring in are often worth printing but would fall rather flat when translated into our less gorgeous tongue. . . .

It is hardest of all for us to hear of the suicides on account of hunger, realizing that we might have helped, but knowing nothing of the existence even of the suicide until it was too late. Only a few weeks ago a young, nice-looking widow hung her two children and then herself, leaving a letter to a friend in which she said she had looked in vain for work and could no longer bear hearing her children cry from hunger.

Work in a village is easy enough for the priests always know who need help the most but in a city the priest does not have the opportunity to know the lives of his parishioners so well and there are all the hundreds of refugees who have no connection with any parish. The old Polish (Catholic) priest, however, knows his flock well and on the rare occasions when he sends one of them to us for help we are perfectly assured that the person sent is absolutely down and out.

We take a great deal of interest in the Kappel School in Nikolsk where there are one hundred and fifty-six children of various ages. We help as we can with clothing and send them monthly two cases of milk, two of lard, a case of steero and any other nourishing thing we happen to have at the time. Col. Bermin, a tall, quizzical-looking invalid officer, is at the head of the organization of the Kappel invalids, widows and orphans, and his troubles are sometimes laughable. In May we gave him the last of our layettes [outfits of clothes, toilet articles, etc., for newborn children], which proved just enough (with the usual division) to go around, and he was so pleased to think no one would be without the needed garments for the coming baby. When he came down this month he was in despair as, on account of the fighting between the Chinese factions in Northern Manchuria, the Kappel women and children from Grodekovo (not far from the border) had been shipped up to him and there were several crying needs for layettes. No matter where or how these people are disabled, nothing on earth seems to interfere with the advent of the annual baby. All we could give this time was shirts, a square of canton [cotton] for a blanket and four flour sacks for diapers.

Let me end this document by introducing to you a few, out of the hundreds of really destitute people, who, thanks to the American Red Cross, are receiving a little assistance once a fortnight, for which they are very grateful, as it is oftener than not all that stands between them and starvation in the actual sense of the word—something very hard for us to understand. I should like you to meet . . . ELIZAVETA MARKOVA, the widow of one of the thousands of Nikolaevsk murdered, who has five daughters to bring up, the eldest only fourteen. She is a good seamstress and asks for nothing better than to have work but there are hundreds of other good seamstresses in town and next to no work to be had as people have no money for hired sewing in these times; ANNA ZAITSEVA and PRASKOVIA IUDCHITS, both widows of murdered Vladivostok militiamen, each left with four small children, the latter with an old sick mother to support as well; they have a pension of four yen monthly; IUSTINIA DOROKHOVA, ninety-three years old, who crosses herself devoutly over her little allowance of flour, sugar and tea, mumbling toothless blessings on the American Red Cross, both for the food and for the warm gray sweater she wears; ARINA NEGREI, a little wisp of a Tatar with four small hungry boys on her hands and only an occasional day's washing; she is happy to have a little green garden and the seeds we gave her are already coming up; delicate old Madame KLIMOVICH and her daughter, Polish gentlewomen, who seek day in and day out for work they cannot find, and which, even if they could find, they would not be strong enough to do; they have paid no rent for months and live in constant terror of being ejected from their damp corner onto the street; NATALIA NOVIKOVA, whose husband was run over and killed in December and who has five children, the last one born in February; she lives in a dugout in Second River and in spite of her cough (a nasty one), baby in her arms, walks twice a week to Sedanka— five miles away—to wash up a floor for which she gets fifty sen. The eldest son, a nice boy of twelve, who sometimes earns a little money, has been laid up in the hospital for over three weeks now with inflammation of the lungs; EVDOKSIA SOBORSKAIA, also from Second River, an officer's widow with eight children, and they never by any chance have eight pairs of shoes; the eldest daughter is a widow with a baby and had one leg cut off by a train two years ago; Mrs. Soborskaia gets thinner every day but makes little of tramping five miles with thirty-six pounds of flour flung over her shoulder, the lard, sugar and tea in her hands; IVAN BELKIN, an artist, with long, finely shaped hands, who lost his sight in the war and who has five children; when he earns six yen a month selling papers, he is the happiest man one could ask to meet, for those six yen pay the rent of the cuddy hole he and his live in; MARIA CHUMAKOVA, whose hands are so crippled by rheumatism that she cannot use her fingers and yet must feed three children; poor IDA ROSE, a deserted wife, whose face got so badly burned last year that her husband could not bear to look at her any longer and took French leave; she wants to give her baby away for adoption and always assures me that he is "such a good baby"; blind ANNA IUSTINTSEVA, who, for a wonder, has no children, and apathetic DARIA KOZLOVA, a deaf and dumb woman who has a swarm of them; and last of all to one-eyed PELAGEIA KAPUSTINA, who, having told the age of four children, and having been asked "Is that all?" replied "Of course not, *barynia* [my lady]!" and went on with the ages of the other six.

Roughly speaking, out of the ten thousand dollars sent from Washington in April, four thousand have been spent for provisions, three thousand for field and garden seeds, and one thousand for materials. With the two thousand we have left, we can continue the sewing two months and the distribution of food one month longer, as it has been agreed to divide the money evenly. Detailed accounts will be sent in next week—also Mrs. Macgowan's report on seeds, Mrs. Newhard's on sewing, and mine on food. Our chapter hopes you can see your way to render us further financial aid, perhaps instructing us as to what lines you would wish us to continue.

CHAPTER 9

A Window Flung Open

New Beginnings

IN EARLY SPRING 1927, ELEANOR PRAY DESCRIBED THE VIEW OVER
the Amur Bay from the Nielsens' *dacha* at 19th Verst: "If I could only lend
you my eyes for a moment—the big window is flung wide open, in the foreground is the . . . purplish brown of the still bare trees, with the background
of hazy blue hills, each crest outlined by itself, . . . and over it all this glorious
spring sunshine—the birds are singing, too, but a freight train coughing its
way out of Okeanskaia station less than a mile away, rather drowns their
music" (24 April 1927 to Dorothy).[1] In Mrs. Pray's own life and that of her
beloved Vladivostok, nature's colors and sounds remained vibrant, sometimes hidden by the noise of civilization, yet patiently continuing to offer
comfort and beauty. That the Russian Empire had become the Soviet Union
immeasurably influenced the lives of everyone living in Vladivostok, including Eleanor Pray, but she kept on writing her letters, continuing to open up
the windows and doors into Vladivostok.

Two far-reaching events occurred within half a year of each other. On
25 October 1922, troops of the People's Revolutionary Army marched victorious into Vladivostok, signaling the end of the Civil War and the victory
of the October Revolution. Then, on 2 April 1923, after weeks of suffering an
unusual cold, recurring boils, and blood poisoning, Frederick Pray died.
Now a widow without an income in a perplexingly changed socioeconomic
climate, Eleanor had to create a new strategy for her existence. Despite her
grief but with her customary pluck, she began dealing with the ever-increas-
ing property taxes, the shortages of food and fuel, and the innovative but to
her distressing housing regulations. She was a bourgeois lady trying to find

her way in a socialist society: "Of course I have been spoiled with all these easy years and no responsibility, so every molehill seems a mountain" (4 June 1923 to Sarah). Contrasting the Prays' first Vladivostok decades in their large, elegant home with servants, money, and festivities, Eleanor Pray now saw almost every facet of her life contracting. Sharing Dom Smith with numerous other tenants, she occupied just one of its rooms for her own; instead of intricate dinners dramatically unveiled by the kitchen staff, she cooked her own frugal meals; and without the support of a husband and relatives, she had to find salaried work. The turn her life had taken was daunting.

While the next few years were to become a tapestry of complex beginnings, highlighted with occasional splashes of both exuberance and conflict, one thread remained unbroken throughout: the joys and concerns of faithful friendships and human contact. Eleanor Pray supported those who were in need: "Yesterday [I went] to congratulate Mrs. Piankova [on her name-day], though there is precious little to congratulate her upon. All our acquaintances were there and it was really very jolly . . . for knowing what a hole the Piankovs are in, their friends made an extra effort to come" (1 October 1929 to Sarah).[2] And in a stroke of great kindness, Alfred Albers removed more than Mrs. Pray's financial instability by offering her a position as translator at the firm of Kunst and Albers.[3] Far from a sinecure, this connection with intelligent colleagues and shared professional tasks gave her life a steady rhythm that she liked and that helped her heal. During her seven years at Kunst and Albers, Eleanor's relief at having an occupation and a regular albeit small income deepened into true affection: "The office work does not tire me and I am always glad when it is time to go in the morning" (9 November 1923 to Sarah). Best of all, the beauty and solace of Vladivostok still stretched out all around her.

Life's difficulties became almost insurmountable for the old bourgeoisie. The Piankovs were among Eleanor Pray's closest friends, once among the wealthiest families in Vladivostok. In 1924, their town house on Svetlanskaia was "municipalized," that is, made public property,[4] but their *dacha* at 19th Verst continued to be a welcoming weekend refuge for many friends, with its offer of tennis and bridge, walks along the sea, and skiing and sledding in winter.[5] When, for much of 1927, the Piankovs disappeared from Eleanor Pray's epistolary horizon, one might wonder what rift had broken the friendship. Only letters hand-carried from Russia by a visitor the following year explain what had happened: "Last June [1927] about three hundred people were arrested in one week—without rhyme or reason, and clapped into the

GPU (Cheka) jail on Aleutskaia, a month or so later being removed to the ordinary prison. . . . Mr. Piankov was detained five months—and for what? Neither he nor anyone else knows, but as most of those arrested had more or less connection with foreigners, the arrests were attributed to that" (29 February 1928 to Dorothy).[6] Eleanor Pray also observed, "Those nights were horrible, for one heard the motor lorries all night long and knew what they were out for" (25 February 1928 to Clara).

That Mrs. Pray clung so stubbornly to Vladivostok and the wrecked pieces of her former life was not easy for her family to understand. Soon after the October Revolution, Clara expressed her view in an uninhibited, run-on outburst of sibling annoyance: "Why on earth do you stay in Vladivostok is what puzzles everyone I suppose you know your business best" (10 March 1918 from Clara to Eleanor). When Ted died, the family thought that she would return home, but Eleanor hoped instead that, remaining in Vladivostok, she could salvage Dom Smith, and even send part of the rental income to Sarah, who still owned the buildings.[7]

The strongest familial admonition was to come from this most unexpected source. Beleaguered by news reports on the increasing shortages of foodstuff and coal in Vladivostok, gentle, soft-spoken Sarah's patience finally evaporated, and she fired off a letter filled with such quick-tempered frustration that Eleanor, in a winsome Victorian euphemism, found it necessary to refer to its "inelegant language" (17 March 1930 to Sarah). Mrs. Smith demanded that her sister-in-law leave for Shanghai immediately, outlining what boat to take and what to do with Dom Smith: "Your [letter] No. 143 has just come and I feel like swearing, that is a fact. I was tempted to go straight to the Telegraph and send you a cable saying 'Come, damn the [return] visa.' . . . I feel much better this morning but am still furious. I see by the paper that *Nancy Moller* is leaving for the North. I hope this gets there before she leaves and you pack your things and leave as if you never intended to go back. I will not have you stay there any longer—going through what you have the past year. Isn't there some man in the firm you could get to look after the place, collect the rent and attend to the repairs, and you come down here and live like a Christian. . . . Why you should stay up there and waste your life in misery is more than I can see. Take what books you want and the things you use and come and let the rest go hang" (7 March 1930 from Sarah to Eleanor). Eleanor's answer was a match in frankness, stating unequivocally, "But I can't bear to leave now. Of course I have thought of coming in the autumn if things continue to toboggan the way they are going now. It will make me feel like a quitter, for most of my friends have a much harder time than I do" (17 March 1930 to Sarah).

THE SOVIET VICTORY

After the People's Revolutionary Army troops finally marched into the city, even Eleanor was impressed: "There is good order in the town and it is a great relief after the sort of thing we have been living through" (12 November 1922 to Sarah). Instead of feeling elated by the bravery of patriotic armies, she had seen men massacred and families brought to inordinate suffering. She longed for simplicity and straightforward human values, where people could be trusted so completely that, similar to the lines of Swedish poet Ulf Lundell, "yes is yes and no is no, and doubts keep calmly still."[8] In the month before the Soviet takeover, Eleanor Pray described a movie presented at the YMCA Hut as an example of words having lost their normal meanings, and human feelings having become inured even to violence: "Tuesday I went to see a comedy called *On the High Seas* and please excuse me from any such comedies—the most facetious thing that happened was somebody shooting the captain, and dropping a heavy pulley on the head of the mate who murdered his superior officer, and the less facetious ones included a burial at sea and a deathbed confession. Quite a comedy" (28 September 1922 to Home).[9]

Eleanor Pray thus observed the final countdown of days to 25 October 1922 not with bated breath but with sorrow for her Russian friends yet relief that order would now be imposed. The eyewitness accounts of the last few days' chaos are gripping, often emphasizing people's rush to escape before the advancing army, with or without their possessions. A French friend, Mademoiselle Thomasine, recalled similar experiences: "She had gone out of her home town in front of the Germans in nineteen fourteen, in exactly that fashion, and she had gone out of [western] Russia in front of the reds four years later practically the same way—now she had nowhere to run and nothing to run with" (20 October 1922 to Home). And Shura Zhebrovskaia, the fourteen-year-old daughter of a Vladivostok merchant, was stunned by the odd spectacle of a young woman running in front of the advancing troops, "barefoot, in a dirty skirt, and holding a small bouquet of flowers."[10]

20 October 1922 to Sarah
After Ted came home at half past three and we had dinner, I went out for a walk to see what the streets were like and . . . cart after cart was coming down

the Svetlanskaia loaded with trunks, boxes or household goods, and, on top of each, women and children, occasionally a pet dog. It was one of the saddest things I have ever seen—they were all fleeing for life to the boats to get out of the country where they were born and which many of them will never see again.

22 October 1922 to Home
As the S.S. *Lorestan* was supposed to leave soon after ten, we had an early breakfast and . . . got over to Churkin, where the boat was lying, without any trouble [to say goodbye to friends]. There were dozens of *sampans* around it and dozens of Chinese peddlers, offering almost anything in the food and fruit line, and it was like pandemonium let loose. On board one could not move for the people, and the broad deck was so littered up with baggage that there wasn't a place to put a cat down. And it was so pitiful to see human beings so terrified and nervous, on a British ship though they were. . . . I wondered how some of those people must feel—people like Peter [Unter-berger], who all their lives have served Russia, their country, to the best of their ability—who, in fear of their lives, are forced to go abroad, and . . . I wondered what their thoughts were as they looked on these magnificent hills which encircle the harbor and knew they had to leave it all.

26 October 1922 to Sarah
By this time I hope you have the news that the change of government is over and that it passed off quietly. The reds marched in from Ugolnaia and the interim was so short that there was no trouble and we breathe once more. . . . All the shops are open again, lights on and things going on as usual, excepting the telephones—these are not yet working.

28 October 1922 to National Headquarters, American Red Cross [no specific addressee]
Excellent order was established at once and for a time at least the horrible tension of the last two weeks is over.

KUNST AND ALBERS TO THE RESCUE

Through Eleanor Pray's descriptions of her work at Kunst and Albers (K&A), we are privileged to peek in at the flow of regular office life in 1923–30 in Vladivostok's largest department store. Mrs. Pray's information about secretarial tasks, blended with a little gossip and news, highlights that most potent cure for those damaged by life's upheavals: the joy of ordinary days. Everyone in the office had suffered insecurity and trauma, and everyone now needed routines and regular tasks—in Mrs. Pray's case, translations, bookkeeping, tax-related lists, and indexes. She realized that, as a friend of the Albers, she had to prove her worth before her possibly critical co-workers. Only when Mr. Albers was about to return to the city after an absence of several years did she allow herself a small pat on the back: "I am earning my salt in better shape than when he went away, because I am really useful in the office now instead of an ornament on account of age, like a worn-out rug" (27 June 1926 to Sarah).

Even more beneficial than the precise work assignments was the relationship with her new colleagues. One senses a kind of old-fashioned *Gemütlichkeit*, a good-natured atmosphere, among people who saw each other every workday and had established congenial professional habits. Their names and glimpses of their lives pop up in the letters: "Max Ivanovich" Limberg, Mr. Brandt, Miss Blinova. This was a kind of collective to which Eleanor Pray had never before belonged, and of which she now appreciated being part. Occasionally the current of work was broken by political or human events—a protest here, a funeral there—but kindness and steady support reigned in their midst: "I am continually in contact with others, and am continually amused and stimulated. I do work among such pleasant sympathetic people and I hope they like me as well as I like them" (15 January 1927 to Sarah). From beyond this office, sounds and images wafted in from the bustling store: customers clattering through from the street, icy-white and woolly winter breaths by the main doors, the hum of shop assistants describing their goods. These images form a small tribute to a bourgeois store soon to be shut.

12 May 1923 to Sarah
On the twenty-first, if all goes well, I enter K&A's office as an English correspondent at one hundred yen a month.[11] A good bit of that magnificent sum will have to go in taxes, but never mind—at least I shall be earning a little. Mr. Albers wrote yesterday, offering me the place.

27 October 1923 to Sarah
The other day Mrs. B. came into the office very angry as she had been in the K&A Club (Mr. Albers gave the Club to the clerks to do what they pleased with) and had found on the table a paper full of salacious caricatures of

Christ and the disciples and saints, so the next time the *tovarishch* in charge of the library came up, she pitched into him—ably assisted by two other women—and said that that sort of paper was not to be lying around where their children were running in and out and could see it, also demanding why the Club subscribed to such a vile thing. The librarian said that he himself did not approve of the paper but if they did not subscribe to it they would get into trouble with the union, so the only thing to do was to keep it out of sight so there would be no chance of the children seeing it.

13 December 1923 to Sarah
Do you know I have come to the conclusion that one of my greatest causes of thankfulness ought to be the ability of getting so much real amusement out of my work. Yesterday all day long I was typing papers relating to the trip to Kamchatka and Nikolaevsk of a certain steamer and I enjoyed getting away from the North with the fish, lived through the sour looks of the passengers when the pig-headed captain had to stand in the *liman* eight days,[12] felt the cold, and experienced the mad rush to get the ships out of Nikolaevsk in time, etc., etc. When the last line was typed I actually felt that I had been through it all.

27 June 1926 to Sarah
My immediate boss, Mr. Brandt, brought me five [strawberries] from his garden Thursday—the first of the season and they were delicious. They are for sale already, but at sixty kopeks a pound, a berry . . . is not tasty.

4 July 1926 to Sarah
Tomorrow I begin acting as cashier on the second floor, while the real one, Mrs. Strauting, the widow of a colonel of engineers, is having her holiday. And the management fondly thinks it is a "rest" for me? Rest? To sit there and twiddle my fingers seven and a half hours a day while an occasional *dacha* husband drifts in for a lamp chimney, or a *tovarishch* for a belted shirt— deliver me! But this year they have promised to arrange a lamp wherever I want it, so I can read, write, or embroider if I care to.

15 January 1927 to Sarah
What a day! No sun, wind blowing a gale and the temperature—to state it mildly—about a hundred and seventy-five below zero. We were comfortable

in the office but in the shop with all the doors flying it was something awful. The cashier in the grocery department sat there in fur coat and cap, and in buying a quarter of a pound of sausage my feet and hands got so cold they ached!

27 January 1927 to Sarah
The unpacking room, a part of our office, is so gay this morning with a big consignment of wooden toys and dishes from Viatka—all lacquered in red and gold and some of them quite pretty, though the work is not so fine.

29 March 1927 to Sarah
A sad morning in the office and none of us with our mind on our work, but on the empty desk opposite, where Mr. Limberg always sat. He died last evening at six o'clock [from typhus]. . . . Besides being an excellent office man, Max Ivanovich, as we always called him, was a number one horticulturist and forester, and their little *dacha* not far from the Lindholm mine had a garden and orchard that was a model for the whole countryside, and they were so happy when they could move out there in the spring.

1 April 1927 to Sarah
Mr. Limberg was buried yesterday. The office was closed at half past four and we all went to the (city) hospital where he was lying in the outhouse set aside for such purposes. After a short service the procession started, and at the corner of Kitaiskaia all the people from the shop joined in and so we walked to the cemetery on Egersheld which took just an hour by my watch.

6 April 1927 to Home
That cemetery is magnificently situated on a bluff over the Amur Bay, but is the most God-forsaken, crude-looking place of its kind I ever saw. By the time we got there it was sunset, not a clear one, but the sky and the bay were all in deep rose and turquoise blue, with the deeper blue of the far-off mountains against the horizon, and the ice of the bay, but for its stillness looking like a street of open water, so blue was it. Mr. Limberg so loved beautiful things that I hope his spirit was more cognizant of the beauty of ice field and sky rather than the ugliness of the place where his body was to rest, rough and unkempt, just barely softened by the smoke arising from two or three other graves which were being prepared—that is, thawed out for digging.

22 April 1927 to Sarah

The grocery department is full of people buying things for Easter, and that of course means more work for the office as new goods are constantly coming in and being distributed to the various departments.

19 September 1927 to Aunt Anna

Last week I had such a nasty piece of work, the like of which I hope will not come my way again. . . . I had to translate an account of the way they took up the body of an Italian captain who died here about a year ago, and cleaned and embalmed it preparatory to sending it to Italy, one of the people who was present meanwhile adding personal impressions to those set forth in the official documents. And I sat here over the typewriter and gagged and gagged and gagged as I have not done for years. The minuteness of the description was in its way worthy of a master of prose like Dickens in that it left little to the imagination.

25 July 1928 to Aunt Anna

Here in our end of the office we have been wickedly enjoying ourselves for the past few days at the expense of the manager of the Technical Department whose desk is in the other end of the room with only a tall bookcase in lieu of a partition—that, however, is enough to conceal our smiles when, as happens several times a day, someone comes in and asks Mr. M., "Why have you got your eye bandaged?" and he barks out "A sty." We happen to know that his brother-in-law beat him up last week, and that in the presence of ladies. He was taken on only a year or two ago and is the most unpleasant person in the firm, consequently we are enjoying all this.

19 October 1928 to Home

Day before yesterday I was at my desk, my nose running like a stream, and I cursing under my breath every time I had to wipe it. . . . Everyone else was as well as usual, and jolly, especially our chief, Mr. Brandt—and yesterday morning he dropped dead of heart disease. I can't believe it even now—a man under fifty leading a healthy, normal life, albeit worried with debts as most family people are in these days. It is such a loss to the firm and to us who worked under him—for in over five years I have never heard an unpleasant word from him addressed to any of us. Strange thing—last Saturday or Sunday night, I can't remember which, I dreamed of his coming around to each of us and saying goodbye, as he was going on a fortnight's holiday and I wondered when he was going that he should do that—a custom only followed when one is taking one's holiday either abroad or in Russia itself.

23 February 1929 to Sarah
Big changes are imminent in K&A, and I do not yet know whether I shall be out of work or not. They are being pushed out of the *magazin* building—such a rent for it having been demanded that it was impossible to pay it, so that leaves just the grocery, hardware and paint departments, and the others will have to be scattered about wherever they can find place for them.

13 March 1929 to SES, DAP, VN, EEP, JU, then to be returned to SES:[13] The firm gave up most of [its property], including the three-story *magazin* building, the three-story bath house for the employees, the old Singing Club and the bowling alley and a lot more. . . . And the staff of employees has to be reduced by twenty-five persons. . . . The bath house . . . is to be made into a hydropathic hospital—doubtless "The First Hydropathic Hospital of Vladivostok" which will look very pretty on paper.[14]

4 February 1930 to Aunt Anna
Maria Ivanovna Blinova is reading *Aunt Jane* and enjoying it very much[15]— she is a little cranky pockmarked old maid as finicky as they make them—the dean of the women in the K&A firm, and she loves reading English. Evenings our manager's mother-in-law comes to see her, and she tells her all about what she has read so far and they both enjoy it.

28 May 1930 to Sarah
Maria Ivanovna . . . won a hundred rubles, and we are all so glad for her as she has an invalid brother and his wife practically on her hands. She is . . . the delight of my soul—I'm the only one in the office that dares talk straight to her. Last week I gave her nine volumes of her beloved Dickens, and wasn't she happy to have them.

13 June 1930 to Sarah
Friday and the thirteenth—and the fiat has gone forth—a tax of one million three hundred thousand which must be paid by the twenty-sixth (this in addition to hundreds of thousands paid already), or else everything will be taken. . . . We shall have three months' salary given us when the firm closes and I shall of course stay on here till autumn as rubles are of no earthly use

anywhere else, so I may as well live on them here as long as they last. This crash for me is not the tragedy it is for others—people who have grown up with the firm, as it were, and feel a loyalty to it only second to what they feel for their own families—and that is what is held up against them.

26 June 1930 to Sarah
Today saw Kunst & Albers out—that is, from tomorrow morning, Mr. Albers is no longer the owner—it has all been taken and the liquidation begins—we shall all probably be out in a few days—two weeks at the outside, as soon as the inventory is made.

SAME HOME, DIFFERENT TIMES

In many ways, Eleanor Pray's life as a widow at Dom Smith became a domestic counterpart to her world at Kunst and Albers, a gradual flow of well-known routines, yet both more complex and simpler than before. Difficulties abounded—taxes, occasional burglaries, drunken brawls—but more often than not, Dom Smith's new tenants turned out to be trustworthy and kind neighbors, even good friends. From August 1924 to July 1928, the Tyrtovs rented the second floor of the main house, an arrangement useful to both parties. The high status of the extended Lindholm family had been shattered: "I was out to Tullie yesterday and it made me absolutely sick to see the rooms stripped of so many of their beautiful things, as she is selling everything that can be turned into money in order to live. . . . Tullie sold her beautiful Peking Rug yesterday for fifty rubles—it was just like new as all her things are, cost a hundred and fifty five years ago and could not be bought in Peking now for less than two hundred and fifty" (9 April 1924 to Home). After they moved to Harbin in the summer of 1928, Mrs. Pray was lucky to have as main renters Ebba and Mats Andersen, of the Danish Telegraph, who were solicitous of her comfort and always ready to suggest a meal or an outing together. And, like children looking after their aged parents, Dom Smith's faithful servants took Mrs. Pray under their wings when her grief was heavy: "Nastia is going out to Platform to spend the day and she made me promise not to work [in the house]. What I should do without her and He Fa I don't know, and Tetia Sasha . . . is a good old standby" (22 April 1923 to Sarah).

At the same time as the new social conditions forced Eleanor Pray's attention toward a workaday existence, her old life was not simply obliterated. Vladivostok's bourgeoisie had shrunk, but it had not disappeared. The Danish Telegraph remained active, and some of Mrs. Pray's old friends from the merchant class, including the Leonid Bryners and the Christian Nielsens, stayed in the city at least through the 1920s. A succession of German consuls—Wagner, Sommer, Balser—entertained in grand style, often with masquerades for Vladivostok's intelligentsia: "Whatever Mr. Sommer does, he does wonderfully. . . . There were over sixty guests and some of the costumes were lovely. Prof. Arseniev and his wife came as an Indian chief with his squaw, he in the real costume of a chief, and they were splendid, their faces really going with the costumes though in everyday life, neither of them looks to be of an Indian type. . . . Dr. Moltrecht was a plump old rajah, very well got up . . . Junghändel [a Spanish brigand]" (20 March 1927 to Sarah).[16] Eleanor Pray appreciated being included in such events, so unlike her private domestic situation in the late 1920s: "You can't think how I appreciate now a dinner at a well laid table among pleasant people—when it was an everyday affair even at home one took it as a matter of course—now it is the biggest kind of a treat" (19 November 1927 to Aunt Anna).

Despite her own struggles (and excepting a few letters hand-carried from Vladivostok by friends), Eleanor's descriptions of the Soviet 1920s are remarkably balanced. She was well aware that officers of the secret police, the GPU, read both her outgoing and incoming mail, but noted with amusement that her daughter Dorothy's letters were rarely opened, protected, perhaps, by the girl's almost illegible handwriting. Ted's death had liberated his wife from her deepest fear—because the worst had already happened—and, although grieving deeply, she slowly began to recreate her life. At Dom Smith, she was now a member of the *dvor*, the "courtyard" or neighborhood around her home, and while the elegant ease of the old home was absent, the achievement of paring down one's needs and sharing material hardship, as well as special treats, with others was gratifying. As never before, Eleanor Pray followed the changing fortunes of the city's food supplies, and when tasty Russian products were available, she sent presents to Sarah in Shanghai: smoked fish, chicken pâté, cheese, honey, even bragging a little about the Russian "soul foods" that she loved: "How I wish you and the girlie could have a good tuck-out on the best things Russia has given the world—viz., *kulich, paskha, pirozhki,* [beef] *Stroganov!*" (22 April 1927 to Sarah). Bureaucratic entanglements flourished, but they also strengthened Eleanor's talent of identifying the amusing angle. Besides, there were good times in Soviet Russia: accessibility to outstanding operas and concerts, the views from Eleanor Pray's windows, excursions around town, and visits with friends. With old traditions continuing on a reduced scale, the scenes and conversations in Vladivostok still supported Eleanor Pray's joie de vivre—and her survival.

7 January 1923 to Mrs. John Allen Dougherty, American Red Cross
The streets are alive with people asking for help—the lame, the halt and the blind, among them such wrecks of humanity as one could not have dreamed of a few years ago. By the entryway to the Post Office, there are always eight or ten thinly clad people hugging the radiators, and inside little hungry, whining boys are standing at every stamp window hoping to get a small coin from the people buying stamps. Officers' wives and daughters are selling newspapers on the street, vainly trying to compete with the more nimble newsboys.

12 May 1923 to Sarah
This morning, as it is the fortieth day since my boy left us, Nastia, Tetia Sasha, Mrs. Krasikova, Mrs. Gavrilova and some other poor women had a mass for the repose of his soul; and it was in the cathedral at half past nine. Of course I went, to please them; even if we don't believe in it, they do.

15 May 1923 to Sarah
The soldiers during the maneuvers Sunday guarded the Chinese Consulate so well that Consul Gen. Fan, who was out for a walk when it happened, was not allowed to get into his own house!

22 July 1923 to Sarah
Summer has now come with a vengeance but when we got back to town [from a friend's *dacha*], there was a fresh, cool fog which was very welcome. But I envied every family I saw on the train—fathers and mothers and little and big children—seemingly no one alone as I was, to come back to empty echoing rooms with no one to talk to about the pleasant afternoon. I wonder if I shall ever get used to that sort of thing and take loneliness as a matter of course. And I looked at the children on the train, the little tots sleepy and nestling up to their fathers and mothers as Dorothy used to do; there was a little curly-head sitting opposite me and she went to sleep in her mother's arms—a little girl about two years old. When we got to town her father took her from the mother and there was that pride in his face and tenderness that one always saw on Ted's face when he had Dorothy in his arms. And it was amazing in that crowded

uncomfortable car that all the way to town there was not so much as a whimper from a single child, and there were several very small ones. The larger ones most of them insisted on leaning out of the window to extract the last possible grain of enjoyment out of the day's outing. . . . I never see a Russian child in these days but I wonder what will come out of that little head in the years to come and what he will do for his country.

29 September 1923 to Sarah
Upon meeting one's friends just now, one makes no inquiry about their health or that of their relations, but inquires if the taxes have been paid or "What has been attached [to cover the taxes]?" It is no joke but one might as well laugh as cry.

30 May 1926 to Dorothy, Sunday
Madame Bryner . . . died Thursday evening, and as she is an old acquaintance of ours I went to the mass Friday afternoon and to the funeral Saturday morning. There were four priests to conduct the service and a church choir with wonderful voices—it just took one along with it, and ever since it has echoed and echoed in my ears. . . . When the doctor told Mrs. Bryner last Monday that she must stay in bed for a few days, she said she couldn't because she was going to Sidemi. And yesterday, in the rain, we stood on the pier by the old Hut and watched a big tug boat take her there, but not as she expected to go. I am so glad for her that she is at rest—she has had six years of loneliness since her husband died and now her body is beside his in their beautiful family tomb near their *dacha* at her beloved Sidemi.[17]

30 September 1926 to Dorothy
We have been laughing over something that occurred at Nineteenth Verst not long ago. It seems that Dr. Moltrecht, coming out from town, saw such a cloud of moths around the arc-light at the station, that, elderly and plump though he is, he could not resist shimmying up the pole and trying to capture some of them, as he always has a butterfly net in his pocket. So up he went. Some of the other passengers, already some distance down the track, happening to look back, got a terrible shock to see a bear half-way up the electric light pole, and you may be sure it speeded up the pace with which they were making for their happy homes. Of course the following morning Platform was buzzing with a "bear scare"—and the impudence of Bruin daring to

appear in thickly populated Nineteenth Verst, climbing a pole at the station itself, was discussed and re-discussed at a great rate until it got as far as Dr. Moltrecht, who nearly died in a fit of laughter—as did many of the others when they heard that the "bear" was Vladivostok's eminent and esteemed scientist!

15 January 1927 to Sarah, Saturday
If I can hold the pen long enough I'll tell you what the house is like—a barn—and a large cold one at that. The stove in the veranda is smoking, the kitchen stove is smoking, and even the kitchen is none too warm. There has been a fire under the boiler all day long and [yet] . . . I don't think I have ever known the whole house so thoroughly uncomfortable as it is today. I lay in bed a good part of the afternoon and now I am going there for the night. And I'm going to put my mittens on and read about the heat of a June Punjab—rather consoling on a night like this.[18]

18 March 1927 to Dorothy
Just now O Ritsa's little grand-nephew was here, the seven-year-old son of the washman, and he is such a quaint little chap. He has decided that he doesn't want to be a washman, and he doesn't want to be a shoemaker, but [will] be the Mikado when he grows up. Of this he dreams all the time. So Auntie Tullie said to him, "How nice. When I go to Tokio again I shall pay you a visit at the palace." He thought things over for a moment, and then said very slowly—as if not wishing to disappoint her—"It isn't sure yet."

21 August 1927 to Sarah
Such a scandal. A man came out of the *dvornik* [Matrena's, our janitor's] room, over to where I sat at the head of the coolie's stairs (there is a bench there), threatened me with all sorts of things, grabbed Tetia Sasha by the arms and tried to drag her off, and when I told him in no very uncertain tones to let her alone, he threw her down bang, turned and struck me in the face twice, knocking me flat on my back and kicking me afterward—if I don't have a black and blue spot under my left eye tomorrow it will be a wonder. [Matrena's] daughter [Liza] called the militia and first aid to her mother, accusing Tetia Sasha of having beaten her, but as they couldn't find any signs of a blow they said that she had had a moral blow! The militiaman was very decent and saw for himself how drunk Mrs. Chichaeva [another neighbor] was—she was telling all kinds of yarns about Tetia Sasha and me.

10 October 1927 to Dorothy

The leaves are like autumn, the grapevines making their glorious splashes of red all over the woods. There was a great orange-colored moon and I stood at the window of the car and looked at it a good part of the way home, as the car was a smoker and the air foul. An old peasant, looking exactly like the pictures of Count Tolstoi, who sat opposite me, got up and opened the window, and I was only too glad to take advantage of it, so we stood there together and discussed apple-growing—of course, I made myself as wise as possible!

3 November 1927 to Sarah

Mr. Spasskii, the head book-keeper in Churin's, moved into the billiard room yesterday and it looked so cheerful there last evening to see lights. He keeps pigeons and has a real cote for them which stands near the gate by the store-house. I don't know either him or his wife, but one hears that they are quiet, respectable people.

7 March 1928 to Dorothy

Thanks to the GPU reading a letter I wrote Auntie in the autumn, that same Liza [Matrena's daughter] is sitting in jail the fifth month already and her husband—the man who knocked me down—has run away, and I'm delighted. They were making our premises a real base for [drugs] contraband, and I knew it but could do nothing because I had no actual, tangible proof. At last I mentioned this in a letter to Auntie . . . and inside two days they began to search Matrena's room, but, finding nothing, they bided their time until they caught her some other way.

4 May 1928 to Home

On pleasant mornings it is delightful to turn over in bed when one awakens and see the silver sails on the little *sampans* plying between the town and Churkin, less than a mile off on the other side of the harbor—I love watching them. And from the West window I can look off over the Amur Bay and see the sunsets.

27 June 1928 to Sarah

Last evening, quite unexpectedly, I fell into a name-day celebration. Walking in the garden after I got home I saw Mrs. Spasskaia . . . and she asked me to tea. I said, "Thanks very much—what time?" and was told six o'clock. Shortly after that time I appeared and . . . we were six guests and it was very jolly. Mr. Spasskii is tall and fat, Mrs. Spasskaia short and fat, the three Russian ladies who I didn't know were all fatter than she—one (and a very charming woman she was) about twice as big, so that I looked, by comparison, like a sylph and Tetia Sasha like a wraith. We had *zakuska*, followed by hot ham and peas— and a name-day *pirog* [a large pie] about 18 × 24 [inches]—um-m-m! Then as soon as the table was cleared it was laid for tea and down we sat again—a big round *senatorskii* ["Senator's type"] torte, and two *pirogs*, of the 18 × 18 size, one with prunes and the other with curds, and I drank four cups of tea and live to tell the tale.

23 September 1928 to Sarah
Long past my bedtime, of course, but you must hear about the concert. Quite unexpectedly this noon the Andersens asked me to go to the Sobinov concert as they had taken three seats in a box.[19] . . . Well, I can truly say I never enjoyed a concert so much in my life. . . . Sobinov himself—an elderly bald-headed man now, and what a greeting he got—the audience clapped and clapped and clapped. He is a tall, big man and must formerly have been a very handsome one. He sang various things unfamiliar to me and then—just think of it—*"Kuda, kuda Vy udalilis"*—which was worth tramping miles to hear. He sang at least half a dozen encores, one of the last being *"Kogda Vy poniali menia"* to violin and piano.[20] . . . The theater was full up, and the applause they repeatedly gave him must have warmed his heartstrings. Five huge baskets of flowers were given him and he stood between them and bowed and bowed, smiling all the time. It was just before ten when finally he refused any more encores, for the audience for the ten o'clock concert (we went to the eight o'clock one) were already pushing in. I wanted to come home and put it all on paper at once, but Mr. Andersen insisted on going to the Zolotoi Rog summer restaurant (in the Admiral's Garden) for beer and ice-cream, and we have only just got home. While sitting there, the orchestra played *"Die Wacht am Rhein"* which I love in spite of its nationality,[21] and then, by radio, we heard a part of the second concert which was of course a repetition of the first.

2 October 1928 to Sarah
[Mrs. Nielsen has paid a visit.] I can tell you feeding a guest at present is not a merry joke. . . . I decided to send down to the Zolotoi Rog for a two-course

dinner as the food there is very good, but to supplement it, I wanted to make some macaroni and cheese. No go. I had macaroni, cheese, and milk, but not a speck of butter or flour. Then I decided to have tomatoes stuffed with eggs and mayonnaise—also no go, because there were no eggs in the house! Cheerful. But the *shchi* [cabbage soup] and cutlets from the restaurant were good and one portion was enough as I only took some of the soup. For dessert we had some gooseberry tart someone sent me—three oblongs—and then a cup of coffee and some peppermints I had boiled before breakfast which were A 1 and then some. Oh, yes, and we each had a bottle of *kvass* [a lightly fermented drink made from grain or fruit]. There was nothing for tea so we drank some more *kvass*.

19 October 1928 to Home
The harbor at night is wonderful—black velvet and diamonds, the lights on Egersheld forming a jeweled sickle like a great brooch.

29 March 1929 to Sarah
[7.40 PM] The woman came with the milk just half an hour ago, having been standing in line at one place or another all day, trying in vain to get some fodder for the cows—they are living on hay, and today, from four of them, they only got twenty bottles of milk when they ought easily to have three times that. When she came in, the coolie said, very politely, "Good morning."

1 May 1929 to Dorothy
This is the great labor holiday and there has been a tremendous celebration—it took the procession quite an hour to pass here and I was watching from the veranda. It was a pure pleasure to see the troops—I have never seen better marching in my life—not a bit of slouching and every boot striking the pavement in unison, it was really a treat to look at it.

20 May 1929 to Sarah
I may be forgiven for writing about food as it is the chief thing in my thoughts and one thinks of little else from morn till dewy eve. . . . What a nasty lot of *burzhui* you people in Shanghai are anyway—fancy being able to buy sugar, rice, flour, and anything else you want. You ought to be ashamed of yourselves!

25 May 1929 to Sarah
You can't think what a pleasant afternoon we have had—the whole compound scratching about in the garden. I have been planting beans and lettuce, Mr. Spasskii superintending the two Chinese who were mucking his part of the garden and putting in seedlings, Matrena, Tetia Sasha, Mr. Chichaev, . . . and the little Rusakov mite dodging about among us and everyone enjoying himself.

11 September 1929 to Sarah
I have had a holiday today and enjoyed myself immensely. . . . I did what I have been promising myself to do for months—took the round trip by tram to Rabochaia *Slobodka* and back, but I couldn't recognize anything—naturally—as it is twenty-five years since we used to walk there, and it was practically all woods then. The tram line is an extension of the one to First River, and goes way up the valley which is all built up now and the trams are always packed full.

15 December 1929 to Sarah
We have been having one of those dry storms you read about—temperature out of sight and the wind blowing a gale straight off the North Pole. . . . On the way home a respectable-looking *tovarishch* stopped in front of me and said very softly *Koshechka* [Kitty]—I was so surprised that before I could pull myself together, he had discovered his mistake and passed on, else I should certainly have addressed him as *sobachka* [doggie].

29 December 1929 to Sarah
Yesterday I heard that Matrena's son-in-law, the man who knocked me down here in the garden two years ago, had been shot—sentenced for some of his various crimes.

29 January 1930 to Sarah
This noon I had to go to see about a five-ruble fine for tardiness of a certain list, but they were very nice about it when I proved that, even if it didn't reach them till three days late, it was sent in ample time, and they said in that case they would not ask me to pay it. This was at an office near the bazaar, and in going back, for some idle fancy or other, I drifted up Pekinskaia, and there happened to see the sign of the office where one can get supplies for broken gold. Having been carrying seven old teeth around in my bag for at least

three months, with this in view, it seemed a real providence that I should blunder across the place. In I went, got twenty-one rubles for them and a receipt which can be exchanged for flour, sugar, butter, oil, etc.

30 January 1930 to Sarah
Matrena got the things today, two *pood* of fairly good, fairly white flour, three quarters of a *pood* of Java sugar, and a kilogram of very good export butter. When we opened up the bag, we were all dancing around it like dervishes. When I went back to the office P. P. [one of the K&A office workers] danced, too, for I brought her some flour and sugar, and there are two or three other friends who must have a share in this good luck—who ever heard of eating teeth before?

3 March 1930 to Dorothy
Really one thinks of so little these days but one's tummy—there is enough to eat but nothing is complete—if you have one thing, its corollary is sure to be missing, and doesn't it sound crazy that one can buy neither bread nor butter in the simple way, but as much caviar and wine as one wants to pay for.

19 May 1930 to Sarah
Such a nice picnic as we [Mrs. Pray and the Andersens] had yesterday, although it was very windy and no sun. . . . We got away about eleven and had to let three trams pass before there was one we could squeeze into. It was twenty to twelve when we got to the terminal and started our hike. . . . We went to the left of the race course and on and on and on along the old military road to Gornostai Bay. . . . The Zoo is about half a mile off the main road and we got there at quarter to one—hungry! There was a *baba* with a samovar, tea and buns, so we each had a glass of tea and some of our sandwiches before starting out to see the sights. For almost two hours we wandered about, and saw very many interesting birds and animals. While we were having tea a crane was wandering around near us, and just behind three lovely swans were swimming in a little brook. At some distance was a netted-in stone pool with wild ducks. Then came the cage of a wild boar—and he *was* wild. . . . Next him were two wolves. . . . The lady was inclined to be friendly, after the first, and I had quite a little understanding conversation with her, but M. le Capitaine was inclined to be sulky and suspicious. Further on was a fox and a cage of pheasants. . . . Our next visit was to a granite bear house— with windows strongly barred and a wire fence to keep the public away from

the windows. In one room was a huge cinnamon bear from Kamchatka . . . looking very disgusted with his accommodations. He poked his muzzle between two of the bars, surveyed us in a bored manner, yawned (and what his breath smelled like!), and went on cleaning his huge paws. . . . The birds were wonderful—five huge owls, three eagles, which were of the prettiest soft colors you can imagine, a buzzard, a falcon, a kite, and various others.

26 May 1930 to Sarah
Instead of going via Aleutskaia [to the German reading-room], I went to the end of Svetlanskaia and along the bluff that way—and never was a more glorious morning. There may be—doubtless are—hundreds of places in the world as beautiful, perhaps many of them undefiled by man, the worm of the universe, but surely none of them exceed in beauty that grand sweep of the Amur Bay. . . . Here and there were fishing boats at anchor, and a big *shalanda* [boat], new red license flag at the stern, its recently patched sails taut-drawn, was lazily clearing the junk harbor. At the foot of the bluff it was so clear that beneath the light ripples one could see the dark branches of the sea weed, a cloud of sage green below them, setting them against the translucent water. And all the town, from the smallest *burzhui* to the greatest commissar, can drink that in for hours without even paying a government tax on amusements.

10 September 1930 to Sarah
This afternoon late we . . . took a *sampan* across to Churkin and landed at the lumber yard. If there is any smell sweeter than new-mown hay it is that of freshly sawn lumber and I sniffed it to my heart's content, for millions of feet of freshly sawn boards were stacked there—I never saw so much lumber in my life. . . . We came back on the ferryboat, just after sunset, and you can imagine the West in a flame of pink, mauve blue and every other color, with the great flank of Tigrovaia, black against it, here and there a light flashing out on its sides—too beautiful for words and it makes me sick to think of leaving this land of sunsets.

3 October 1930 to Sarah
[Matrena is ill.] Another lost day and practically nothing accomplished. Having been told . . . that the health department was in the old [hotel] Moskovskoe Podvorie, I went there, only to find, of course, that it was somewhere else—in that blessed rabbit warren of a Startsev house. There I did some plain

talking and they promised to see that a doctor was sent at once (promised!), then down a couple of flights to the finance department to get one of the preliminary documents for my visa—[which] they couldn't give me because I didn't have with me my documents proving that I had worked in K&A's. "Tomorrow is our day of rest, so come with them Sunday"—*Ladno?* [All right? Okay?]? Then to the State Bank to pay the [health] insurance for poor old Matrena who, for all the good she has got of it, might as well not be insured. That didn't take long. The next was to push on to a crowded tram— just the toes of my feet on the step and hanging on for dear life, a husky militiaman holding on behind me else I should certainly have bounced off. . . . [Then] I went to the Dalbank . . . to buy a book of tickets for the tramway—and in a vision I already saw myself riding any time I wanted to. Vain dream—I was asked to produce a union card which most assuredly I couldn't do, and therefore they couldn't sell me a fifty-trip book, although there is no discount whatever on the price and a book of tickets makes it so much easier for the conductor. From there I went up to the foreign department on Komarovskaia [Street] but couldn't get in—either it was their day of rest, or else they have moved somewhere else—and as my legs could manage no more, I came home. About the middle of the afternoon, as the doctor hadn't come, we telephoned, and were told that he was on the way. He is evidently still on the way, and we have telephoned twice since then, and now they say he will come in the morning!

25 October 1930 to Sarah
Everything downstairs is ready for the [farewell] dinner and the table looks lovely—a huge cut-glass rose bowl of snapdragons in the middle and low bowls of snapdragons, cosmos and white dahlias at the ends—every one of them gathered here in the garden today. The last dinner party in Dom Smith, and there is a lump in my throat every time I think of all the merry ones we have had here. It is dear of the Andersens to go to all the expense and trouble of a dinner for me, but I would have far rather gone without it—giving a dinner in these days is a great task—even a simple one like this.

26 October 1930 to Sarah
Well, it's over, and the last evening was as jolly as its predecessors—everything went off beautifully as they have a way of doing in Dom Smith. . . . We were only fourteen at table and it was all right—Mr. Andersen and I sat on a piano bench close up against the radiator, so there was no going around the

table at that end.... We had soup with *pirozhki*, cold salmon with a rich vegetable salad, pork cutlets with potatoes and red cabbage, topping off with a chocolate layer-cake for dessert.

11 December 1930 to Aunt Anna, on board the Gleniffer, *"getting into the China Sea."*
I love walking on deck and looking up at that towering red funnel, the outstanding mark of the Glen Line and one we are always glad to see rounding Goldobin into the harbor.

Mrs. Pray was traveling away forever, but her heart is still in Vladivostok.

Acknowledgments

BY PATRICIA D. SILVER

I would like to thank my mother, Dorothy Pray Dunn Barringer, for giving me my grandmother's letters.

To my colleague, Birgitta Ingemanson, I give many, many thanks for all her encouragement, research help, writing, proofreading of the book, and excellent knowledge of Vladivostok.

To my niece, Sophie Wadsworth, I give thanks for the wonderful poetry she has written based on her great-grandmother's letters.

I will always be grateful to my Russian friends: Alexander Zemtsov, who organized my first trip to Vladivostok, and Boris I. Vasiliev and his lovely wife Eneida, who made me feel so welcome when I stayed with them in Vladivostok. I also thank Boris for making me an honorary member of the Professors' Club of Vladivostok. Further, I thank Mikhail Maguta, who arranged for me to use the library at the Geographical Society in Vladivostok and made me a member of that society, and Runar Gareyev, who drove me around to see all of the sights of Vladivostok.

To my teachers at Columbia University's Graduate School, New York, professor Marc Raeff and professor Carol Gluck, for all they taught me about Russia and Japan.

I give many thanks to those two dear women, my Russian governesses, Ekaterina Afrakova and Anastasia Artemieva. They began my interest in Russia by teaching me the language and about Russia's history, culture, food, and needlework. Without these early influences, I would not have had my lifelong interest in Russia.

Most of all, I want to thank my dearest husband, Stuart Robinson Silver, MD, for his support, emotionally, financially, and in every other possible way, while I worked on the book.

BY BIRGITTA INGEMANSON

During a walk along Vladivostok's Pushkin Street in 1992, I came across what seemed like a forgotten home. The big house stood there with its curtains closed, the garden in ruins, and no one coming or going. I saw fences fallen down, paths grown over, and a wild profusion of flowers. When stopping and listening, I could imagine the whispers of the past: sounds coming through the open windows of plates being set for summer meals, the cadences of friends chatting on the garden benches, the little voices of children playing under the trees. And I longed to open the gates and look in, to uncover the soul of this city.

It is a great gift that not only Eleanor Pray, with her thousands of letters, but also numerous colleagues, friends, and acquaintances, with their warm, unselfish spirit, have helped open up the windows and gates of Vladivostok. During sixteen visits since the spring of 1990, I have been shown the famous Far Eastern hospitality, the kind interest, and the helpfulness that Mrs. Pray describes so vividly, and that make me feel at home in the city, as if truly I am one of the family. For this bond, which has given my life an inspired new direction, I am deeply honored and grateful.

Firstly, I celebrate the great, thoughtful generosity of Stuart and Patricia Silver in sharing Patricia's grandmother's letters and photo albums, and in discussing their fascinating information about Vladivostok. Coming into contact with Mrs. Silver by the virtually winged messenger of Petr Brovko was a true case of Russian-style *sudba* (fate)—it seems to have simply been "meant." Mrs. Silver made this book possible with her advice, encouragement, and support.

Several reliable and patient assistants helped in transcribing Mrs. Pray's letters to computer files. With all my heart, I thank Tatiana Avdeyeva, Sally Beaton, Gitta Bridges, Marina Tchernokojeva (now Tarasheva), and Shereen Thompson (now Benjamin). They were joyously responsible, and gratifying to work with.

My research on the letters has been augmented with the offerings of numerous Vladivostokians who have given interviews, suggested documents, organized field trips, and participated in research discussions. I am indebted to everyone I have met in Vladivostok, and I thank the following for their direct contributions to this book:

For logistical arrangements, thanks to V. I. Kurilov, L. P. Bondarenko, E. V. Filimonova, M. Grintsevich, and A. G. Zhidkov at Far Eastern Federal (formerly State) University (DVFU/DVGU); and to V. L. Larin, <u>A. P. Derevianko</u>, and B. M. Afonin at the Institute of the History, Ethnography, and Archeology of the Peoples of the Far East, Russian Academy of Sciences; and to G. P. Turmov and P. P. Unru at Far Eastern State Technical University (DVGTU).

For interviews, books, photos, and newspaper clippings pertaining to Mrs. Pray, thanks to V. I. Apanasevich, I. K. Elizariev, L. I. Elizarieva, <u>V. Filatiev</u>, V. V. Gorchakov, N. K. Gorchakova, I. Lindberg, T. I. Prokopova, <u>E. A. Shchebenkova</u>, E. S. Sheremetieva, A. I. Sheveleva, A. G. Tretiakova, and Iu. I. Tretiakov.

For field trips and special excursions, thanks to G. M. Berezina, V. V. Dubeleva, and N. N. Dubelev at today's Dom Smith; Z. D. Fedorets, M. A. Ivashchenko, D. M. Kovalenko, Z. N. Kovylina, G. S. Lopatenko, S. E. Morozova, and A. F. Suvorin on De Vries; and A. S. Doluda, V. A. Kamovskii, <u>M. F. Maguta</u>, A. I. Melnik, V. K. Moor, N. Shakhnazarova, and V. I. Smotrikovskii at other sites in and around Vladivostok.

For discussions with historians, *kraevedy*, and journalists on matters pertaining to Mrs. Pray, thanks to D. A. Ancha, A. V. Borodin, Lothar Deeg, <u>Boris Diachenko</u>, E. V. Ermakova, T. N. Kaliberova, V. I. Kalinin, A. A. Khisamutdinov, A. V. Kolesov, O. B. Lynsha, A. B. Meshcheriakova, Z. G. Proshina, A. Savruev, A. Iu. Sidorov, and <u>Ivan G. Striuchenko</u>.

For work pertaining to Mrs. Pray in museums, archives, and other culture organizations, thanks to G. A. Aleksiuk, V. N. Sokolov, N. B. Kerchelaeva, I. N. Klimenko, R. A. Mordovtseva, S. P. Moskvitina, I. P. Nam, and V. A. Shalay of the Arseniev Museum; A. A. Toporov of the State Archive of the Maritime Territory; L. A. Ermolenko and Maia Mikhailovna of the Russian Geographic Society; and N. F. Balakerskaia, E. M. Nazarenko, T. V. Aleksandrova, and V. M. Pevneva, among many others, at the Association of Book Lovers.

At Washington State University, I received internal grants, course releases, and the Marianna Merritt and Donald S. Matteson Distinguished Professorship. I especially recognize presidents Samuel Smith and Eldon Floyd; the deans of the College of Liberal Arts, John Pierce, Barbara Couture, Marina Tolmacheva, Erich Lear, and Douglas Epperson; the chairs of the Department of Foreign Languages and Cultures, Marianna Matteson, John Brewer, Bonnie Frederick, and Eloy Gonzalez; and colleagues who have read and commented on parts or all of the manuscript, Kathleen Bodley, George Bridges, Rachel Halverson, Béatrice Henrioulle, Sonja Moseley, and Sandra Walsh.

Descendants of Vladivostok's illustrious families have gone out of their way to provide information of various kinds, inspiring meetings and correspondence. Warm thanks to Dorothy Pray Barringer, Peggy Siebens, Beverley Wadsworth, Dyer Wadsworth, and Sophie Wadsworth of the Pray family; Cyril Bryner, Irina Brynner, and Rock Brynner; Dietrich Bernecker, Ingrid Detweiler, Marlen Wilbrand, and Herman Wilbrand of the Dattan family; Ann Findlay Hawkins; Nicholas Davis and Alexander de Haes of the Lindholm family; Tatiana Matveeva; Ted Merkuloff and Vladimir Merkuloff; and Ariadna Belova of the Sollogub family.

Reading the anonymous reviewers' discussions of my manuscript has been gratifying and also humbling. I appreciate their pragmatic, insightful suggestions, and the long hours they must have spent scrutinizing the manuscript and putting together their letters. Thank you warmly for this attention and support.

Finally, I have worked closely with and been generously helped by Larisa Aleksandrovskaia, Nelli Miz, Andrey Sapelkin, Natalia Shinkovskaia, Mikhail Shinkovskii, and Elena Vasileva, as well as by my very dear, intriguingly shaped, six-leaf clover of Nina Velikaia, Alla Priyatkina, Liubov Bobyleva, Oksana Popova, Maria Lebedko, and Tamara Bogolepova.

Too many kind colleagues have died during the years of this book's making, in addition to those whose names are underlined above. I also thank the late Nadezhda Aleksakhina, Nina Berezkina, Andrei Kamalov, Alexandra Kaspers, Sergei Krivshenko, Marina Kulikova, Gertruda Smirnova, Nina Stoliarova, Nina Svetlichnaia, and Riurik Tushkin.

May we always honor and remember those who came before.

Glossary of Uncommon Terms Frequently Used by Eleanor Pray

amah. Japanese maid, nanny
arshin. Russian measure of length, almost thirty inches
baba. Woman (slang)
Bolshevik/i. Member/s of, or sympathizer/s with, the communist party
brusnika. Bilberries (similar to lingonberries)
burzhui. Bourgeois person or persons (pejorative)
coolie. Chinese laborer
dacha. Summer house (cabin; villa)
dolgusha, dolgushka. Cart
dvornik. Janitor, groundkeeper
godown. Storehouse
hoong-hoozi. Chinese brigands
izvozchik. Coachman
kisel. Boiled-fruit dessert
kulich/i. Wheat bun/s baked for Easter
kvass. Lightly fermented drink made from grain or fruit
magazin. Store
manza. Chinese person
Menshevik/i. Opponent/s of Bolshevik ideas; social democrat/s
muzhik. Man, fellow
pirog. Large pie
pirozhok (plural *pirozhki*). Small, covered pie/s with savory or sweet fillings
pood. Russian measure of weight, approximately thirty-six pounds
rod. Old English measure of distance, 5.5 yards
sampan. Small, low-lying boat
-san. Respectful ending of (usually) Japanese name

shalanda. Type of boat
shchi. Cabbage soup
slobodka. Neighborhood, city district
sopka (plural *sopki*). Cone-shaped hill/s (in the Far East)
telega. Cart
tiffin. Midday meal, lunch
tovarishch/i. Comrade/s, friend/s; also address used among communists
verst. Old Russian measure of distance, equaling 3,500 feet (0.6620 miles)
zakuska. Appetizers

Appendix

*Biographical Notes on Persons Frequently
Mentioned in the Letters*

Albers, Alfred (1877–1960; known as Vasilii Gustavovich in Russia). Husband of Margarethe
   Albers. From Hamburg. From 1910, Alfred Albers was a partner, with Adolph Dattan, in
   the department store Kunst and Albers (K&A), and became the sole owner after his partner's death (1924).

Albers, Margarethe (Ita), née Lorenz-Mayer. Wife of Alfred Albers.

Andersen, Ebba Rufinovna. Wife of Mats Andersen. The Andersens rented part of Dom Smith
   in the late 1920s. Their daughter Karin was born in Vladivostok (1928).

Andersen, Marius Petrovich (Mats). Of the Danish Telegraph. Husband of Ebba Andersen.
   Their home address was still 5 Sodom Lane (the former Dom Smith) in 1934.

Arseniev, Vladimir Klavdievich (1872–1930). Military officer, ethnographer, and explorer of
   the Ussuri Territory. Director of the Khabarovsk Regional Museum (1910–19, 1924–25).
   Lecturer in Vladivostok (1926–30).

Artemieva, Anastasia (Nastia). First a seamstress at Dom Smith on a part-time basis (1907),
   then Dorothy Pray's beloved nanny. In the late 1920s she moved to Shanghai, and later to
   Belgium.

Behn, Paul (1863–1924; Pavel-German Fedorovich). Worked at K&A, including in Bla-
   goveshchensk. Married Tina Meyer (sister of Otto) 31 December 1899.

Birk, Ewelina Andreevna (d. 1925). Wife of Ludwig Birk. The Birks' daughter Jenny (Zhenia,
   born in 1889) married Peter Pavlovich Unterberger on 22 December 1910.

Birk, Ludwig (1855–1908). Graduated from the University of Dorpat, served in the Far East
   from 1880 on. Physician in Vladivostok with the rank of major general. Husband of
   Ewelina Birk.

Borisova, Ida Fedorovna (born c. 1854). Sister of Vice Admiral Schultz; widow. Organizer of
   the "Admiral's Sewing Circle" during World War I.

Brandt, Viktor Teodorovich (1849–1907). Rear admiral. Assistant to the commander (from
   1890), and commander of the Siberian Flotilla (1897–1903). An old friend of the
   Lindholms.

Breck, Belle (d. 1947). Originally from Kentucky, worked at the YMCA in Vladivostok
   (1919–20).

Bryner (Russian: Briner), Iulii Ivanovich (1849–1920, originally from Switzerland). Husband of Natalia Bryner. Merchant of the First Guild. The Bryners owned shipping companies, mines, and other enterprises in Vladivostok and Primorie.

Bryner (Russian: Briner), Natalia Iosifovna (1866–1926). Wife of Iulii Bryner. Their son Leonid (1884–1947) first married Therese ("Mika") Williams, an American woman, and later Elena Mikhailovna Brotnovskaia, a Russian actress.

Bushueva, Anna Ioanovna. Member of the Vladivostok Philanthropic Society. Her house was at 33 Pushkin Street.

Butakova, Aina (née Lindholm, b. 1884). Married lieutenant Alexander ("Sashik") Ivanovich Butakov (1882–1914), in 1907. Butakov served on the cruiser *Bogatyr* and, later, on the Tsar's yacht, the *Standart*, in the Baltic Sea.

Chichagova, Olga. Daughter of the military governor Nikolai Mikhailovich Chichagov (1852–1911). Chichagova married prince Pavel Ukhtomskii in 1900.

The Christensens. Of the Danish Telegraph. Mrs. Christensen was Russian, from Siberia.

Clarkson, David M., Jr. (1861–1913). American businessman in Vladivostok from November 1897. Owned mines at Mikha River and at Mys Rechnoi south of Tavrichanka. Husband of Shira Clarkson. Eleanor Pray attended their wedding in 1908.

Clarkson, Shira. The former *amah* O Hiro-san, hailed from an old Japanese samurai family. Wife of David M. Clarkson, Jr.

Cornehls, Anna (known as "Tante Anna" in the family). Mrs. Dattan's sister. Wife of Edward Cornehls.

Cornehls, Edward (Eduard Fedorovich; "Onkel Eddie" in the family). Manager at K&A, merchant of the Second Guild, member of the Vladivostok Duma. Husband of Anna Cornehls.

Crompton, Gladys Mary (1878–1915). The daughter of General Salis-Schwabe, vice-governor of the Royal Hospital Chelsea in London (early 1900s). Wife of Paul Crompton. The Cromptons and their six children perished with approximately 1,190 others on the *Lusitania*, sunk by the German submarine *U-20* on the way from New York to Liverpool, 7 May 1915.

Crompton, Paul. Husband of Gladys Mary, friends with her brother Edgar Salis-Schwabe, with whom he traveled in Siberia (1898).

Dattan, Adolph (1854–1924). From Naumburg. Led K&A from 1882, by 1898 owned 47.5 percent of the firm (Gustav Albers owned 52.5 percent). Husband of Marie Dattan. The Dattans were naturalized Russian subjects.

Dattan, Marie (1866–1924). Wife of Adolph Dattan. They had seven children, two of whom, Alexander (1890–1916) and Adolph (1894–1915), perished in World War I. Mrs. Dattan led the tea party that gave so much joy to Eleanor Pray.

Davidson, William S. (1873–1926). American businessman in Vladivostok, late 1890s. His first wife, Cecilia Genevieve (1880–1900), perished on the SS *Cullenden* catastrophe near Shanghai in September 1900.

Dou Kee. Gardener and jack-of-all-trades at Dom Smith (until April 1913).

Dunn, Thomas Balfour (1886–1948). Physician on the USS *Brooklyn* (1918), then lived and practiced medicine in Shanghai. Widowed in 1927 with two small children, Peggy and Patricia. Married Dorothy Pray in 1929. Together they had twin daughters Beverley and Daphne.

Epstein, Stefan Lvovich. Nobleman and director of the Russo-Chinese Bank in Vladivostok.

Married Evdokiia Vasilievna (Dunia), daughter of Vladivostok entrepreneur Vasilii P. Babintsev (1838–1905), 9 May 1900.

Fedorov, Mikhail Kuzmich (1840–1906). Well-known entrepreneur and public figure in Vladivostok. The city's first "head" (mayor). He and his wife, Emma (an Englishwoman), had one son and five daughters, including Anna (Ania) Gladkaia and Elizaveta (Liza) Ivanova.

Findlay, Dorothy (1890–1979). Wife of John Findlay, both English. The Findlays married in Vladivostok's Lutheran Church (1916), lived first at 15 Pushkin Street, and later at 19th Verst. Both their son James and daughter Ann (Hawkins) were born in Vladivostok (1917 and 1920, respectively).

Findlay, John (1885–1964). Worked for the BECOS company. Husband of Dorothy Findlay.

Goldenstedt, Agafia (Livina, c. 1850–1924). With husband Karl, owners of the Novogeorgievsk Estate, where the Prays and Sarah Smith rented their *dacha*.

Goldenstedt, Karl (c. 1842–1910). Husband of Agafia Goldenstedt.

Greener, Richard Theodore (1844–1922). Jurist, diplomat, educator. First African American graduate of Harvard College (1870). US commercial agent in Vladivostok (1898–1905).

Hansen, Eleonora (born 1859). Wife of Jørgen Hansen. The Hansens' nephew, Woldemar ("Kid") Hansen (born in 1879), worked at K&A until 1914.

Hansen, Jørgen (1856–1928). Of the Danish Telegraph. Husband of Eleonora Hansen.

Mr. Igoni. Nephew of Axel Walldén.

Ivy, Anne E. (d. 1923). Wife of Robert Sutcliffe Ivy. English friend of Charles and Sarah Smith in Shanghai. An accomplished photographer. The Ivys often spent summers in Vladivostok with their children Bessie and Herbert (Bertie).

Ivy, Robert Sutcliffe (1858–1936). Englishman, lived in Shanghai. Dentist. Husband of Anne E. Ivy.

Jan. From Shantung. Compradore at Dom Smith since circa 1900.

Keyserling (Russian: Keizerling), Count Heinrich. Had a house and whaling station at Gaidamak Bay. The first Countess Keyserling was Annie (1878–1910). Children: Cecilia, Henri, and Wendelin.

Khan, He Fa. From Chefoo. The most trusted worker at Dom Smith. Built a house and had his own garden at Novogeorgievsk Estate.

Kizhevich, Frances ("Aunt Kevich," 1869–1925). Wife of Viktor I. Kizhevich.

Kizhevich, Viktor Ieronimovich. Mechanical engineer; sold agricultural machinery. Husband of Frances Kizhevich. They lived at Number 6, Grand Hotel on Railway Station Square.

Klepsch, Carl (Karlovich; 1868–1912). Nephew of Mr. Kunst. Worked at K&A, first in Hamburg, then in Vladivostok and Nagasaki.

Knorring, Fedor Ivanovich (1854–1914). Director-in-chief of the Ussuri Railway, 1895–1907. Husband of Tatiana Konstantinovna Knorring.

Knorring, Tatiana Konstantinovna. Wife of Fedor Ivanovich Knorring.

Kozhevnikov, Vissarion Andreevich. Husband of Ekaterina Alexandrovna Kozhevnikova. The couple married in April 1894 and had their first child only in 1906 (like the Prays).

Kozhevnikova, Ekaterina Alexandrovna. Wife of Vissarion A. Kozhevnikov.

Kravtsov, S. D. Merchant of the Second Guild. Sold sewing machines, bicycles, and typewriters. Husband of Varvara Kravtsova.

Kravtsova, Varvara. Wife of S. D. Kravtsov.

Krüll, Magda (born in 1880, née Peterson). Wife of Maximilian K. Krüll.

Krüll, Maximilian Karlovich (d. 1920). Honorary Swedish consul, 1912–20. Husband of Magda Krüll. After Consul Krüll's death of typhus, the family lived at their *dacha* at 19th Verst. Their daughter Tania died at age seventeen (4 July 1931) from tuberculosis.

Kuster, Olga Josephina (1874–1920). Daughter of Maria Josephina Theresa and Johannes (Ivan Ivanovich) Kuster (1837–1895). Olga married lieutenant Konstantin Alexandrovich Luther in 1898 (he was born in 1874; served on the *Rurik*).

Langelütje (Russian: Langelitie), Johann (Iogann) Mikhailovich (1851–1900). Merchant of the First Guild (1910). Founder and owner of the firm of J. Langelütje and Company, specializing in heavy machinery and furniture. Husband of Elena Egorovna Langelütje.

Langelütje (Russian: Langelitie), Thekla Elena Egorovna (b. 1857). Wife of Johann Mikhailovich Langelütje.

Langschwadt, Wilhelmina (Minni; d. 1902 from diphtheria). Her husband Adolph was with K&A. They lived on Missionerskaia Street, in the House of Langelütje. A second Mrs. Langschwadt was Lidiia Mikhailovna.

Lao Oo. Did carpentry and other handiwork at Dom Smith.

Lindholm, Nathalie (1848–1920, died in Japan). Of Swedish and German background from Finland; her father was Admiral Nordman. Wife of Otto Lindholm. The Lindholms' daughters: Natalia (Tullie) Tyrtova (b. 1878); Helen (Lolla) Millais (b. 1879); and Aina Butakova (b. 1884).

Lindholm, Otto (1832–1914). Swede from Finland. Prominent merchant of the First Guild in Vladivostok. Husband of Nathalie Lindholm.

Loi Glee. Worked at Dom Smith since 1890s, "our old watchman." Loi's son Jan was the compradore for a time.

Macgowan, David. US consul to Vladivostok (1920–22). Husband of Emma Macgowan. The Macgowans' daughter Mary married vice-consul Rollin Winslow (September 1922).

Macgowan, Emma. Wife of David Macgowan.

Maslennikov, Alexander Alekseevich (1867–1917). Nobleman. Director of Russo-Asian Bank in Vladivostok. Married Margarita ("Gretli," 1885–1958), née Bryner, in 1910.

The Mathiasens. Of the Danish Telegraph. Mrs. Mathiasen was Russian. The Mathiasens left Vladivostok in 1930.

Meares, Cecil. In Vladivostok off and on (1903–6). Briefly a member of the Scott expedition (1910).

Merriam, B. E. In charge of the Navy YMCA in Vladivostok (from May 1922). Husband of Carolyn S. Merriam. The Merriams rented rooms in Dom Smith for part of their stay.

Merriam, Carolyn S. Wife of B. E. Merriam.

Merritt, Leon. From New England. Assistant at the American Store (1900–1903).

Meyer, Else (born in 1875, née Wehner). Wife of Paul Meyer.

Meyer, Otto. Meyer's sister Christina ("Tina") was Mrs. Behn.

Meyer, Paul (1862–1945; Pavel Grigorievich). Of K&A. Husband of Else Meyer. Karl Goldenstedt was P. Meyer's uncle.

Mitt, Pavel (Pasha). Grandchild of the Goldenstedts. Pasha married Nina Bryner but perished soon after in the war (April-May 1916).

Mr. Molchanov. Worked in the American Store (from 1905). Had a *dacha* at Sadgorod on the Lianchikhe River (1923).

Morphew, Maud (d. in 1917). Englishwoman teaching art in private Vladivostok homes until 1903.

Nastia. See Artemieva.

Newhard, Harold Frederick ("Newhard-san"; 1877–1930). Agent for Standard Oil working in Mr. Clarkson's office, later at the US consulate in Vladivostok. Husband of Wanda Marie Newhard. The couple married on 8 November 1902.

Newhard, Wanda Marie (1881–1933, from Poland). Wife of Harold F. Newhard. Their daughter Vanda Alice (born in 1905) was good friends with Dorothy Pray.

Nielsen, Christian (1869–1936). Husband of Margrethe Nielsen, both from Denmark. The couple married on 3 April 1902.

Nielsen, Margrethe. One of Mrs. Pray's closest friends, especially in the 1920s when she was often invited to visit the Nielsens' *dacha* at 19th Verst.

Pershina, Alexandra. Probably the "Tetia Sasha" [Auntie Sasha] who worked with Mrs. Pray for the Red Cross and lived at Dom Smith (1920s).

Piankova, Nadezhda Alexandrovna. A close friend of Eleanor Pray, especially in the 1920s. Lived in Dom Piankov at 43 Svetlanskaia Street.

Rasmussen, Anders Karl Markus (Karl Ivanovich). Of the Danish Telegraph. The Rasmussens left Vladivostok with their son Axel on 27 May 1905.

Rumpeter, Avgust Petrovich (1849–1912). Pastor of the Lutheran Church in Vladivostok. Boyhood friends with Dr. Birk in Dorpat.

Schultz, Mikhail Fedorovich (murdered in 1919). Vice admiral. Commander of the Siberian Fleet (1914–17). His sister Ida Fedorovna Borisova wrote to Eleanor Pray about his death.

Smith, Reuben E. (1878–1919, drowned in the River Ulia on Kamchatka). One of Mr. Clarkson's mining engineers. Later, US consulate official. Smith's first wife, Helen (from San Francisco), left Vladivostok in May 1904 to be safe during the Russo-Japanese War, but drowned mid-ocean. His second wife was known as "Mrs. Reuben."

Sommer. German consul (mid-1920s). Lived at K&A, where the consulate and the vice-consul's apartment were also situated.

Späth, E. F. (b. 1865). Danish lieutenant serving in the Russian Navy for several years.

Stark, Fedor Oskarovich (d. 1939). Son of admiral Oskar Viktorovich Stark (1846–1927). Lieutenant Stark's brother Alexander died in the Battle of Tsushima (May 1905).

Stein, Alexander Konstantinovich (1875–1945, died in Leningrad). Physician on the *Gromoboi*. A widower when Mrs. Pray met him. His second wife was Maria Ivanovna. They lived in Saint Petersburg and had two children, "Shurik" and Tamara. Dr. Stein published many scientific books and articles.

Szentgali, Antal Mikhailovich. Hungarian native who worked in Mr. Clarkson's firm. A gifted violin player.

Talko, Maria (d. 1925, in Shanghai, of pneumonia). Russian Sister of Mercy (1904–5 and 1914–18). Volunteered for the Red Cross.

Taube, Georgii Nikolaevich. Baron. Manager of Vladivostok's commercial port (1912–16). Mrs. Taube was from Riga. When arrested in 1917, Taube gave his yacht, the *Minnetonka*, to the Tyrtovs.

"Tetia Sasha." See Pershina.

Tolle, Evgeniia Parfenovna (d. in 1926). Wife of Georg F. Tolle.

Tolle, Georg Fedorovich. Insurance agent and merchant of the First Guild. Served as manager of J. Langelütje & Co. Husband of Evgeniia Tolle.

Tyrtov, Konstantin. Lieutenant on the *Russia*. Married Tullie Lindholm in 1901. Two daughters: Natalia Davis (Tussie, b. 1907) and Vera De Haas (b. 1908).

Unterberger, Pavel Fedorovich (1842–1921, died in Mecklenburg). Military governor of Primorskaia Oblast (1888–97). Governor-general of Priamurie (1905–10).

Unterberger, Peter Pavlovich. Son of Governor Unterberger. Fortress engineer and military officer. A widower, Unterberger married Jenny Birk on 22 December 1910.

Walldén (Russian: Valden), Axel Kirillovich. Swede originally from Finland. Trained as a pharmacist, Walldén became a merchant of the Second Guild (1910), and partnered with Mr. Lindholm, managing O. V. Lindholm and Company. His wife was Selma Augusta (1841–1910); their son Franz (1871–1943) was a lawyer.

Walsham, John (1869–1940). Of Crompton and Schwabe. Helped organize the first golf course in Vladivostok. Son of Sir John Walsham of Radnorshire, the former British minister to Pekin. The family's manor, Knill Court, is situated on a small island in the River Wye, on the Welsh border.

Wang-sama (1900–1914). A chow-chow. Eleanor Pray's special friend, the "gentleman pup."

Wissing, Anna (born in 1884; known as "Ännchenlieb" to her friends). Wife of Nicolai Wissing. The Wissings left Vladivostok in 1913 "for a vacation" but never returned.

Wissing, Nicolai Lauritz. Of the Danish Telegraph. Husband of Anna Wissing.

Wohlfahrt, Rudolph. Of K&A. Merchant of the Second Guild. Husband of Sophie Wohlfahrt. The Wohlfahrts left Vladivostok in 1903.

Wohlfahrt, Sophie. Wife of Rudolph Wohlfahrt.

Notes

NOTES TO INTRODUCTION

1   A. N. Izergina et al., *The Hermitage, Leningrad: French Nineteenth-Century Masters* (Prague: Artia/Leningrad: Sovetsky Khudozhnik, 1968), plate 34. The painting discussed is *Boulevard Montmartre, Paris*.

2   Lewis Mumford, *The City in History: Its Origins, Its Transformations, and Its Prospects* (New York: Harcourt, Brace & World, 1961), 76, 79.

3   Michael F. Hamm, *Kiev: A Portrait, 1800–1917* (Princeton, NJ: Princeton University Press, 1993), xvi. See also Loren Graham and Jean-Michel Kantor, "'Soft' Area Studies versus 'Hard' Social Science: A False Opposition," *Slavic Review* 66, no. 1 (Spring 2007): 1, 17; Jochen Hellbeck, *Revolution on My Mind: Writing a Diary under Stalin* (Cambridge, MA: Harvard University Press, 2006).

4   Examples include David Wolff, *To the Harbin Station: The Liberal Alternative in Russian Manchuria, 1898–1914* (Stanford, CA: Stanford University Press, 1999); Roshanna P. Sylvester, *Tales of Old Odessa: Crime and Civility in a City of Thieves* (DeKalb: Northern Illinois University Press, 2005); and Hamm, *Kiev: A Portrait*, note 3.

5   Today, East Siberia is a different administrative region within the Russian Federation. Mrs. Pray was referring to the area now known as the Russian Far East.

6   The term "Old Vladivostok" usually indicates the prerevolutionary period, as, for example, in Boris D'iachenko's book *Staryi Vladivostok/Old Vladivostok*, trans. Alexander Mel'nikov (Vladivostok: Utro Rossii, 1992). I include most of Mrs. Pray's Vladivostok period in the term "Old Vladivostok."

7   The memoirs of Otto W. Lindholm, merchant of the First Guild, are another invaluable source on early Vladivostok. See his *Beyond the Frontiers of Imperial Russia: From the Memoirs of Otto W. Lindholm*, ed. Alexander de Haes Tyrtoff and Nicholas Tyrtoff Davis (Javea, Spain: A. de Haes OWL Publishing, 2008). Writing in Nice in 1908, Mr. Lindholm recalled events from the mid-nineteenth century in his native Finland through the early 1900s in Vladivostok.

8   This phrase, translated as "Nothing human is alien to me," from Terentius, the Roman playwright (d. 159 BC), suggests compassion for human failings; *Heauton Timorumenos* I. 1, 25.

9   Dorothy Findlay, an Englishwoman, wrote on 21 November 1923 that Mrs. Pray was the

"only . . . American here now." John and Dorothy Findlay, "Letters from Vladivostok, 1918–1923," ed. Dorothy Galton and John Keep, *Slavonic Review* 45 (July 1967): 530.

10 Konstantin Iasnov, "Pis'ma iz proshloi zhizni: Segodnia sostoitsia prezentatsiia unikal'nogo kul'turnogo proekta" [Letters from another life: A unique culture project will be presented today], *Rossiiskaia gazeta: Primorskii krai*, no. 4780, October 24, 2008. See also Liubov' Berchanskaia, "Samyi istinnyi portret Vladivostoka" [The most truthful portrait of Vladivostok], *Vladivostok*, no. 2428, October 28, 2008, p. 6.

11 Now and then, Mrs. Pray considered transforming her letters into a book, but, finding her talent for pithy letters greater than for publishable stories, she did not ultimately pursue this idea.

12 Mumford likens cities to "theater, in which common life itself takes on the features of a drama, heightened by every device of costume and scenery," *City in History*, 115, 200. While such spectacles, including Stalin's "rituals of theater," are usually created to boost the image of political leaders, Eleanor Pray wanted both to watch and to be *in* them, herself. The Stalin quote is from Jeffrey Brooks, *Thank You, Comrade Stalin! Soviet Public Culture from Revolution to Cold War* (Princeton, NJ: Princeton University Press, 2000), xvi; see also 66.

13 The Prays graduated from Great Falls High School in New Hampshire on 17 June 1887. They visited friends in China and Japan several times and traveled around the world in 1902–3 (their only visit home to New England), but when in Russia they always remained in and around Vladivostok.

14 For information on Russia's ethnic diversity, see Andreas Kappeler, *The Russian Empire: A Multiethnic History* (Harlow, UK: Pearson Education Limited, 2001).

15 The regular recipients of Mrs. Pray's letters are identified at the end of this introduction. Square brackets within quotations are used for brief editorial clarifications, while parentheses within quotations contain the writer's own remarks.

16 Birgitta Ingemanson, "Portrait of a City: Impressions of Vladivostok among English-Speaking Visitors," *Rossiia i ATR* 3 (1995): 107–14.

17 Lidiia Ginzburg is quoted by Julian Graffy, "Unshelving Stalin after the Period of Stagnation," in *Stalinism and the Soviet Cinema*, ed. Richard Taylor and Derek Spring (London: Routledge, 1993), 226, 266–67.

18 G. I. Ponomarchuk, "Rastitel'nost' i zhivotnyi mir" [Flora and fauna], in *Fizicheskaia geografiia Primorskogo kraia: Uchebnoe posobie* [Physical geography of the Maritime Territory: Textbook], ed. G. V. Svinukhov (DVGU, 1990), 4, 156. (Abbreviated names of publishers are given in full at the start of the bibliography.)

19 This kind of observation—e.g., "Dal'nii Vostok—eto krai porazitel'nykh kontrastov" [The Far East is a region of striking contrasts]—is found in many publications, here D. I. Boiko-Pavlov and E. P. Sodorchuk, *Tak bylo na Dal'nem Vostoke* [It was like this in the Far East] (Moscow: Mysl', 1964), 5. In a letter to Boris Lazarevskii on 13 April 1904, Anton Chekhov suggested that the "joy and suffering" in the region is a positive trait; *Letters of Anton Chekhov*, trans. Michael Henry Heim with Simon Karlinsky, selection, commentary, and introduction by Simon Karlinsky (New York: Harper & Row, 1973), 470.

20 While the terms "anorexia" and "body art" were not used in 1907 and 1915, the phenomena were known.

21 See, for example, the entry of 13 March 1929 in chapter 9.

22 To show her disdain for Russia's new political path, Eleanor Pray did not capitalize Bolshevism or Bolshevik.

23 The relationship of the Russian merchants, *kuptsy*, with the new entrepreneurs that often originated in the nobility is discussed in Alfred J. Rieber, *Merchants and Entrepreneurs in Imperial Russia* (Chapel Hill: University of North Carolina Press, 1982).

24 A. I. Krushanov, ed., *Istoriia Sovetskogo Primor'ia: Uchebnoe posobie dlia uchashchikhsia VIII-X klassov shkol Primorskogo kraia* [History of Soviet Primorie: Textbook for students of classes eight through ten in the schools of the Maritime Territory] (Vladivostok: Dal'nevostochnoe Knizhnoe Izdatel'stvo, 1970), 42.

25 Ivan G. Striuchenko, ed., *Zabytye imena: Istoriia Dal'nego Vostoka Rossii v litsakh: Stat'i i ocherki*, vyp. I [Forgotten names: History of Russia's Far East through individuals: Articles and essays, part I] (Vladivostok: Dal'nauka, 1994); Nelli G. Miz' and Gennadii P. Turmov, *Stranitsy zabytoi istorii: K 140-letiiu Vladivostoka* [Pages of forgotten history: To Vladivostok's 140th anniversary], book 1 (DVGTU, 2000).

CHAPTER 1

1 In Russian, the name would be either Dom Smita ("the House of Smith") or Dom Smitov ("the Smiths' House").

2 The name of their lane commemorates the early reputation of this city block as a veritable "Sodom" of immorality and crime. Sodom Hill was renamed Aleksei Hill in connection with the visit of Aleksei, son of Tsar Alexander II, in 1873, and the street name was changed in the Soviet period to Post Lane (Pochtovyi Pereulok). The role of the American Store in prerevolutionary Vladivostok will be the subject of separate writings.

3 Oscar and Charles Smith are among the examples given, not without scorn, of foreign investors benefiting from the lucrative land deals, in Nikolai P. Matveev, *Kratkii istoricheskii ocherk g. Vladivostoka* [Brief historical essay about the city of Vladivostok] (1910; repr., Vladivostok: Rubezh, 2010), 160–62. For some background to the rancor, see Thomas C. Owen, "Impediments to a Bourgeois Consciousness in Russia, 1880–1905: The Estate Structure, Ethnic Diversity, and Economic Regionalism," in *Between Tsar and People: Educated Society and the Quest for Public Identity in Late Imperial Russia*, ed. Edith W. Clowes, Samuel D. Kassow, and James L. West (Princeton, NJ: Princeton University Press, 1991), 79, 82, 85. For a portrait of the new Russian merchants operating in the quarter century before World War I, including their proclivity for European consumer goods and manners, see James L. West and Iurii A. Petrov, eds., *Merchant Moscow: Images of Russia's Vanished Bourgeoisie* (Princeton, NJ: Princeton University Press, 1998); also Richard Stites, *Serfdom, Society, and the Arts in Imperial Russia: The Pleasure and the Power* (New Haven, CT: Yale University Press, 2005), 22–23.

4 Harvey Green with Mary-Ellen Perry, *The Light of the Home: An Intimate View of the Lives of Women in Victorian America* (New York: Pantheon Books, 1983), 145. This book was praised as a "landmark study" about Victorian women by Ellen M. Plante, in *Women at Home in Victorian America: A Social History* (New York: Facts on File, 1997), xiii.

5 The idea of the home as a safe haven was widespread. See, for example, Shirley Murphy,

Our Homes and How to Make Them Healthy (1883): "A clean, fresh, and well-ordered house exercises over its inmates a moral, no less than physical influence, and has a direct tendency to make members of the family sober, peaceable, and considerate of the feelings and happiness of each other"; quoted in Green with Perry, *Light of the Home*, 59.

6 See, for example, Sibylle Meyer, "The Tiresome Work of Conspicuous Leisure: On the Domestic Duties of the Wives of Civil Servants in the German Empire, 1871–1918," in *Connecting Spheres: European Women in a Globalizing World, 1500 to the Present*, ed. Marilyn Boxer and Jean H. Quataert, 2nd ed. (New York: Oxford University Press, 2000), 185–93.

7 The first quote concerns the title figure of Mary J. Straw Cook, ed., *Immortal Summer: A Victorian Woman's Travels in the Southwest: The 1897 Letters and Photographs of Amelia Hollenback* (Santa Fe: Museum of New Mexico Press, 2002), xi. The second quote is from Christine Hill Smith, *Reading "A Victorian Gentlewoman in the Far West: The Reminiscences of Mary Hallock Foote"* (Boise, ID: Boise State University, 2002), 16, 39.

8 There were no municipal waterworks in Vladivostok until the hydrocomplex of the Sedanka Reservoir was constructed in 1928–38; V. A. Obertas, V. K. Moor, and E. A. Erysheva, *Pamiatniki istorii i kul'tury goroda Vladivostoka: Materialy k svodu* [Monuments of the history and culture of the city of Vladivostok: Materials] (Vladivostok: Svetlana, 2012), 89. Before this project, people used wells and also collected rain water.

9 Walter Scott's novel *Kenilworth* was published in 1821.

10 For the time being, Sarah Smith remained in Vladivostok, although she also traveled regularly to New England, including in 1900 when she brought her husband's ashes home to be buried and bought the headstone for the family grave at the New Glade Cemetery in Somersworth.

11 Aggravating other factors, the sinking of the US battleship *Maine* in the harbor of Havana on 15 February 1898, when 260 men were killed, precipitated the Spanish-American War (1898). On 1 May, a US squadron led by the *Olympia* under admiral George Dewey defeated the Spanish fleet in Manila; this ship had participated in Vladivostok's coronation festivities in May 1896, where Eleanor saw it. The slogan was "Remember the *Maine*!"

12 These were geological expeditions prospecting for Siberia's natural resources.

13 For the importance of potted plants and indoor "gardens" in Victorian society, see, for example, Catharine E. Beecher and Harriet Beecher Stowe, *The American Woman's Home, or, Principles of Domestic Science, Being a Guide to the Formation and Maintenance of Economical, Healthful, Beautiful, and Christian Homes* (1869; repr., Watkins Glen, NY: Library of Victorian Culture, American Life Foundation, 1979), 94–103; Plante, *Women at Home*, 172–75; and Elan Zingman-Leith and Susan Zingman-Leith, *Creating Authentic Victorian Rooms* (Washington, DC: Elliott & Clark Publishing, 1995), 121–22.

14 Mrs. Pray used these terms loosely. The *hoong-hoozi* were Chinese bandits roaming the region; the Boxers were members of the uprising in China.

15 The ruble, divided into one hundred kopeks, was worth approximately fifty cents before World War I.

16 Mrs. Pray has misunderstood the essence of feng shui, which is not an "evil wind" but a system of placing buildings and furniture to benefit from the life-giving force of the *qi* (or *chi*).

17 Finland was a grand duchy in the Russian Empire, from 1815 to 1918. Additional information and numerous photos of the Lindholm family, including from the Eleanor L. Pray
Collection, can be found in Larisa Aleksandrovskaia and Birgitta Ingemanson,
Udivitel'naia zhizn' Otto Lindgol'ma: Dokumental'no-istoricheskoe povestvovanie [The
remarkable life of Otto Lindholm: A documentary-historical narrative] (OIAK, PGOM,
2003); and L. Aleksandrovskaia and B. Ingemanson, *Fotografiia na pamiat': Otto
Lindgol'm i ego okruzhenie, 1890-e-1920-e gody/Photos for the Memories: Otto Lindholm
and His Circle, 1890s-1920s* (PGOM, 2005).

18 Chup-chup, sometimes called "chow-chow," a savory relish, was popular in nineteenth-
century India and China, in US Mennonite communities, and generally in the US South.
It combines chopped vegetables—e.g., cucumbers, tomatoes, green peppers, and peas—
in a vinegar-and-sugar marinade flavored with mustard and other spices. I am indebted
to Michael Hamm, Gregory Polgar, and one of the (anonymous) peer reviewers for this
information.

19 This "poetry" consisted of rhymed jokes intended to make the recipient of each wrapped
package guess what it contained.

20 This dinner was in celebration of the Lindholms' nineteenth wedding anniversary.

CHAPTER 2

1 Although the word *antebellum* (before the war) often refers to life in the US South before
the Civil War, here I use it for life in Vladivostok before mid-1914 and the beginning of
the so-called Great War.

2 For a history of Kunst and Albers, see Lothar Deeg, *Kunst und Albers in Wladivostok: Die
Geschichte eines deutschen Handelshauses im russischen Fernen Osten, 1864-1924* [Kunst
and Albers in Vladivostok: The history of a German trading house in the Russian Far
East, 1864-1924] (Essen: Klartext Verlag, 1996). This book was recently published in Eng-
lish translation as Lothar Deeg, *Kunst and Albers Vladivostok: The History of a German
Trading Company in the Russian Far East (1864-1924)*, trans. Sarah Bohnet (DVFU, 2012).

3 The Great Northern Telegraph Company (Det Store Nordiske Telegrafselskab) began its
operations in East Asia in 1869. The marriages of the Danish Princesses Alexandra (in 1863)
and Dagmar (in 1866) to the heirs of the British and Russian thrones favored Denmark's role
in establishing Russia's telegraphic connections with England. This accomplished, the more
complex endeavor of connecting Hong Kong, Shanghai, and Japan with Scandinavia and
Great Britain ensued. The headquarters of the "Danish Telegraph," as the company was pop-
ularly known, were in Nagasaki, and its Vladivostok office, the "Danish House," was
located on Aleutskaia Street where the apartment complex "the Gray Horse" now stands.

4 Mr. Bushuev's murder is mentioned in Matveev, *Kratkii istoricheskii ocherk*, 304–05. Paul
Dattan, although ailing, was to live until 1945.

5 This was a straight-brimmed straw hat with a low, flat crown, also called a "boater"; see
Alison Gernsheim, *Fashion and Reality* (London: Faber and Faber, 1963), plate 204.

6 For more information on Victorian clothing care, see Christina Walkley and Vanda Foster, *Crinolines and Crimping Irons: Victorian Clothes: How They Were Cleaned and Cared
For* (1978; repr., London: Peter Owen, 1985).

7   A basque is a close-fitting bodice.

8   The Tsar's younger brother, Georgii Alexandrovich, died from tuberculosis on 10 July 1899, at the age of twenty-eight. Aleksei, the son of Nikolai II and Empress Alexandra Fedorovna, was born only in 1904.

9   Vladivostok's beatific status as a "porto franco" or duty-free port, established in 1872, was abolished in 1900; David Wolff, *To the Harbin Station*, 56; John J. Stephan, *The Russian Far East: A History* (Stanford, CA: Stanford University Press, 1994), 90. While the decree restoring the free port was dated 1 May 1904, in practice it lasted only from 1906 to early 1909, when import duties were again imposed.

10 Corsets were both the boon and the scourge of Victorian ladies. For a captivating overview, see Valerie Steele, *The Corset: A Cultural History* (New Haven, CT: Yale University Press, 2001). For corset problems, see Leigh Summers, *Bound to Please: A History of the Victorian Corset* (Oxford, NY: Berg, 2001).

11 Dorothy was born on 26 June 1906, in Dom Smith, and died on 7 August 2006, in Sarasota, Florida.

12 In 1915, the Amoskeag Mills in Manchester, New Hampshire, was the largest producer of cotton textiles in the world, employing more than 17,000 workers. After World War I, the Mills lost the competitive edge to the cotton-growing areas of the South, where labor was less expensive. Layoffs prompted a long strike during 1922, and the Mills permanently closed in 1935.

13 For an introduction to some of Vladivostok's grander examples of financial philanthropy, see A. A. Belousov, "Dushi prekrasnye poryvy . . . " [Beautiful impulses of the soul . . .], in *Na altar' otechestva: Iz istorii metsenatstva i blagotvoritel'nosti v Rossii* [On the altar of the Fatherland: From the history of patronage and philanthropy in Russia] (DVGU, 1996), 101–59.

14 Nikolai Petrovich Linevich (1839–1908) led the storming of Peking in 1900, helping to quell the Boxer Rebellion. His military contributions were to become further noticed during the Russo-Japanese War. Both the *Petropavlovsk* and the *Navarin* mentioned in this passage were destroyed in that war.

15 Korean children were often available to run errands for a small fee, and this boy and his friends were regularly employed by the Prays as caddies during golf.

16 As kindly pointed out by Andrei Sidorov, Dr. Popov was the head physician at the Naval Hospital.

17 This may be a writing slip; elsewhere, the tennis assistants are described as Korean children.

CHAPTER 3

1   The former residence of the prominent First Guild merchant Iulii (Jules) Bryner and his family, at 15 Aleutskaia Street, was built in 1913 (by architect Georg Junghändel). Bryner's grandson Iulii, actor Yul Brynner (who, along with his sister Vera, spelled the family name with two *n*'s), was born here in 1920. Another relation carrying this illustrious name has written a fascinating family history: Rock Brynner, *Empire and Odyssey: The Brynners in Far East Russia and Beyond* (Hanover, NH: Steerforth Press, 2006).

2   The Nikolai Triumphal Arch was created in memory of Tsesarevich Nikolai Alexandrov-ich's visit to Vladivostok in 1891. It was razed in the 1930s but was rebuilt in full splendor in 2003 (by architects V. Moor, V. Obertas, and A. Gavrilov).

3   V. A. Obertas's writings on Vladivostok's architecture are particularly insightful, e.g., "Formirovanie planirovochnoi struktury Vladivostoka v XIX v." [Formation of Vladivo-stok's urban structure in the nineteenth century], *Arkhitekturnoe nasledstvo* 25 (1976): 85–93; "Arkhitektura starogo Vladivostoka" [Architecture of old Vladivostok], *Arkhitek-turnoe nasledstvo* 28 (1980): 107–18. Monuments still standing are catalogued in V. A. Obertas et al, *Pamiatniki istorii i kul'tury goroda Vladivostoka.* Crisply beautiful photos by Dmitrii Ancha and others can be found in A. V. Mialk and V. I. Kalinin, *Vladivostok: Pamiatniki arkhitektury* [Vladivostok: Monuments of architecture], trans. Z. Proshina (Vladivostok: Dal'press, 2005). A handy reference guide on the Internet is Maria Lebed'ko's *Vladivostok: A Historic Walking Tour,* ed. Birgitta Ingemanson, web prepara-tion by Donna McCool, 1999, available at http://www.wsulibs.wsu.edu/Vladivostok.

4   The cathedral's towers were toppled on 17 April 1937 (near that year's Orthodox Easter on 2 May), and photos of the event were published in 1990. See Sergei Chesunov, "Lomat'—ne stroit'" [To break is not to build], *Vechernii Vladivostok,* July 17, 1990, 7. These images have been seen repeatedly since then, for example, in D'iachenko, *Staryi Vladivostok/Old Vladivostok,* 359–61. The building itself was torn down in 1938.

5   Zakhar L. Dicharov, *Rasskaz o gorode i cheloveke* [Story of a city and a person] (Vladivo-stok: Primorskoe Knizhnoe Izdatel'stvo, 1960), 12. I have borrowed the amphitheater image from Viacheslav M. Elesh, *Na beregakh Volgi i Tikhogo okeana* [On the shores of the Volga and the Pacific Ocean] (Moscow: Sovetskaia Rossiia, 1970), 42.

6   A good photo of the terrace formations along Patrice Lumumba (today Admiral Kuznetsov) Street can be found in A. Il'in, ed., *Vladivostok: Spravochnik-putevoditel'* [A directory-guidebook] (Vladivostok: Dal'nevostochnoe Knizhnoe Izdatel'stvo, 1972), 87. For further developments of the city's architecture, see, for example, Latkin, A. P., ed., *Perspektivy razvitiia g. Vladivostoka (Materialy k proektu kontseptsii)* [Perspectives on Vladivostok's development (Materials toward conceptualizing the project)] (Vladivostok: Vladivostokskii Gorodskoi Sovet Narodnykh Deputatov, 1990); I am grateful to V. K. Moor for giving me this book. See also, for instance, William Richardson, "Stalinist Vladivostok: Architecture and Urban Planning, 1928–1953," *The Soviet and Post-Soviet Review* 27, no. 2–3 (2000): 293–314.

7   Chekhov saw a whale in the Bay of the Golden Horn in October 1890, and noted this in his 13 April 1904 letter to Boris A. Lazarevskii; Anton Chekhov, *Letters,* 470. The book is cited in full in note 20 of the introduction.

8   Fridtjof Nansen, *Through Siberia, the Land of the Future,* trans. Arthur G. Chater (Lon-don: William Heineman, 1914), 342. Nansen's visit is recounted by Vladimir Shcherbak, "Norvezhskii gost'" [A Norwegian guest], in *Znamenitye gosti Vladivostoka* [Famous guests of Vladivostok] (Vladivostok: Dal'press, 2005), 87–89.

9   Tamara N. Kaliberova, "Slushaia gorod" [Listening to the city], *Krasnoe znamia,* Novem-ber 9, 1985; Amir A. Khisamutdinov, "Vladivostok: Window or Fortress?" in *The Russian Far East: Historical Essays* (Honolulu: N.p., 1993), 132.

10 Information from the newspaper *Dalekaia okraina,* May 3, 1909, OS; D. Bogdanov, *Pute-

voditel' po Vladivostoku i Promyslu Primorskoi oblasti, Kamchatki i Sakhalina [Guidebook on Vladivostok and on trade in the Primorie oblast', Kamchatka and Sakhalin] (Vladivostok: Izd. Bogdanova i Drobinskogo, 1909), 16, 23; E. J. Harrison, *Peace or War East of Baikal?* (Yokohama: Kelly & Walsh, [1910]), 144.

11 Marshall Everett, *Exciting Experiences in the Japanese-Russian War* (N.p.: Henry Neil, 1904), 180, quoting a man from Kansas City; Emil Lengyel, *Siberia* (Garden City, NY: Garden City Publishing, 1943), 300. For an engrossing scholarly account of the Vladivostok Fortress, see N. B. Aiushin, V. I. Kalinin, S. A. Vorob'ev, and N. V. Gavrilkin, *Vladivostokskaia krepost'* [The Fortress of Vladivostok] (Vladivostok: Dal'nauka, 2006).

12 J. Oswald Forsyth, Vladivostok, to his father in Sydney, 30 July 1913, in J. Oswald Forsyth's archive, file 9, "Private Correspondence, 1913–20," Riksarkivet [National Archives], Stockholm.

13 Sedanka soon became a center of Vladivostok's *dacha* region, as well as the administrative headquarters of the Vladivostok and Kamchatka diocese. The Archbishop's Residence was built in 1900–1901, and the Alexander Nevskii Chapel in 1910–11. From 1926 on, the chapel was used variously as a rest home, as a reading room, and as housing; and from 1934 on, the residence was used as a school and a cinema. The ensemble was returned to the Russian Orthodox Church in 1989–90; Obertas et al., *Pamiatniki istorii i kul'tury*, 130, 136.

14 Russian New Year's Eve in the nineteenth century was on January 12, and the Blessing of the Waters on January 18 (i.e., January 6, OS). The discrepancy between the dates occurs because the Orthodox Church used (and still uses) the Julian Calendar.

15 This simple hall of worship was located near the lot between Svetlanskaia and Pushkin Streets where the Gothic-style Lutheran Church of St. Paul's was built in 1907–9 (funded privately, including by the Dattan and Lindholm families). St. Paul's was given to the Pacific Fleet in 1935 to be used as a club and, from 1951 on, served as Vladivostok's museum of military history (Obertas et al., *Pamiatniki istorii i kul'tury*, 140–41). From the mid-1990s it serves again as the meeting place of Vladivostok's Lutheran congregation, offering both religious services and cultural events such as concerts under the leadership of Pastor Manfred Brockmann.

16 The governor-general was Lieutenant General S. M. Dukhovskoi, who served from 1893 to 1898. I thank Vladimir Kalinin for this identification.

17 At this time, General Linevich was, rather, the commander of the southern Ussuri district.

18 Andrei Labinskii (1871–1941) was a well-known Russian tenor, Maria Mikhailova (1864–1943) a soloist at the Mariinskii Theater in Petersburg.

19 The location for the outpost Vladivostok was determined on 2 July 1860, but the fiftieth anniversary was celebrated on 2 (15 NS) November 1910 in memory of the Treaty of Peking (2 November 1860, OS), which confirmed the Russian-Chinese borders in the Far East and officially allowed the settlement.

20 Fernsicht was the building to the immediate west of Dom Smith, owned by Kunst and Albers and serving as a home for bachelors working at the company. The words in italics mean "fire" in German and Russian, respectively.

21 This refers to those in charge of the regional government, whose political views Mrs. Pray did not agree with.

22 Admiral Gennadii I. Nevel'skoi (1813–76) explored the eastern shores of Russia, confirming in 1849 that Sakhalin was an island rather than a peninsula. The Nevel'skoi Monument was unveiled on 7 November 1897. The two-headed imperial eagle atop the monument was replaced in 1923 with the five-pointed Soviet star, but by 1960 the eagle was returned; Lebed'ko, *Vladivostok: A Historic Walking Tour*, 28.

CHAPTER 4

1 Much has been written about the Trans-Siberian Railway, including in English, e.g., Steven G. Marks, *Road to Power: The Trans-Siberian Railroad and the Colonization of Asian Russia, 1850–1917* (Ithaca, NY: Cornell University Press, 1991); and Harmon Tupper, *To the Great Ocean: Siberia and the Trans-Siberian Railway* (Boston: Little, Brown, 1965).

2 The prince was probably Don Jaime (1870–1931), son of Don Carlos of Bourbon, Duke of Madrid (1848–1909), who was educated in Austrian and British military schools, and became a colonel of dragoons in the Russian army. Admiral Evgenii Ivanovich Alekseev (1843–1917) was the viceroy for the Russian Far East during the Russo-Japanese War. Despite his patronymic, he was the natural son of Tsar Alexander II, and thus an uncle of Nikolai II.

3 Namely, in alphabetical order, China, France, Germany, Great Britain, Greece, Holland, Italy, Japan, Norway, Sweden, Turkey, and the United States, Bogdanov; *Putevoditel' po Vladivostoku*, 49–51. Sweden's consulate, which this publication does not mention, was opened in May 1909; n.a., *Dalekaia okraina*, May 28, 1909, OS, 4.

4 The American inventor R. J. Gatling (1818–1903) created this early type of machine gun.

5 Even in English, the title Tsesarevich, "son of the tsar," is preferred to the more common form Tsarevich; Charlotte Zeepvat, *Romanov Autumn: Stories from the Last Century of Imperial Russia* (Stroud, UK: Sutton, 2000), xii. The memoirs of German-born Alfred Keyserling (1861–1939), who served under governor-general A. N. Korf, include the Tsesarevich's visit to Vladivostok and East Siberia; Al'fred Keizerling, *Vospominaniia o russkoi sluzhbe* [Memories of Russian service] (Moscow: Akademkniga, 2001).

6 This ring was later lost, possibly pawned in China during the 1920s. Fedor N. Merkuloff, son of the captain, interview by Birgitta Ingemanson, 23 November 1993, San Francisco. For Merkulov's connection with the steamship company, see E. V. Ermakova et al., eds., *Primorskii Krai: Kratkii entsiklopedicheskii spravochnik* [The Maritime Territory: Brief encyclopedic reference work] (DVGU, 1997), 300. A similar ring was given to "Mr. Yaneovich Yanevsky" (14 July 1895 to Home), Eleanor Pray's Polish relative by marriage. He was the second husband of Emily (Cooper) Smith, the widow of Charles Smith's brother Oscar (who died in Vladivostok in 1889).

7 Greg King, *The Last Empress: The Life and Times of Alexandra Feodorovna, Tsarina of Russia* (Secaucus, NJ: Carol Pub. Group, 1994), 109. This description is based on that of Mathilda Kschessinska in H. S. H. the Princess Romanovsky-Krassinsky, *Dancing in Petersburg: The Memoirs of Kschessinska*, trans. from French by Arnold Haskell (New York: Da Capo Press, 1977), 59. Already, at the imperial couple's wedding in 1894, electric lights were used effectively; Penelope Hunter-Stiebel, *Hesse: A Princely German Collection* (Portland, OR: Portland Art Museum, 2005), 159.

8   Mrs. Pray has in mind the Cathedral of the Assumption.

9   Alexander III died on 1 November 1894.

10 The former Princess Alix's sentiments were very similar. After the wedding, she wrote to her sister Victoria, "One's feelings one can imagine. One day in deepest mourning lamenting a beloved one, the next in smartest clothes being married. There cannot be a greater contrast, but it drew us more together if possible." Quoted in Sophie Buxhoevden, *The Life and Tragedy of Alexandra Feodorovna, Empress of Russia* (New York: Longmans, Green, 1928), 44.

11 Eleanor L. Pray, "Coronation Week in Vladivostok," *Somersworth Free Press* (New Hampshire), July 17, 1896. The article is dated 3 June 1896.

12 This is "The President's March" by Philip Phile, with words by Joseph Hopkinson (1798).

13 Pristan' Lindgol'ma [Lindholm's pier] is outlined on *Plan goroda Vladivostok v 1900 godu* [City plan Vladivostok, 1900], MPK 4397 [Museum of the Maritime Territory, map 4397], PGOM, Vladivostok. I am grateful to Rimma Mordovtseva for showing me this map.

14 The rebuilt house was sold in the 1920s to the city, which used it for a medical clinic. The Vladivostok fishery firm More [the sea], renovated it in a modern style in 2004. A plaque with a portrait of Otto Lindholm by Vladivostok sculptor Eduard V. Barsegov is by the main entrance.

15 This information (which can be found at www.alexanderpalace.org/letterstsaritsa/december14.html) was supplied by Nicholas Davis, son of Natal'ia ("Tussie") Davis, née Tyrtova (daughter of Tullie and Konstantin Tyrtov), on 9 July 2006. I am very grateful for his help.

16 Petr Rimskii-Korsakov (1861–1927), rear admiral since 1913, was commander of Vladivostok's military port. He was a cousin of Nikolai Rimsky-Korsakov (1844–1908), the composer.

17 The empress dowager was Maria Fedorovna, the tsar's mother, formerly Princess Dagmar of Denmark (1847–1928); the queen dowager of Greece was the former Olga Konstantinovna (1851–1926), a niece of Alexander II; and the tsar's two sisters were Ksenia (1875–1960) and Olga (1882–1960).

18 The officers serving on the *Standart* "were chosen for their social gifts. Their task was to create on board the atmosphere of a fairy-tale, a charming idyll"; A. A. Mossolov, *At the Court of the Last Tsar: Being the Memoirs of A. A. Mossolov, Head of the Court Chancellery, 1900-1916*, ed. A. A. Pilenco, trans. E. W. Dickes (London: Methuen, 1935), 249.

19 In 1917, the Lithuanian city of Kovno was renamed Kaunas.

20 Empress Alexandra Fedorovna's mother was Alice, princess of Great Britain and grand duchess of Hesse and by Rhine (1845–75), the second daughter of Queen Victoria and Prince Albert.

21 The new palace at Livadia in the Crimea was finished in 1911.

22 For a pretty exposé in watercolors of the Kamenka Estate, see Mariamna Davydoff, *Memoirs of a Russian Lady: Drawings and Tales of Life before the Revolution* (New York: Harry N. Abrams, 1986).

23 For her own account of the visit, see Isabella Bird Bishop, *Korea and Her Neighbors: A Narrative of Travel, with an Account of the Recent Vicissitudes and Present Position of the Country* (New York: Fleming H. Revell, 1898), 213–45.

24 Bishop, *Korea and Her Neighbors,* plate by page 214. While the title page acknowledges "Illustrations from Photos by the Author," Mrs. Pray's copy of this Vladivostok panorama is clearly marked A. E. I. (Anne E. Ivy). Eleanor Pray attempted always to credit the photographers whose snapshots she accepted, and it is unlikely that she would have acknowledged this as Mrs. Ivy's if Mrs. Bishop were the author. One must assume a mistake by the publisher.

25 For background information on Isabella Bird Bishop, see, for example, Pat Barr, *A Curious Life for a Lady: The Story of Isabella Bird* [sic] (London: Macmillan, John Murray, 1970).

26 Martha Elizabeth Powers (d. in 1892) and John Greenleaf Whittier (1807–92) were Quakers, and the latter was a great favorite of Eleanor Pray's. *The Christian's Secret of a Happy Life,* by Hanna Whitall Smith (1832–1911), a popular self-help book, was published in 1875.

27 The Duke of York was the future George V (grandfather of Queen Elizabeth II), whose wedding to Mary of Teck was celebrated in 1893.

28 Now Shantou, this Chinese city is a major port on the South China Sea, about two hundred miles east of Hong Kong.

29 [Richard T. Greener], "Despatches [sic] from United States Consuls in Vladivostok, [20 June] 1898–[17 August] 1906" (Lawrence: University of Kansas Libraries, 1963), microform.

30 "Greener, Richard Theodore," *Harvard Class of 1870, 25th Anniversary Report* (Cambridge, MA: Harvard College, 1895), 25–28, and *50th Anniversary Report* (Cambridge, MA: Harvard College, 1920), 66–67. See also Allison Blakely, "Richard T. Greener and the 'Talented Tenth's' Dilemma," *Journal of Negro History* 59, no. 4 (October 1974): 305–21; Allison Blakely, "Black US Consuls and Diplomats and Black Leadership, 1880–1920," *Umoja: A Scholarly Journal of Black Studies* 1, no. 1 (Spring 1977): 1–16; and Nonna Chernyakova, "Harvard's First Black Graduate Left Imprint on Far East," *Vladivostok News: Focus* 197, October 8, 1999, 1.

31 From the article "For Good Government and Urban Politics: The Career of R. T. Greener '70," *Harvard Alumni Bulletin* (12 December 1964): 267. The ensuing quote is from Horace G. Dawson, Jr., "From the Director's Desk," *The Globe: A Ralph J. Bunche International Affairs Center* 2, no. 1 (Summer 1998): 7.

32 Quoted by Chernyakova, in "Harvard's First Black Graduate," 1.

33 Mr. Bechtel had arrived in Vladivostok in April 1898 and worked at the office of David Clarkson, where the twenty-one-year-old Harold Newhard was also employed.

34 In his book *Sesame and Lilies* (1865), John Ruskin (1819–1900), the English art critic, discusses his perception of the differences between men and women.

35 Marie Corelli (1855–1924), a very popular writer at this time, was a favorite of both the Russian empress and her grandmother, Queen Victoria; King, *Last Empress,* 40, 71.

36 The pawnshop was located at the Russo-Chinese Bank, whose director was A. A. Maslennikov.

37 President McKinley died on 14 September 1901, after being shot in Buffalo on 6 September.

38 The Japanese ending -san, which when added to a name indicates respect, was sometimes used to honor friends of other nationalities, too.

1   See, for example, S. N. Razgonov, ed., *Pamiatniki Otechestva: Mir russkoi usad'by* [Monuments of the Fatherland: The world of the Russian country estate] (Moscow: Russkaia kniga, 1992); and Priscilla Roosevelt, *Life on the Russian Country Estate: A Social and Cultural History*, with photographs by William Brumfield (New Haven, CT: Yale University Press, 1995).

2   Miz' and Turmov, *Stranitsy*, 68–73; Ermakova, *Primorskii Krai*, 127–28.

3   Some of the information in this chapter was included in Birgitta Ingemanson, "Poteriannyi rai: Imenie Novogeorgievskoe, 1892–1922" [A paradise lost: The Novogeorgievsk estate, 1892–1922], trans. Elena Smith and Vladimir I. Kalinin, *Rossiia i ATR* 4 (2001): 22–33.

4   The word means "it is boring" or "[one is] bored," but it may be better understood here as "lonely."

5   Tsintau, or Tsingtao (today Qingdao), in China's Shandong Province on the Yellow Sea, was leased to Germany from 1898 to 1914, and became a center of the Far Eastern beer industry.

6   Mrs. Pray was referring to a braying donkey. The phrase comes from a fairy tale by the Brothers Grimm, "The Bremen Town Musicians," where a donkey, a dog, a cat, and a rooster play music together but scare those who hear them. Jamie and John Rea Caldwell, sons of the American consul, were spending the summer with Mrs. Pray.

7   *The Poetry of T'ao Ch'ien*, trans. James Robert Hightower, with commentary and annotations (Oxford, UK: Clarendon Press, 1970); A. R. Davis, *T'ao Yüan-ming, AD 365-427: His Works and Their Meaning* (Cambridge, UK: Cambridge University Press, 1983). The two different names refer to the same poet. I am grateful to Dong Zheng-min for clarifying the Chinese words.

8   Mrs. Pray's birthday book shows that He Fa was born on 14/26 April. He was so loved by everyone on the estate that one year when he returned from winter in Chefoo (where his family lived), "about half the Chinese on the place went down to the pier to meet him, hardly allowing him to carry a pound of his baggage himself" (14 May 1915 to Aunt Anna). When Mr. Pray died, He Fa was one of the pallbearers.

9   Much of Russia experienced a severe drought in the summer of 1921, causing widespread famine the following winter.

10 Roosevelt, *Life*, xiii; Stephen Lovell, *Summerfolk: A History of the Dacha, 1710-2000* (Ithaca, NY: Cornell University Press, 2003), 31, 95.

11 A "capote" is a cloak, a kind of long jacket, sometimes with a hood.

12 The usual size of a corset's waist was from eighteen to thirty inches, but "the W. B. Reduso Corset, 'a boon for large women,' went up to 36 inches," Steele, *Corset*, 102.

13 The inhabitants of Novogeorgievsk gave the German name Irishain ("Iris grove") to a pleasant beach on the western side of the peninsula, where wild iris still grew in large numbers when I walked along it in the early 2000s.

14 Mr. Pray was reading a popular detective novel by Mary Roberts Rinehart (1876–1958), published in 1906. The title refers to the lower berth and compartment number of a train's sleeping car.

15 The day described was Dorothy's seventh birthday. The two little Goldenstedt children were probably Vera and "Idochka" [Ida], both born in 1910, daughters of Mrs. Goldenstedt's sons Pavel and Vladimir, respectively.

16 Maharishi Mahesh Yogi, *On the Bhagavad-Gita: A New Translation and Commentary, Chapters 1–6* (Harmondsworth, UK: Penguin Books, 1969), 447–50; William James, *The Varieties of Religious Experience: A Study in Human Nature* (London: Longmans, Green, 1902); C. N. Alexander et al., "Growth of Higher Stages of Consciousness: Maharishi's Vedic Psychology of Human Development," in *Higher Stages of Human Development: Perspectives on Adult Growth,* ed. Charles N. Alexander and Ellen J. Langer (New York: Oxford University Press, 1990), 307–27. From the twentieth century on, recorded testimonies of Unity Consciousness include those by Albert Einstein and Eugene Ionesco. I am grateful to Ronald E. Openshaw and Michael Delahoyde for these references.

17 Vladivostok newspapers at this time regularly ran stories on Chinese gambling, prostitution, and opium rings; see, for example, *Dalekaia okraina,* April 3, 1907, OS. Two well-known writers were to confirm the anti-Chinese prejudice: Vladimir Arsen'ev, *Kitaitsy v Ussuriiskom Krae: Ocherk istorichesko-etnograficheskii* [The Chinese in the Ussuri Territory: A historical-ethnographic essay] (Khabarovsk: Zapiski Priamurskogo Otdela Imperatorskogo Russkogo Geograficheskogo Obshchestva, 1914); and Nansen, *Through Siberia,* 328–31.

18 Otto Lagerfeldt was to become the father of fashion designer Karl Otto Lagerfeld (who simplified the spelling of the family name), born in Hamburg in 1933.

19 Information from Andrei Iu. Sidorov.

20 Pasha was twenty years old at this time, born on the cusp of two calendar years: 22 December 1893, OS/3 January 1894, NS. I am grateful to Nelli G. Miz' for this and for the information in the next note.

21 Pasha's mother was Mrs. Goldenstedt's daughter Elizaveta Fedorovna (b. 1868). Her husband, Vladimir Martynovich Mitt, a veterinarian, had died in 1901.

22 Kolaika was Pasha's younger brother, Nikolai Mitt. The original letter is handwritten in Russian by Pasha and dated 18 September 1914, OS.

23 Another date has been suggested for Pavel Mitt's death, albeit not conclusively. According to archive information connected with his studies at the Military Aviation School in Gatchina, near Petersburg, and published in a Russian history journal, Pavel Mitt died on 10/23 April 1916; Ian Borisovich Ianush, "Avarii 1915–1916 gg. v Gatchinskoi Voennoi aviatsionnoi shkole" [Accidents at the Gatchina Military Aviation School, 1915–16], *ZhUK: Zhurnal liubitelei otkrytok* [Journal for lovers of postcards] 4 (2009): 37–41. The article includes two small photos of Pavel Mitt's plane after the accident. I am grateful to historian Elena N. Sergeeva for generously sharing this information.

24 Nina Bryner, born in 1895, was the sister of Boris Bryner (thus an aunt of actor Yul Bryner), their parents being Iulii (Jules) and Natal'ia Bryner. Nina's sister, mentioned in connection with the funeral, was Margarita, nicknamed Gretli.

25 Nina did not have a child with Pasha, but had two children with her second husband, Alexander S. Ostroumov, a lawyer. They were married in September 1918; their first child was named Pavel. (Information from Elena N. Sergeeva.)

26 Pasha's uncles were Georgii, Vladimir, and Pavel Goldenstedt. Excepting Nikolai, still a

teenager, Pasha's brothers were all engaged in the war. In April 1915, Vladimir Karlovich Goldenstedt petitioned officially to reclaim his father's last name, Livin, rather than using that of his stepfather, Karl Goldenstedt, and in June 1916 he thus became Vladimir Fedorovich Livin. I am grateful to Elena V. Vasil'eva for our Livin discussions.

CHAPTER 6

1   Usually called the Baltic Fleet, its official name was the Second Pacific Squadron (the ships at Port Arthur comprised the First Pacific Squadron).

2   See, for example, Oleg R. Airapetov, "The Russian Army's Fatal Flaws," in *The Russo-Japanese War in Global Perspective: World War Zero*, ed. John W. Steinberg, Bruce W. Manning, David Schimmelpenninck van der Oye, David Wolff, and Shinji Yokote (Leiden: Brill, 2005), 157–78; I. I. Rostunov, *Istoriia russko-iaponskoi voiny, 1904-05 gg.* [History of the Russo-Japanese War, 1904–5] (Moscow: Nauka, 1977); and Julian S. Corbett, *Maritime Operations in the Russo-Japanese War, 1904-5,* intr. John B. Hattendorf and Donald M. Shurman (1905; repr., Annapolis, MD: Naval Institute Press/Newport, RI: Naval War College Press, 1994).

3   Many war correspondents flocked to Manchuria for first-hand observations. See, for example, Peter Slattery, *Reporting the Russo-Japanese War, 1904-5: Lionel James's First Wireless Transmissions to "The Times"* (Folkestone, UK: Global Oriental, 2004); and Torsten Bergman, *Svensk opinion och diplomati under rysk-japanska kriget, 1904-5* [Swedish opinion and diplomacy during the Russo-Japanese War, 1904–5] (Stockholm: Svenska bokförlaget/Norstedts, 1965). Tom Standage, *The Victorian Internet: The Remarkable Story of the Telegraph and the Nineteenth Century's On-Line Pioneers* (New York: Berkley Books, 1998) offers an engaging overview of the swift news-sharing possibilities of that time. Still, Vice Admiral Togo's wife did not know where her husband was until she read it in the newspapers; Denis Warner and Peggy Warner, *The Tide at Sunrise: A History of the Russo-Japanese War, 1904-5* (New York: Charterhouse, 1974), 203. And after the Battle of Tsushima, Sarah Smith wrote in exasperation from Shanghai to Eleanor in Vladivostok: "Received your No. 9 postcard on Monday last. . . . I see your postal was dated May 30th and you never mentioned the loss of the Baltic fleet. I really wonder if they had not given you the news then? The battle was on the 27th" (12 July 1905 from Sarah to Eleanor).

4   Edwin Sharpe Grew, *The War in the Far East, 1904-5, by the Military Correspondent of "The Times"* (New York: E. P. Dutton, 1905), 25.

5   Sarah had gone to see her friends the Ivys in Shanghai in February 1905, and was unable to return to Vladivostok until mid-December 1905, more than three months after peace was declared.

6   Ivanov is a very common Russian last name, and this was a different Ivanov family than that of Engineer Ivan Vasilievich Ivanov of the *Rurik*.

7   The deadline for answers to Japan's proposals of August 1903, concerning Russian and Japanese positions in Manchuria and Korea, was set for October 1903. The two countries were completely unable to come to terms: "In this highly charged atmosphere it was scarcely possible that war could be avoided"; Corbett, *Maritime Operations*, 42.

8   Japan broke off diplomatic relations with Russia at 4 PM on 5 February 1904 (Saint Peters-

burg time; almost midnight in Japan), but the attacks on Port Arthur and at Chemulpo occurred before war was declared. Russia's declaration against Japan came on 9 February; Japan's against Russia followed the next day.

9 Corbett, *Maritime Operations*, 48.

10 Lieutenant Vladimir Semenov of the *Diana*, who saw the *Petropavlovsk* go down, cited in Warner, *Tide at Sunrise*, 240.

11 Rostunov, *Istoriia russko-iaponskoi voiny*, 248; Warner, *Tide at Sunrise*, 440.

12 War correspondent Robert L. Dunn was one of very few taking photos of the destroyed Russian ships at Chemulpo; *The Russo-Japanese War: A Photographic and Descriptive Review of the Great Conflict in the Far East, Gathered from the Reports, Records, Cable Despatches* [sic], *Photographs, etc., etc., of Collier's War Correspondents*, Richard Harding Davis, Frederick Palmer, James F. J. Archibald, Robert L. Dunn, Ellis Ashmead Bartlett, James H. Hare, Henry James Whigham, and Victor K. Bulla (New York: P. F. Collier & Son, 1905). The Battle of Chemulpo Bay took place in the afternoon of 9 February 1904. The gunboat *Koreets* was blown up, but the protected cruiser *Variag*, although scuttled, was not. Her captain of the first rank, Vsevolod Rudnev (1855–1913), was the last to leave the ship, injured but alive.

13 Mrs. Pray is confusing the use of semaphores (signaling messages with flags) with that of megaphones (shouting messages).

14 The merchantmen were the *Nakamaura-Maru* and the *Goye-Maru*; the transport the *Kinsiu-Maru*.

15 Sydney Tyler, *The Japan-Russia War: An Illustrated History of the War in the Far East: The Greatest Conflict of Modern Times* (Philadelphia: P. W. Ziegler, 1905), 104.

16 Sydney Tyler mentions the same calculation; Tyler, *Japan-Russia War*, 106.

17 Two of the Japanese transports were the *Idzumi-Maru* and the *Hitachi*; Corbett, *Maritime Operations*, 284–87.

18 Dr. Stein's note refers to the battle described in the next entry; his letter is in Russian and dated 4 August 1904, OS.

19 This was the Battle of the Korea Strait (not the more famous Battle of Tsushima).

20 The *Novik* could do twenty-five knots, compared to, for example, the twenty-three knots of the similarly-sized *Variag* or the twenty knots of the *Pallada*; Rostunov, *Istoriia russko-iaponskoi voiny*, 81; Tyler, *Japan-Russia War*, 44.

21 Aleksei Nikolaevich Kuropatkin (1848–1925) was Russia's minister of war, and the Russian commander in Manchuria. His counterpart in the Battle of Liao-yang was general Kuroki Tamemoto (1844–1923), commander of the Imperial Japanese First Army.

22 The lyrics by "Skitalets" (Stepan Petrov) were added later and have been rewritten (by others) several times. This waltz is used prominently in Nikita Mikhal'kov's 1993 film *Urga* (in English, *Close to Eden*).

23 After the enormous losses at Mukden, General Kuropatkin was replaced on 17 March 1905 by General Linevich.

24 Admiral Fel'kerzam was ill through most of the voyage from Russia, and died on 25 May on board the *Osliabia*. His body was kept frozen and went down with his ship in the battle.

25 The toast to Sarah's "glorious twin Teddy" referred to the fact that she and president Teddy Roosevelt were born on the same day, 27 October 1858. Mr. Clarkson loved one of Dom

Smith's former *amahs*, O Hiro-san, whom he married in 1908; thus his special enthusiasm for the Japanese toasts.

26 Translation from German: "But it was not dear God, Dad, it was Linevich!"

27 Rear admiral Karl von Iessen (1852–1918) commanded the Vladivostok squadron after Skrydlov.

28 See also Vadim L. Agapov, "Sdany bez boia: Razoruzhenie i internirovanie korablei ros- siiskogo flota v inostrannykh portakh, 1904–5 gg." [Surrendered without a fight: Disarma- ment and internment of the Russian Navy's ships in foreign ports, 1904–5], *Rossiia i ATR* 3 (2000): 148–55.

CHAPTER 7

1 Several times in this chapter, Mrs. Pray uses the Russian word for "store," *magazin*. For a few years the American Store was in the P'iankov House on the corner of Svetlanskaia and the stairs leading up to Dom Smith (rather than in Dom Smith itself, as it had been before and would be again later). The Prays were worried about general ransacking, as well as about the possible theft of arms.

2 This circus, named the Boroviks, was located on the south side of Tiger Hill.

3 The English translation of Lothar Deeg's book about K&A contains an impressive gallery of sixty (unnumbered) pages of photos, including some that show the enormous destruction suffered by the store in the riots; *Kunst and Albers Vladivostok: The History of a German Trading Company in the Russian Far East (1864–1924)*, trans. Sarah Bohnet (DVFU, 2012).

4 All the stores mentioned were in the same general area of central Vladivostok as Dom Smith.

5 This faithful old servant was referring to Mr. Lindholm, the master of the house.

6 A. I. Krushanov, ed., *Istoriia Dal'nego Vostoka SSSR v epokhu fedodalizma i kapitalizma (XVII v.-fevral' 1917 g.)* [History of the Far East of the USSR during the epoch of feudalism and capitalism (seventeenth century–February 1917)] (Moscow: Nauka, 1991), 340–47; Stephan, *Russian Far East*, 101–3.

7 Liudmila Alexandrovna Vol'kenstein (1857–1906) was active in revolutionary groups in the late 1870s, including the People's Will movement, and was implicated in the 1879 murder of prince Dmitrii Kropotkin, the governor of Kharkov Province. After exile in Europe, she returned to Russia and was almost immediately included in the "Trial of 14" (1884) for People's Will activities led by Vera Figner (1852–1942). Their death sentences were commuted to fifteen years of hard labor at the notorious Schlüsselburg Fortress, situ- ated in the Neva near Lake Ladoga. (The Peter and Paul Fortress, where Mrs. Vol'kenstein was not confined, is in Saint Petersburg).

CHAPTER 8

1 German troops invaded neutral Belgium on 4 August, prompting Britain's entry into the war.

2 Affectionately called by her patronymic, "daughter of Grigorii," Grigorievna was a servant at the Novogeorgievsk Estate.

3   Eleanor Pray's assessment was hauntingly prescient, but with a peaceful twist. This was the very day when just a few hours later (accounting for the different time zones), French, British, and German troops near Ypres in Belgium would step across the muddy fields between their trenches, share Christmas greetings, and sing "Silent Night" together. This brief cessation of hostilities, known as "The Christmas Truce," has been portrayed in books and films, for example, in *Joyeux Noël* (by French director Christian Carion, 2005).

4   This city, today called Pila, is located in northwestern Poland.

5   Music, often practiced by choirs or amateur orchestras, became an acknowledged tool in the fight for survival both at the front lines and in the rapidly growing refugee and prisoner-of-war camps; Frederick Harris, ed., *Service with Fighting Men: An Account of the Work of the American Young Men's Christian Association in the World War*, vol. 2 (New York: Association Press, 1922), 272.

6   The names of the two revolutions reflect their dates according to the Julian Calendar: 23–27 February and 25 October.

7   The German-sounding name of Russia's northern capital, Sankt-Peterburg, was translated into the Russian Petrograd at the beginning of the war; but Eleanor Pray, like many, continued to call it Petersburg.

8   One of three ships named the USS *Brooklyn*, this armored cruiser was launched in October 1895 and had participated in the Spanish-American War of 1898. It was the flagship of the US Pacific Fleet from 1915 until its decommission in early 1921.

9   Khromov, S. S., ed., "Interventsiia Antanty na Dal'nem Vostoke" [Intervention of the Entente in the Far East], in *Grazhdanskaia voina i voennaia interventsiia v SSSR: Entsiklopediia* [The Civil War and the military intervention in the USSR: An encyclopedia], 2nd ed. (Moscow: Sovetskaia Entsiklopediia, 1987), 229.

10   Stephan, *Russian Far East*, 111.

11   Taking into account his son Aleksei's hemophilia, Nikolai II abdicated in favor of his brother Mikhail. The first Mikhail Romanov had gained the Russian throne in 1613. The Russian and French words mean "citizen" and "citizeness."

12   That is, the public prosecutor of the district (*okrug*) military court.

13   Almost thirty thousand people participated in this demonstration after a mass in the cathedral. It was offered in memory of those fallen in protest against the tsar's government, especially in the upheavals of 1905–6.

14   The Industrial Workers of the World were organized in Chicago in 1905 as a joint labor union of skilled and unskilled manual workers. Its objective was to overthrow capitalism in order to build a new society based on socialist principles.

15   An admiral in the US Navy, Austin M. Knight (1854–1927) was commander in chief of the US Asiatic Fleet from 1917 to 1918.

16   W. Bruce Lincoln, *Red Victory: A History of the Russian Civil War* (New York: Simon and Schuster, 1989), 236.

17   William S. Graves, *America's Siberian Adventure, 1918-1920* (New York: Jonathan Cape & Harrison Smith, 1931), 5, 7, 8, 9. The Aide-Mémoire, issued by Secretary of State Lansing, was written by President Wilson. The abbreviation "MOOTW" (military operations other than war), occasionally used in Iraq, reflected a similar situation. I thank lieutenant colonel Charles Ramsay for this point, shared with me in 2006.

18 George F. Kennan's belief that President Wilson had neither interest in nor knowledge about Russia is refuted by David S. Foglesong. See George F. Kennan, *Soviet-American Relations, 1917-20: Russia Leaves the War* (Princeton, NJ: Princeton University Press, 1956), 28; and David S. Foglesong, *America's Secret War against Bolshevism: US Intervention in the Russian Civil War* (Chapel Hill: University of North Carolina Press, 1995).

19 Graves, *America's Siberian Adventure*, 354.

20 This Mrs. C. H. Smith was the wife of the US representative on the Inter-Allied Railway Committee (not Sarah, whose husband Charles had the same initials). Before leaving in 1922, the Smiths rented part of the Lindholm house from the Tyrtovs.

21 Ekaterina K. Breshko-Breshkovskaia (1844–1934) was a leader of Russia's Socialist Revolutionary Party (the SRs), who was leaving Russia at this time. Referring to Breshko-Breshkovskaia's time in prison, labor camp, and internal exile from 1874 to 1896, Eleanor added: "The 'Grandmother of the Russian Revolution' must be pretty well disgusted with her grandchild—the old régime only kept her in prison but this *bolsheviki* outfit would kill her if they could get hold of her" (6 December 1918 to Clara).

22 Speculating sarcastically that "A. R. Williams, John Reed and Louise whoever she is" would approve of bullets dipped in poison, Mrs. Pray called them traitors (11 July 1919 to Aunt Anna). John Reed's common-law wife, Louise Bryant, was a journalist. For Williams's account of his visit to Vladivostok, see Albert Rhys Williams, *Through the Russian Revolution* (New York: Monthly Review Press, 1921), 218–67.

23 For biographies of the famous Josip Broz, see, for example, Vladimir Dedijer, *Tito* (New York: Simon & Schuster, 1953); Phyllis Auty, *Tito: A Biography* (New York: McGraw-Hill, 1970); and Svetolik Mitic, *Mladost Josipa Broza* [Josip Broz's youth] (Beograd: NIP Mladost, 1978). Because there is a gap in Tito's biography during late 1919 and into January 1920 (known as his "Kirghiz" period), one might wonder if he made his way to Vladivostok then. He had worked on the Trans-Siberian Railway, had certain Red Cross connections, and might have been able to travel back and forth with the help of old acquaintances. However, despite Mrs. Pray's later identification of Tito as the Josip Broz whom she knew and met, with his wife (e.g., 10 November 1919, and 24 February 1920), she herself clearly gave this man's nationality as Czech, his title as "the Czech High Commissioner," and his civil status as married, whereas Tito was Croatian and married (the first time) only in January 1920. Professor doctor Anton Bebler of the University of Ljubljana, who "accompanied President Tito as a secretary of the Yugoslav state delegation to Moscow, Japan, Siberia, Mongolia and Central Asia" in 1968, confirms: "During the trip [Tito] mentioned his stay almost 50 years earlier in Eastern Siberia and in what is now N. Kazakhstan, but never in Far East [sic] and Vladivostok"; Anton Bebler to Birgitta Ingemanson, letter, 25 March 1998. I am very grateful to Professor Bebler, as well as to Professors Charles Jelavich and Peter Vodopivec, who kindly discussed this question with me.

24 D. A. Ancha, V. I. Kalinin, and T. Z. Pozniak, *Vladivostok v fotografiiakh Merrilla Khaskella, 11 avgusta 1919–23 fevralia 1920/Vladivostok in the Photos of Merrill Haskell, August 11, 1919–February 23, 1920*, trans. Z. Proshina, English text ed. B. Ingemanson ([Khabarovsk:] RIOTIP, 2009), 12–13 (Russian), 15–16 (English).

25 A thank-you letter from Admiral Knight, 18 June 1918, reads,

I am writing to thank you for the translations you have made for us and to assure you of my very high appreciation of your kindness and consideration with them and your willingness to be of further assistance. I am sure there is no one else in Vladivostok as well qualified as you are for this work—certainly there is no one else who could put the material into such good English.

I have a man in view who will, I think, be able to translate the current news for me but I do not think he could give me anything that I should care to send to Washington without re-writing it, whereas your material can be put on the typewriter as it stands and go to the President himself, if necessary. For this reason I shall continue to call for your help in cases of special importance.

I hope to have the pleasure of thanking you in person as soon as you return to town [from the *dacha*].

With kind regards
very cordially y[ours]
Austin M. Knight.

26 Terence Emmons, ed., *Time of Troubles: The Diary of Iurii Vladimirovich Got'e, Moscow, 8 July 1917 to 23 July 1922* (Princeton, NJ: Princeton University Press, 1988), 222. Eleanor Pray did not know Professor Got'e [Gautier], chief librarian of the Rumiantsev Museum in Moscow, but she would have liked his erudite, droll, often sarcastic style. His views on Russia's fate were very similar to hers.

27 This was the *Iwami*, soon followed by the British HMS *Suffolk*, and, on 18 January 1918, the Japanese *Asahi*.

28 Mrs. Pray refers here to the phrase "between the devil [i.e., the socialists] and the deep blue sea."

29 A few days earlier, on 13 February 1918, Professor Got'e had noted, facetiously, that "All the talk is about Mr. Trotsky's notorious 'peace,'" and expressed dismay with its ratification on this day; Emmons, *Time of Troubles*, 106, 111. The very first words of his diary, on 8 July 1917, are *"Finis Russiae"* (Latin for "Russia's End, " or "Russia is finished"), 27.

30 Robert Hodgson (1874–1956), British diplomat, was appointed commercial agent to Vladivostok in 1906, vice-consul in 1908, and served as consul in 1911–19. His wife Olga was Russian.

31 By contrast, Albert Rhys-Williams was friendly with Sukhanov: "He was small in stature, but great in energy"; Williams, *Through the Russian Revolution*, 222–23. The Czechs arrested Sukhanov on 29 June; he was shot on 17 November 1918.

32 Alexander Kerenskii (1881–1970) was Prime Minister of Russia from July 1917 until the October Revolution 1917.

33 See similar information in, e.g., Rex A. Wade, *The Triumph of Bolshevism, 1917-19*, vol. 1, *Documents of Soviet History* (Gulf Breeze, FL: Academic International Press, 1991), 419–20; and Viktor Agoshkov, "Kolchakovskie 'Sibirki' (Iz istorii obestsenivaniia deneg)" [Kolchak's "sibirki" (From the history of the depreciation of money)], *Vladivostok*, April 8, 1993.

34 Unique photos of the Gaida uprising taken by the YMCA secretary Merrill Haskell can be found in Ancha et al., *Vladivostok v fotografiiakh*, 250–67.

35 This program with Rudolf Karel (1880–1945) included pieces by Tchaikovsky, the overture to *Tannhäuser*, Smetana's "Vltava," and Moussorgsky's "Night on Bald Mountain."

36 This elegant structure is now the Administration Building of Far Eastern Federal [formerly State] University.

37 Canfield F. Smith, *Vladivostok under Red and White Rule: Revolution and Counterrevolution in the Russian Far East, 1920-22* (Seattle: University of Washington Press, 1975), xiv.

38 Letter from Warren H. Langdon to Helen J. Fitzgerald, 15 July 1919; USS *Albany* web site managed by L. D. Mayo, "Mayo Postal History." Commas added by Birgitta Ingemanson.

39 The hugely popular adventure story set during the French Revolution, *The Scarlet Pimpernel* (1903) by Hungarian-born Baroness Orczy (1865–1947), was followed in 1919 by *The League of the Scarlet Pimpernel*. The French phrase *faute de mieux* translates as "for lack of anything better to do."

40 Mrs. Pray did mean to use the abbreviated form of "Japanese" to show her condescension and disdain.

41 This was the Merkulov uprising. Spiridon and Nikolai Merkulov, co-owners of the match factory at Sedanka, came to power in what became known as the Provisional Government of Priamur'e.

42 Grigorii Mikhailovich Semenov (1890–1946), a Cossack supported by the Japanese, was known for his extraordinary cruelty.

43 By "Gruzians" Mrs. Pray means the inhabitants of the now independent country on the Black Sea, Georgia (in Russian, Gruzia).

CHAPTER 9

1 The 19th Verst station was so named due to its being located nineteen *verst* (approximately 12.5 miles) from Vladivostok.

2 Mrs. P'iankova's first name was Nadezhda; her name-day was on 30 September.

3 After Adolph Dattan's death in 1924, Alfred Albers became the store's sole owner; Deeg, *Kunst and Albers Vladivostok*, 344.

4 On "municipalization," see Sheila Fitzpatrick, *Everyday Stalinism: Ordinary Life in Extraordinary Times: Soviet Russia in the 1930s* (New York: Oxford University Press, 1999), 46.

5 The *dacha* was registered to N. A. P'iankova, address Proseka [the path through the woods], house 9/11; I. S. Klark, ed., *Ves' delovoi i torgovyi Vladivostok na 1924 g.* [All of Vladivostok's business and trade for 1924] (Vladivostok: *Krasnoe znamia*, 1924), 105.

6 The GPU was the Gosudarstvennoe Politicheskoe Upravlenie, the State Political Directorate, or "secret police."

7 Documents in the Eleanor L. Pray Collection suggest that Dorothy was eventually reimbursed by the US Department of State for the loss of Dom Smith.

8 Ulf Lundell, "Öppna landskap" [Open landscapes] (Stockholm: EMI Svenska AB, 1982) The Swedish line is *Ja är ja, och nej är nej, och tvivlet tiger still*.

9 Here, Mrs. Pray used the word "facetious" in its meaning of "droll, funny." The film *On the High Seas*, directed by Irvin Willat (USA, 1922), was billed as an adventure-romance.

10 Interview with Alexandra ("Shura") Stefanovna Kaspars, née Zhebrovskaia, by Birgitta

Ingemanson, 29 May 1993, Seattle. After recounting this memory, Alexandra Stefanovna paused, then said, "I couldn't imagine that twenty years later I would arrive in L'vov in Poland, barefoot, and as ragged as she was." I am grateful to Marina Tolmacheva and L. Tret'iakova for arranging this meeting.

11 Along with all the variations of Russian money, Japanese yen (and sen) were also used at this time.

12 A *liman* is a lake by a river's estuary.

13 These initials indicate Sarah, Dorothy, Vanda Newhard, and Jenny Unterberger (EEP remains unidentified).

14 The building became an institute of physical therapy, 1930–56, and from 1957 a hospital devoted to physical healing methods; Obertas et al., *Pamiatniki istorii i kul'tury*, 32.

15 This was probably one of the ten novels for young women depicting the adventures of "Aunt Jane's Nieces." They were written by L. Frank Baum under the pseudonym Edith Van Dyne between 1906 and 1918.

16 Eleanor Pray met the famous scientist Vladimir K. Arsen'ev several times: "I love to meet him in company" (6 June 1929 to Home). Georg K. Junghändel, a German-born, naturalized Russian subject, was a prominent architect in Vladivostok, designing, among other buildings, the Kunst and Albers department store, the Lutheran Church, and the Bryner mansion.

17 The buildings at the Bryner estate in Sidemi were eventually destroyed, and only ruins remain of the mausoleum. However, some of the old photographs are included in Rock Brynner's book *Empire and Odyssey*.

18 Mrs. Pray often sought comfort in the novels of Maud Diver (1867–1945), with whom she also corresponded. Taking place in India under British rule, they include *The Great Amulet* (1909) and *Desmond's Daughter* (1916).

19 Leonid Sobinov (1872–1934) was a beloved Russian tenor.

20 The aria "Where, Oh, Where Did You Go?" is from *Eugene Onegin* by Peter Tchaikovsky, and "When You Understood Me" is a romance by L. Dentsa.

21 A German patriotic song from the mid-1800s, "The Watch on the Rhine" reflects the military rivalries between Germany and France. It was particularly popular during the Franco-Prussian War of 1870–71 and during World War I.

Bibliography

DVGU Far Eastern State University, Vladivostok (name changed in 2010 to DVFU Far Eastern Federal University)
DVGTU Far Eastern State Technological University, Vladivostok
OIAK Society for the Study of the Amur Territory, Vladivostok
PGOM The Vladimir K. Arseniev State Museum of Primorie

PRIMARY SOURCES

Forsyth, J. Oswald. Archive. J. Oswald Forsyth, Vladivostok. File 9, "Private Correspondence, 1913–1920." Riksarkivet [National Archives], Stockholm.
[Greener, Richard T.] "Despatches [sic] from United States Consuls in Vladivostok, 1898–1906." Lawrence: University of Kansas Libraries, 1963. Microform.
Pray, Eleanor Lord. Collection. Letters and diaries, 1894–1930. Library of Congress.
———. Collection. Photo albums, scrapbooks, birthday book, 1894–1931. Family archives of Patricia Dunn Silver, Sarasota, Florida.
———. Photo album, 1899. Library of Congress.
———. Two photo albums, 1899, 1904. PGOM.
State Archive of the Maritime Territory. Newspapers *Dalekaia okraina* and *Dal'nii Vostok*, 1890s–1900s.
Vladimir K. Arseniev State Museum, Vladivostok. Maps of Vladivostok and Primorie, 1860s–1930.

SECONDARY SOURCES

Agapov, Vadim L. "Sdany bez boia: Razoruzhenie i internirovanie korablei rossiiskogo flota v inostrannykh portakh, 1904–1905 gg." [Surrendered without a fight: Disarmament and internment of the Russian Navy's ships in foreign ports, 1904–1905]. *Rossiia i ATR* 3 (2000): 148–55.
Agoshkov, Viktor. "Kolchakovskie 'Sibirki' (Iz istorii obestsenivaniia deneg)" [Kolchak's "sibirki" (From the history of the depreciation of money)]. *Vladivostok*, April 8, 1993.

Airapetov, Oleg R. "The Russian Army's Fatal Flaws." In *The Russo-Japanese War in Global Perspective: World War Zero,* edited by John W. Steinberg, Bruce W. Manning, David Schimmelpenninck van der Oye, David Wolff, and Shinji Yokote. Leiden: Brill, 2005.

Aiushin, N. *Zhemchuzhina Zolotogo roga/The Golden Horn Pearl.* In Russian and English. Translated by M. Nemtsov. Vladivostok: Ussuri, 1992.

Aiushin, N. B., V. I. Kalinin, S. A. Vorob'ev, and N. V. Gavrilkin. *Vladivostokskaia krepost'* [The Vladivostok Fortress]. Vladivostok: Dal'nauka, 2006.

Alexander, C. N., et al. "Growth of Higher Stages of Consciousness: Maharishi's Vedic Psychology of Human Development." In *Higher Stages of Human Development: Perspectives on Adult Growth,* edited by Charles N. Alexander and Ellen J. Langer. New York: Oxford University Press, 1990.

Aleksandrovskaia, Larisa V. *Mgnoveniia Karla Shul'tsa* [Moments of Carl Schoultz]. Katalog, 22–28 noiabria 2001 goda [Catalogue, 22–28 November, 2001]. OIAK, 2002.

———. *Odisseia Fridol'fa Geka* [The odyssey of Fridolf Höök]. Vladivostok: Russkoe Geograficheskoe Obshchestvo, 1999.

———. *Opyt pervogo morskogo pereseleniia v Iuzhno-Ussuriiskii krai v 60–kh godakh XIX veka* [Experiences of the first migration by sea to the South Ussuri Territory in the 1860s]. DVGU, 1990.

———. *Tikhookeanskaia trilogiia. Knigi 1 i 2* [Pacific trilogy, books 1–2]. OIAK, 2003. One-volume reprint of *Opyt pervogo morskogo pereseleniia v Iuzhno-Ussuriiskii krai v 60–kh godakh XIX veka* and *Odisseia Fridol'fa Geka.* [Experiences of the first migration by sea to the South Ussuri Territory in the 1860s; The odyssey of Fridolf Höök].

———. *Vladivostok: Nachalo biografii* [Beginning of a biography]. DVGU, OIAK, 2010.

Aleksandrovskaia, L[arisa], and B[irgitta] Ingemanson. *Fotografiia na pamiat': Otto Lindgol'm i ego okruzhenie, 1890-e-1920-e gody/Photos for the Memories: Otto Lindholm and His Circle, 1890s–1920s.* Exhibit catalogue, in Russian and English by the authors. PGOM, 2005.

Aleksandrovskaia, Larisa, and Birgitta Ingemanson. *Udivitel'naia zhizn' Otto Lindgol'ma: Dokumental'no-istoricheskoe povestvovanie* [The remarkable life of Otto Lindholm: A documentary-historical narrative]. OIAK, PGOM, 2003.

Aleksiuk, Galina, ed. *Iankovskie chteniia: Materialy IV-V mezhdunarodnykh nauchno-prakticheskikh konferentsii, 1998–2000 gg.* [Jankowski readings: Materials from the fourth and fifth international scientific-practical conferences, 1998–2000]. PGOM, DVGU, 2003.

Ancha, D. A., V. I. Kalinin, and T. Z. Pozniak. *Vladivostok v fotografiiakh Merrilla Khaskella, 11 avgusta 1919–23 fevralia 1920/Vladivostok in the Photos of Merrill Haskell, August 11, 1919–February 23, 1920.* In Russian and English. Translated by Z. Proshina. English text edited by B. Ingemanson. [Khabarovsk:] RIOTIP, 2009.

Arsen'ev, Vladimir. *Kitaitsy v Ussuriiskom Krae: Ocherk istoricheshко-etnograficheskii* [The Chinese in the Ussuri Territory: A historical-ethnographic essay]. Khabarovsk: Zapiski Priamurskogo Otdela Imperatorskogo Russkogo Geograficheskogo Obshchestva, 1914.

Auty, Phyllis. *Tito: A Biography.* New York: McGraw-Hill, 1970.

Azulay, Erik, and Allegra Azulay. *The Russian Far East.* New York: Hippocrene Books, 1995.

Back to the Future. Edited by Michael Lennikov. Vladivostok: Far-Eastern Shipping Company, n.d. [c. 1992].

Barr, Pat. *A Curious Life for a Lady: The Story of Isabella Bird.* London: Macmillan, John Murray, 1970.

Beecher, Catharine E., and Harriet Beecher Stowe. *The American Woman's Home, or, Principles of Domestic Science, Being a Guide to the Formation and Maintenance of Economical, Healthful, Beautiful, and Christian Homes.* 1869. Reprint, Watkins Glen, NY: Library of Victorian Culture, American Life Foundation, 1979.

Belousov, A. A. *Na altar' otechestva: Iz istorii metsenatstva i blagotvoritel'nosti v Rossii* [On the altar of the Fatherland: From the history of patronage and philanthropy in Russia]. DVGU, 1996.

Berchanskaia, Liubov'. "Samyi istinnyi portret Vladivostoka" [The most truthful portrait of Vladivostok]. *Vladivostok*, no. 2428, October 28, 2008, 6.

Bergman, Torsten. *Svensk opinion och diplomati under rysk-japanska kriget, 1904–5* [Swedish opinion and diplomacy during the Russo-Japanese War, 1904–5]. Stockholm: Svenska bokförlaget/Norstedts, 1965.

Bishop, Isabella Bird. *Korea and Her Neighbors: A Narrative of Travel, with an Account of the Recent Vicissitudes and Present Position of the Country.* New York: Fleming H. Revell, 1898.

Blakely, Allison. "Richard T. Greener and the 'Talented Tenth's' Dilemma." *Journal of Negro History* 59, no. 4 (October 1974): 305–21.

———. "Black US Consuls and Diplomats and Black Leadership, 1880–1920." *Umoja: A Scholarly Journal of Black Studies* 1, no. 1 (Spring 1977): 1–16.

Bogdanov, D. *Putevoditel' po Vladivostoku i Promyslu Primorskoi oblasti, Kamchatki i Sakhalina* [Guidebook on Vladivostok and on trade in the Primorie Oblast', Kamchatka and Sakhalin]. Vladivostok: Izd. Bogdanova i Drobinskogo, 1909.

Boiko-Pavlov, D. I., and E. P. Sodorchuk. *Tak bylo na Dal'nem Vostoke* [It was like this in the Far East]. Moscow: Mysl', 1964.

Brooks, Jeffrey. *Thank You, Comrade Stalin! Soviet Public Culture from Revolution to Cold War.* Princeton, NJ: Princeton University Press, 2000.

Brynner, Rock. *Empire and Odyssey: The Brynners in Far East Russia and Beyond.* Hanover, NH: Steerforth Press, 2006.

Buxhoevden, Sophie. *The Life and Tragedy of Alexandra Feodorovna, Empress of Russia.* New York: Longmans, Green, 1928.

Chekhov, Anton. *Letters of Anton Chekhov.* Translated by Michael Henry Heim, with Simon Karlinsky; selection, commentary, and introduction by Simon Karlinsky. New York: Harper & Row, 1973.

Chernyakova, Nonna. "Harvard's First Black Graduate Left Imprint on Far East." *Vladivostok News: Focus* 197, October 8, 1999, 1.

Chesunov, Sergei. "Lomat'—ne stroit'" [To break is not to build]. *Vechernii Vladivostok*, July 17, 1990, 7.

Cook, Mary J. Straw, ed. *Immortal Summer: A Victorian Woman's Travels in the Southwest: The 1897 Letters and Photographs of Amelia Hollenback.* Santa Fe: Museum of New Mexico Press, 2002.

Corbett, Julian S. *Maritime Operations in the Russo-Japanese War, 1904–5.* Introduction by John B. Hattendorf and Donald M. Shurman. 1905. Reprint, Annapolis, MD: Naval Institute Press/Newport, RI: Naval War College Press, 1994.

Dal'nevostochnyi gosudarstvennyi universitet: Istoriia i sovremennost', 1899–1999 [Far Eastern State University: History and the present, 1899–1999]. Edited by Vladimir I. Kurilov, E. V. Ermakova, and R. M. Samigulin. DVGU, 1999.

Davis, A. R. *T'ao Yüan-ming, AD 365–427: His Works and Their Meaning.* Cambridge, UK: Cambridge University Press, 1983.

Davydoff, Mariamna. *Memoirs of a Russian Lady: Drawings and Tales of Life before the Revolution.* New York: Harry N. Abrams, 1986.

Dawson, Horace G., Jr. "From the Director's Desk." *The Globe: A Ralph J. Bunche International Affairs Center* 2, no. 1 (Summer 1998): 7.

Dedijer, Vladimir. *Tito.* New York: Simon & Schuster, 1953.

Deeg, Lothar. *Kunst und Albers in Wladiwostok: Die Geschichte eines deutschen Handelshauses im russischen Fernen Osten, 1864–1924* [Kunst and Albers in Vladivostok: The history of a German trading house in the Russian Far East, 1864–1924]. Essen: Klartext-Verlag, 1996. Published in English, with an additional sixty pages of remarkable photos, as Lothar Deeg, *Kunst and Albers Vladivostok: The History of a German Trading Company in the Russian Far East (1864–1924),* translated by Sarah Bohnet, DVFU, 2012.

D'iachenko, Boris A. *Krai Rossii: Vladivostok/Vladivostok: The Edge of Russia.* In Russian and English. Translated by Max Nemtsov. Vladivostok: Voron, 1994.

———. *Staryi Vladivostok/Old Vladivostok.* In Russian and English. Translated by Alexander Mel'nikov. Vladivostok: Utro Rossii, 1992.

Dicharov, Zakhar L. *Rasskaz o gorode i cheloveke* [Story of a city and a person]. Vladivostok: Primorskoe Knizhnoe Izdatel'stvo, 1960.

Diment, Galya, and Yuri Slezkine, eds. *Between Heaven and Hell: The Myth of Siberia in Russian Culture.* New York: St. Martin's Press, 1993.

Eleonora Lord Prei: Pis'ma iz Vladivostoka, 1894–1930 [Eleanor Lord Pray: Letters from Vladivostok, 1894–1930]. Edited, with introductions, by Birgitta Ingemanson. Translated by A. A. Sapelkin. Vladivostok: Rubezh, 2008. Citations from 3rd ed., 2011. This book was translated into Russian from the first manuscript of *Letters from Vladivostok.* The present English volume is substantially revised and abbreviated.

Elesh, Viacheslav M. *Na beregakh Volgi i Tikhogo okeana* [On the shores of the Volga and the Pacific Ocean]. Moscow: Sovetskaia Rossiia, 1970.

Emmons, Terence, ed. *Time of Troubles: The Diary of Iurii Vladimirovich Got'e, Moscow, 8 July 1917 to 23 July 1922.* Princeton, NJ: Princeton University Press, 1988.

Ermakova, E. V., et al., eds. *Primorskii Krai: Kratkii entsiklopedicheskii spravochnik* [The Maritime Territory: Brief encyclopedic reference work]. DVGU, 1997.

Everett, Marshall. *Exciting Experiences in the Japanese-Russian War.* N.p.: Henry Neil, 1904.

Findlay, John, and Dorothy Findlay. "Letters from Vladivostok, 1918–1923." Edited by Dorothy Galton and John Keep. *Slavonic Review* 45 (July 1967): 497–530.

Fitzpatrick, Sheila. *Everyday Stalinism: Ordinary Life in Extraordinary Times: Soviet Russia in the 1930s.* New York: Oxford University Press, 1999.

Foglesong, David S. *America's Secret War against Bolshevism: US Intervention in the Russian Civil War.* Chapel Hill: University of North Carolina Press, 1995.

Gernsheim, Alison. *Fashion and Reality.* London: Faber and Faber, 1963.

Graffy, Julian. "Unshelving Stalin after the Period of Stagnation." In *Stalinism and the Soviet Cinema*, edited by Richard Taylor and Derek Spring. London: Routledge, 1993.

Graham, Loren, and Jean-Michel Kantor. "'Soft' Area Studies versus 'Hard' Social Science: A False Opposition." *Slavic Review* 66, no. 1 (Spring 2007): 1, 17.

Graves, William S. *America's Siberian Adventure, 1918–1920*. New York: Jonathan Cape & Harrison Smith, 1931.

Grazhdanskaia voina i voennaia interventsiia v SSSR: Entsiklopediia [The civil war and military intervention in the USSR: Encyclopedia]. Edited by S. S. Khromov. 2nd ed. Moscow: Sovetskaia Entsiklopediia, 1987.

Green, Harvey, with Mary-Ellen Perry. *The Light of the Home: An Intimate View of the Lives of Women in Victorian America*. New York: Pantheon Books, 1983.

"Greener, Richard Theodore." *Harvard Class of 1870, 25th Anniversary Report* (Cambridge, MA: Harvard College, 1895), 25–28.

———. *50th Anniversary Report* (Cambridge, MA: Harvard College, 1920), 66–67.

[Greener, R. T.]. "For Good Government and Urban Politics: The Career of R. T. Greener '70." *Harvard Alumni Bulletin* (12 December 1964): 267.

Grew, Edwin Sharpe. *The War in the Far East, 1904–5. By the military correspondent of "The Times."* New York: E. P. Dutton, 1905.

Hamm, Michael F. *Kiev: A Portrait, 1800–1917*. Princeton, NJ: Princeton University Press, 1993.

Harris, Frederick, ed. *Service with Fighting Men: An Account of the Work of the American Young Men's Christian Association in the World War*. Vol. 2. New York: Association Press, 1922.

Harrison, E. J. *Peace or War East of Baikal?* Yokohama: Kelly & Walsh, [1910].

Hellbeck, Jochen. *Revolution on My Mind: Writing a Diary under Stalin*. Cambridge, MA: Harvard University Press, 2006.

Hudgins, Sharon. *The Other Side of Russia: A Slice of Life in Siberia and the Russian Far East*. College Station: Texas A&M University Press, 2003.

Hunter-Stiebel, Penelope. *Hesse: A Princely German Collection*. Portland, OR: Portland Art Museum, 2005.

Iankovskaia, Viktoriia. *Po stranam rasseianiia: Stikhotvoreniia, proza* [Around scattered countries: Poems, prose]. Vladivostok: Rubezh, 1993.

Iankovskie, Iurii i Valerii. *Nenuni: Dal'nevostochnaia odisseia* [Nenuni: A Far Eastern odyssey]. One-volume reprint of Iurii Iankovskii, *Polveka okhoty na tigrov* [A half-century of tiger hunts], and Valerii Iankovskii, *Nenuni* [Nenuni] and *Koreiskie novelly* [Korean stories]. Vladivostok: Rubezh, 2007.

Iankovskii, Iurii M. *Polveka okhoty na tigrov* [A half-century of tiger hunts]. Vladivostok: Ussuri, 1990.

Ianush, Ian Borisovich. "Avarii 1915–1916 gg. v Gatchinskoi Voennoi aviatsionnoi shkole" [Accidents at the Gatchina Military Aviation School, 1915–16]. *ZhUK: Zhurnal liubitelei otkrytok* [Journal for lovers of postcards] 4 (2009): 37–41.

Iasnov, Konstantin. "Pis'ma iz proshloi zhizni: Segodnia sostoitsia prezentatsiia unikal'nogo kul'turnogo proekta" [Letters from another life: A unique culture project will be presented today]. *Rossiiskaia gazeta: Primorskii krai*, no. 4780, October 24, 2008.

Il'in, A., ed. *Vladivostok: Spravochnik-putevoditel'* [A directory-guidebook]. Vladivostok: Dal'nevostochnoe Knizhnoe Izdatel'stvo, 1972.

Ingemanson, Birgitta. "Cosmopolitan Vladivostok: Swedish Glimpses, 1908–1923." *Scando-Slavica* 42 (1996): 36–57; "Kosmopoliticheskii Vladivostok: Shvedskie otbleski, 1908–1923." Translated by Tamara Bogolepova. *Rubezh Al'manakh* 4 (2003): 362–78; and in Aleksiuk, ed., *Iankovskie chtenia*, 119–37.

———. "Portrait of a City: Impressions of Vladivostok among English-Speaking Visitors." *Rossiia i ATR* 3 (1995): 107–14.

———. "Poteriannyi rai: Imenie Novogeorgievskoe, 1892–1922" [A paradise lost: The Novogeorgievsk estate, 1892–1922]. Translated by Elena Smith and Vladimir I. Kalinin. *Rossiia i ATR* 4 (2001): 22–33.

———. *The Sunny Neighborhood: A Vladivostok Tale/Solnechnyi dvorik: Vladivostokskaia povest'*. In English and Russian. Translated by Max Nemtsov. Vladivostok: Rubezh, 2011.

———. "Vladivostok: Russia's Frontier Town on the Pacific." In *The Siberian Saga: A History of Russia's Wild East*. Edited by Eva-Maria Stolberg. Frankfurt am Main: Peter Lang, 2005: 119–30; "Vladivostok: Pogranichnyi gorod na Tikhom Okeane." Translated by A. A. Sapelkin. *Sotsial'nye i gumanitarnye nauki na Dal'nem Vostoke* 8, no. 4 (2005): 86–93 (Russian), 94–100 (English).

Izergina, A. N., et al. *The Hermitage, Leningrad: French Nineteenth-Century Masters*. Prague: Artia/Leningrad: Sovetsky Khudozhnik, 1968.

James, William. *The Varieties of Religious Experience: A Study in Human Nature*. London: Longmans, Green, 1902.

Kaliberova, Tamara N. "Avtograf na l'nianoi skaterti, ili Roman o Vladivostoke v pis'makh" [Autograph on a linen table-cloth, or a novel of Vladivostok in letters]. In Tamara Kaliberova, *Progulki po Vladivostoku* [Walks Around Vladivostok]. DVGTU, 2002.

———. "Slushaia gorod" [Listening to the city]. *Krasnoe znamia*, November 9, 1985.

Kappeler, Andreas. *The Russian Empire: A Multiethnic History*. Harlow, UK: Pearson Education Limited, 2001.

Keizerling, Al'fred. *Vospominaniia o russkoi sluzhbe* [Memories of Russian service]. Moscow: Akademkniga, 2001.

Kennan, George F. *Soviet-American Relations, 1917–1920: Russia Leaves the War*. Princeton, NJ: Princeton University Press, 1956.

Khisamutdinov, Amir A. *The Russian Far East: Historical Essays*. Honolulu: N.p., 1993.

———. *Vladivostok: Etiudy k istorii starogo goroda* [Vladivostok: Etudes toward the history of an old city]. DVGU, 1992.

Khromov, S. S., ed. "Interventsiia Antanty na Dal'nem Vostoke" [Intervention of the Entente in the Far East]. In *Grazhdanskaia voina i voennaia interventsiia v SSSR: Entsiklopediia* [The Civil War and the military intervention in the USSR: Encyclopedia]. Moscow: Sovetskaia Entsiklopediia, 1987.

King, Greg. *The Last Empress: The Life and Times of Alexandra Feodorovna, Tsarina of Russia*. Secaucus, NJ: Carol Pub. Group [sic], 1994.

Klark, I. S., ed. *Ves' delovoi i torgovyi Vladivostok na 1924 g.* [All of Vladivostok's business and trade for 1924]. Vladivostok: *Krasnoe znamia*, 1924.

Klimenko, I. N. *Mig mezhdu proshlym i budushchim: Fotosalony Vladivostoka kontsa XIX-*

nachala XX veka: Katalog fotografii [A moment between past and future: Vladivostok's photo salons, end of the nineteenth and beginning of the twentieth century: Catalogue of photographs]. PGOM, 2001.

Kotkin, Stephen, and David Wolff, eds. *Rediscovering Russia in Asia: Siberia and the Russian Far East*. Armonk, NY/London, England: M. E. Sharpe, 1995.

Krai otkrytyi miru: 70 let Primorskomu kraiu, 1938–2008 [A territory open to the world: Seventy years of the Maritime Territory, 1938–2008]. Krasnoiarsk: Platina, 2008.

Krushanov, A. I., ed. *Istoriia Dal'nego Vostoka SSSR v epokhu feodalizma i kapitalizma (XVII v.-fevral' 1917 g.)* [History of the Far East of the USSR during the epoch of feudalism and capitalism (seventeenth century-February 1917)]. Moscow: Nauka, 1991.

———. *Istoriia Sovetskogo Primor'ia: Uchebnoe posobie dlia uchashchikhsia VIII-X klassov shkol Primorskogo kraia* [History of Soviet Primorie: Textbook for students of classes eight through ten in the schools of the Maritime Territory]. Vladivostok: Dal'nevostochnoe Knizhnoe Izdatel'stvo, 1970.

Kschessinska, Mathilda, H. S. H. the Princess Romanovsky-Krassinsky. *Dancing in Petersburg: The Memoirs of Kschessinska*. Translated from the French by Arnold Haskell. New York: Da Capo Press, 1977.

Kungurov, Gennadii, and Boris D'iachenko, eds. *Vladivostok: Skrepy pamiati* [Bonds of memory]. In Russian and English. Translated by Tat'iana Pisareva. Vladivostok: Svetlana, 2001.

Latkin, A. P., ed. *Perspektivy razvitiia g. Vladivostoka (Materialy k proektu kontseptsii)* [Perspectives on Vladivostok's development (Materials toward conceptualizing the project)]. Vladivostok: Vladivostokskii Gorodskoi Sovet Narodnykh Deputatov, 1990.

Lebed'ko, Maria. *Vladivostok Downtown: Historic Walking Tour*. DVGU, 1995.

———. *Vladivostok: A Historic Walking Tour*. Updated online edition of *Vladivostok Downtown*. Edited by Birgitta Ingemanson. Web preparation by Donna McCool. 1999. Available at http://www.wsulibs.wsu.edu/Vladivostok.

Lengyel, Emil. *Siberia*. Garden City, NY: Garden City Publishing, 1943.

Levitskii, V. L., ed. *Vladivostok, 1860–1960*. Vladivostok: Primorskoe Knizhnoe Izdatel'stvo, 1960.

Lincoln, W. Bruce. *Red Victory: A History of the Russian Civil War*. New York: Simon and Schuster, 1989.

Lindholm, Otto W. *Beyond the Frontiers of Imperial Russia: From the Memoirs of Otto W. Lindholm*. Edited by Alexander de Haes Tyrtoff and Nicholas Tyrtoff Davis. Javea, Spain: A. de Haes OWL Publishing, 2008.

Lomakin, V. L. *Primor'e vchera, segodnia, zavtra* [Primorie yesterday, today, tomorrow]. Moscow: Politizdat, 1981.

Lovell, Stephen. *Summerfolk: A History of the Dacha, 1710–2000*. Ithaca, NY: Cornell University Press, 2003.

Luganskii, Iurii. *Vladimir Klavdievich Arsen'ev: Biografiia v fotografiiakh, vospominaniiakh druzei, svidetel'stvakh epokhi/A Biography in Photographs and Eyewitness Accounts*. In Russian and English. Edited by G. Aleksiuk. Translated by Nonna Chernyakova. Vladivostok: Ussuri, 1997.

Lundell, Ulf. "Öppna landskap" [Open landscapes]. Stockholm: EMI Svenska AB, 1982.

Maharishi Mahesh Yogi. *On the Bhagavad-Gita: A New Translation and Commentary, Chapters 1–6*. Harmondsworth, UK: Penguin Books, 1969.

Markov, V. *Vladivostok: Poltora veka na karte Rossii: Putevoditel'* [A century and a half on the map of Russia: A Guidebook]. In Russian and English. Translated by Z. Proshina. Vladivostok: Dal'press, 2010.

Marks, Steven G. *Road to Power: The Trans-Siberian Railroad and the Colonization of Asian Russia, 1850–1917.* Ithaca, NY: Cornell University Press, 1991.

Matveev, Nikolai P. *Kratkii istoricheskii ocherk g. Vladivostoka* [Brief historical essay about the city of Vladivostok]. 1910. Reprint, Vladivostok: Rubezh, 2010.

Meyer, Sibylle. "The Tiresome Work of Conspicuous Leisure: On the Domestic Duties of the Wives of Civil Servants in the German Empire, 1871–1918." In *Connecting Spheres: European Women in a Globalizing World, 1500 to the Present.* Edited by Marilyn Boxer and Jean H. Quataert. 2nd ed. New York: Oxford University Press, 2000.

Mialk, A. V., and V. I. Kalinin. *Vladivostok: Pamiatniki arkhitektury* [Vladivostok: Monuments of architecture]. In Russian and English. Translated by Z. Proshina. Vladivostok: Dal'press, 2005.

Mitic, Svetolik. *Mladost Josipa Broza* [Josip Broz's youth]. Beograd: NIP Mladost, 1978.

Miz', Nelli G., and Gennadii P. Turmov. *Stranitsy zabytoi istorii: K 140-letiiu Vladivostoka* [Pages of forgotten history: To Vladivostok's 140th anniversary]. DVGTU, 2000.

Miz', N. G. *Pokrovskii nekropol' Vladivostoka* [The Pokrovskoe cemetery of Vladivostok]. Vladivostok: Dal'nevostochnyi Afon, 2002.

Mossolov, A. A. *At the Court of the Last Tsar: Being the Memoirs of A. A. Mossolov, Head of the Court Chancellery, 1900–1916.* Edited by A. A. Pilenco. Translated by E. W. Dickes. London: Methuen, 1935.

Mukhachev, B. I., ed. *Istoriia Dal'nego Vostoka Rossii* [History of Russia's Far East]. Book 1, *Dal'nii Vostok Rossii v period revoliutsii 1917 goda i grazhdanskoi voiny* [Russia's Far East during the 1917 revolutions and the Civil War]. Vladivostok: Dal'nauka, 2003.

Mumford, Lewis. *The City in History: Its Origins, Its Transformations, and Its Prospects.* New York: Harcourt, Brace & World, 1961.

Nansen, Fridtjof. *Through Siberia, the Land of the Future.* Translated by Arthur G. Chater. London: William Heineman, 1914.

Obertas, V. A. "Arkhitektura starogo Vladivostoka" [Architecture of old Vladivostok]. *Arkhitekturnoe nasledstvo* 28 (1980): 107–18.

———. "Formirovanie planirovochnoi struktury Vladivostoka v XIX v." [Formation of Vladivostok's urban structure in the nineteenth century]. *Arkhitekturnoe nasledstvo* 25 (1976): 85–93.

Obertas, V. A., V. K. Moor, and E. A. Erysheva. *Pamiatniki istorii i kul'tury goroda Vladivostoka: Materialy k svodu* [Monuments of the history and culture of the city of Vladivostok: Materials]. Vladivostok: Svetlana, 2012.

Owen, Thomas C. "Impediments to a Bourgeois Consciousness in Russia, 1880–1905: The Estate Structure, Ethnic Diversity, and Economic Regionalism." In *Between Tsar and People: Educated Society and the Quest for Public Identity in Late Imperial Russia,* edited by Edith W. Clowes, Samuel D. Kassow, and James L. West, 75–89. Princeton, NJ: Princeton University Press, 1991.

Pecheritsa, V. F. *Vostochnaia vetv' russkoi emigratsii* [The Eastern branch of Russian emigration]. DVGU, 1994.

Petrov, Viktor P. *Rossiia na Dal'nem Vostoke* [Russia in the Far East]. Tenafly, NJ: Hermitage Publishers, 1996.

Plante, Ellen M. *Women at Home in Victorian America: A Social History.* New York: Facts on File, 1997.

The Poetry of T'ao Ch'ien. Translated by James Robert Hightower, with commentary and annotations. Oxford, UK: Clarendon Press, 1970.

Ponomarchuk, G. I. "Rastitel'nost' i zhivotnyi mir" [Flora and fauna]. In *Fizicheskaia geografiia Primorskogo kraia: Uchebnoe posobie* [Physical geography of the Maritime Territory: Textbook], edited by G. V. Svinukhov, 135–65. DVGU, 1990.

Pray, Eleanor L. "Coronation Week in Vladivostok." *Somersworth Free Press* (New Hampshire), July 17, 1896.

Razgonov, S. N., ed. *Pamiatniki otechestva: Mir russkoi usad'by* [Monuments of the fatherland: The world of the Russian country estate]. Moscow: Russkaia Kniga, 1992.

Richardson, William. "Stalinist Vladivostok: Architecture and Urban Planning, 1928–1953." *The Soviet and Post-Soviet Review* 27, no. 2–3 (2000): 293–314.

Rieber, Alfred J. *Merchants and Entrepreneurs in Imperial Russia.* Chapel Hill: University of North Carolina Press, 1982.

Roosevelt, Priscilla. *Life on the Russian Country Estate: A Social and Cultural History.* Photographs by William Brumfield. New Haven, CT: Yale University Press, 1995.

Rostunov, I. I., ed. *Istoriia russko-iaponskoi voiny, 1904–1905 gg.* [History of the Russo-Japanese War, 1904–5]. Moscow: Nauka, 1977.

The Russo-Japanese War: A Photographic and Descriptive Review of the Great Conflict in the Far East, Gathered from the Reports, Records, Cable Despatches [sic], *Photographs, etc., etc., of Collier's War Correspondents*: Richard Harding Davis, Frederick Palmer, James F. J. Archibald, Robert L. Dunn, Ellis Ashmead Bartlett, James H. Hare, Henry James Whigham, and Victor K. Bulla. New York: P. F. Collier & Son, 1905.

Shalay, Victor. *Vladivostok 1860–2010: Vzgliad sovremennika/Views of a Contemporary.* In Russian and English. Edited by Marina Barinova (Russian) and Birgitta Ingemanson (English). Vladivostok: Sobranie-Exclusive, 2010.

Shcheben'kova, Elena. *Vladivostok: Moia sud'ba* [Vladivostok: My destiny]. Vladivostok: Dal'press, 2004.

Shcherbak, Vladimir. *Znamenitye gosti Vladivostoka* [Famous guests of Vladivostok]. Vladivostok: Dal'press, 2005.

Slattery, Peter. *Reporting the Russo-Japanese War, 1904–5: Lionel James's First Wireless Transmissions to "The Times."* Folkestone, UK: Global Oriental, 2004.

Smith, Canfield F. *Vladivostok under Red and White Rule: Revolution and Counterrevolution in the Russian Far East, 1920–22.* Seattle: University of Washington Press, 1975.

Smith, Christine Hill. *Reading "A Victorian Gentlewoman in the Far West: The Reminiscences of Mary Hallock Foote."* Boise, ID: Boise State University, 2002.

Standage, Tom. *The Victorian Internet: The Remarkable Story of the Telegraph and the Nineteenth Century's On-Line Pioneers.* New York: Berkley Books, 1998.

Startsev, Aleksei, and Aleksei Shereshev. *Khronika trekh pokolenii: Istoricheskii ocherk* [Chronicle of three generations: A historical essay]. Vladivostok: TINRO-Tsentr, 2006.

Steele, Valerie. *The Corset: A Cultural History.* New Haven, CT: Yale University Press, 2001.

Stephan, John J. *The Russian Far East: A History*. Stanford, CA: Stanford University Press, 1994.

Stephan, John J., and V. P. Chichkanov, eds. *Soviet-American Horizons on the Pacific*. Honolulu: University of Hawai'i Press, 1986.

Stites, Richard. *Serfdom, Society, and the Arts in Imperial Russia: The Pleasure and the Power*. New Haven, CT: Yale University Press, 2005.

Stratievskii, O. B., N. G. Miz', and I. A. Avduevskaia. *Kto v imeni tvoem? Ulitsy goroda Vladivostoka* [Who's in your name? Vladivostok's streets]. Vladivostok: Dal'press, 2005.

Striuchenko, Ivan G., ed. *Zabytye imena: Istoriia Dal'nego Vostoka Rossii v litsakh. Stat'i i ocherki, vyp. I* [Forgotten names: History of Russia's Far East through individuals: Articles and essays, part 1]. Vladivostok: Dal'nauka, 1994.

Summers, Leigh. *Bound to Please: A History of the Victorian Corset*. Oxford, NY: Berg, 2001.

Sylvester, Roshanna P. *Tales of Old Odessa: Crime and Civility in a City of Thieves*. DeKalb: Northern Illinois University Press, 2005.

Tupper, Harmon. *To the Great Ocean: Siberia and the Trans-Siberian Railway*. Boston: Little, Brown, 1965.

Turmov, G. P., and A. A. Khisamutdinov. *Vladivostok: Istoricheskii putevoditel'* [Historical guidebook]. Moscow: Veche, 2010.

Tyler, Sydney. *The Japan-Russia War: An Illustrated History of the War in the Far East: The Greatest Conflict of Modern Times*. Philadelphia: P. W. Ziegler, 1905.

Wade, Rex A. *The Triumph of Bolshevism, 1917–1919*. Vol. 1, *Documents of Soviet History*. Gulf Breeze, FL: Academic International Press, 1991.

Walkley, Christina, and Vanda Foster. *Crinolines and Crimping Irons: Victorian Clothes: How They Were Cleaned and Cared For*. 1978. Reprint, London: Peter Owen, 1985.

Warner, Denis, and Peggy Warner. *The Tide at Sunrise: A History of the Russo-Japanese War, 1904–5*. New York: Charterhouse, 1974.

West, James L., and Iurii A. Petrov, eds. *Merchant Moscow: Images of Russia's Vanished Bourgeoisie*. Princeton, NJ: Princeton University Press, 1998.

White, Christine A. *British and American Commercial Relations with Soviet Russia, 1918–1924*. Chapel Hill: University of North Carolina Press, 1992.

Williams, Albert Rhys. *Through the Russian Revolution*. New York: Monthly Review Press, 1921.

Wolff, David. *To the Harbin Station: The Liberal Alternative in Russian Manchuria, 1898–1914*. Stanford, CA: Stanford University Press, 1999.

Zeepvat, Charlotte. *Romanov Autumn: Stories from the Last Century of Imperial Russia*. Stroud, UK: Sutton, 2000.

Zingman-Leith, Elan, and Susan Zingman-Leith. *Creating Authentic Victorian Rooms*. Washington, DC: Elliott & Clark Publishing, 1995.

Index

Note: page numbers in *italics* refer to illustrations or captions; those followed by "n" indicate endnotes. "ELP" stands for Eleanor Lord Pray.

Arseniev Museum (Vladimir K. Arseniev State Museum of Primorie), xviii, xix

Artemieva, Anastasia (Nastia): biography, 223; hiring of, 18–19; Japanese occupation and, 180, 183; mentioned, 53, 206; Merkulov uprising and, 185; at Novo-georgievsk, 89; reliance on, 204; as seamstress, 35

Atkinson, Mrs., 152

Australia, emigrants returned from, 167

Azov, 40

Babintsev, Vasilii P., 225

Balser, Mr., 205

Baltic Fleet, 125, 141–43, 242n1, 242n3

Barrett, Mr., 61–62

Barringer, Dorothy Pray Dunn. *See* Pray, Dorothy

bashlyk (Russian hood), 31

Bayard, 67

Bay of the Golden Horn, 47, *111*, *116*, *120*, 126

bazaars, 32, 36–38

Bebler, Anton, 246n23

Bechtel, Mr., 82, 239n33

Behn, Christina (Tina) (née Meyer), 33, 223

Behn, Paul (Pavel-German Fedorovich), 33, 76, 223

Belkin, Ivan, 192

Berg, Dr., 13–14

Bermin, Colonel, 191

Berner, Mr., 157

Bezuslavina, Maria, 186

bicycling, 42

billiards, 12

Birk, Dr. Ludwig, 58–59, 142, 223, 227

Birk, Ewelina Andreevna, 9, 223

Birk, Jenny, 39, 228

birthday celebrations, 26

Bishop, Isabella Bird, 77–80, *116*

Biurgen, Mr. and Mrs., 57–58

Blessing of the Waters, 236n14

Blinova, Maria Ivanovna, 199, 203

Blok, Lieutenant, 126, 127–28

Bloody Sunday (St. Petersburg, 1905), 154–55

Bloody Sunday (Vladivostok, 1906), 154–59

boating: canoeing, 41–42; Clarkson's *Samson*, 151; ELP's seasickness, 85, 98; on the Lindholms' *Siberia*, 49, 50; at Novo-georgievsk, 98; *sampans*, 52, 137, 198, 214

Boesch, Mrs., 32–33

Bogatyr, 66, 127, 130–31, 144

Bolsheviks: expelled from "nests," 174; Merkulov uprising, 184–85; October Revolution (1917), 163–64, 167–68; spread of Bolshevism, xxiii–xxiv; on the tram, 61; *Uprava* (city council) chased out by, 173

Bonsdorf, Madame, 9

Borisova, Ida Fedorovna (née Schultz), *122*, 163, 223, 227

Borodino, 142

Boxer Rebellion, 17–18, 234n14

Brandt, Mr., 199, 200, 202–3

Brandt, Viktor Teodorovich, 14, 24, 223

Bravyi, 142

Breck, Belle, 178–79, 223

Breshko-Breshkovskaia, Ekaterina K., 170, 246n21

bridge group, 25

Brockmann, Pastor Manfred, 236n15

Brooklyn (ship), 164, 168, 169–70, 245n8

Brotnovskaia, Elena Mikhailovna, 205, 224

Brown, Mr., 43

Broz, Josip, 169–70, 178, 181, 246n23

Bryant, Louise, 246n22

Bryner, Elena Mikhailovna (née Brotnovs-kaia), 205, 224

Bryner, Iulii Ivanovich, 64, 128, 224, 234n1, 241n24

Bryner, Kiriusha, 97

Bryner, Leonid, 205, 224

Bryner, Margarita ("Gretli"), 226, 241n24

Bryner, Natalia Iosifovna, 224, 241n24

Bryner, Nina, 101–2, 226, 241nn24–25

Bryner, Therese ("Mika") (née Williams), 97, 224

Bryner family: art nouveau mansion of, 47, 234n1; Sidemi estate, 207, 249n17

paddling, 41–42
parades, 53, 54–55, 56, 167, 174
Parenago, Dr., 40
parties, masquerade, 22
Pastukhova, Maria, 188
Patterson, Lieutenant, 175
pawn shop, 82–83, 239n36
pension payments, 62
People's Revolutionary Army, 194, 197
People's Will movement, 244n7
Peresvet, 145
Pershina, Alexandra ("Tetia Sasha" [Auntie
  Sasha]), 172, 188, 204, 206, 210, 212, 227
Pestrikova, Elizaveta Gustavovna, 122
Petropavlovsk, 38, 130, 132, 234n14
Petrov (Chief of Police), 55
Piankov, Mr., 195–96
Piankova, Nadezhda Alexandrovna, 195,
  227, 248n2, 248n5
picnics, 50–51, 98, 112, 116, 213
Pissarro, Camille, xvii
Plarr, M., 135
Poe, Mrs., 179–80
Poltava, 145
Popov, Dr., 40
Port Arthur squadron, 126, 136–39, 141, 145
Powers, Martha Elizabeth, 78, 239n26
Pray, Dorothy (daughter), 105, 121; birthday
  at Novogeorgievsk, 97, 241n15; birth of,
  xxx, 19, 234n11; Civil War and, 174; death
  of, 234n11; dog Tylo of, 97; Eleanor Lord
  Pray Collection and, xxv; mentioned,
  35, 74, 167, 206; Nastia as governess for,
  19; at Novogeorgievsk, 89, 92–93, 96–
  98; at parade, 56; plans for birth of, 34;
  Russian language use, as child, 19–20;
  secret police not opening letters from,
  205; sent to Shanghai American School,
  xxx; sleighing and, 53
Pray, Eleanor Lord (Eleonora Georgievna
  or Roxy): arrival in Vladivostok, xviii, 5,
  21; biographical sketch, xxix–xxxi; death
  of, xxxi; dieting by, 34; economic rise
  and fall of, 28–29; education and mind

of, xx–xxi; English lessons given by, 10;
gratitude prayers at Cathedral for, 186;
name of, xxviii; out-of-body experience
at Novogeorgievsk, 99; photography by,
108, 115, 120; Russian language studies
and accent, xxi; Sarah, relationship with,
8; Shanghai, move to, xxxi, 28; tea circle
and, 28; wedding, xxx. *See also specific
persons and topics*
Pray, Eleanor Lord, photographs of: with
  friends, 103; in Lindholms' garden, 114;
  at Novogeorgievsk, 118; picnicking, 112,
  116; at Sewing Circle at the Admiral's,
  122; with tea circle, 109, 117; at tennis,
  105; in veranda room, 104
Pray, Frederick (Fred or Ted) (husband):
  arrival in Vladivostok, xviii, 5, 21;
  billiards and, 12; biography, xxx–xxxi;
  birthdays, 90, 98; Bloody Sunday and,
  156–57; at bridge group, 25; on *Brooklyn*
  farewell supper, 169–70; business taken
  over by, 15; at Christmas, 24; Civil War
  and, 173–74; at Czech concert, 178; death
  of, xxxi, 7, 20, 91, 161, 194, 196, 205, 206,
  240n8; death of Charles Smith and, 13–
  14; death of Otto Lindholm and, 73;
  engraving by, 7, 10; fireside companionship with ELP, 7–8; gardening by, 17;
  at *Gromoboi* performance, 128; health
  issues, 7; Japanese occupation and,
  182; Langdon and, 183; mentioned, 55,
  74, 129, 197, 206; Merritt mistaken for,
  17; November (1905) riots and, 147–53;
  at Novogeorgievsk, 88, 90, 92–93, 95–
  98; outings with, 51–52, 82, 112; photographs of, 103, 104, 105, 106, 112, 114, 116,
  118, 121; revolutions of 1917 and, 165,
  166; Russo-Japanese War and, 133, 135–
  36, 137, 141, 144; as secretary of meeting
  of Americans, 83; shopping with, 54;
  social calls by, 8–9; sports and recre-
  ation, 43; suits, new, 33; typewriter, 18;
  US consulate position, 160; whale sight-
  ing, 48

Unterberger, Gori, 51
Unterberger, Jenny (née Birk), 39, 228
Unterberger, Mania, 51
Unterberger, Pavel Fedorovich, 55, 94, 228
Unterberger, Peter Pavlovich, 51, 198, 228
uprava (city council), 170–71, 173
Ural (ship), 142
Ussuri Bay, 47
Ussuri Railway, 54

Variag, 145, 243n12
Vasilieva, Elena V., xxiv
Vereshchagin, Vasilii, 130
Victoria, Queen of the United Kingdom,
  75, 79
Victoria Melita, Princess of Saxe-Coburg
  and Gotha, 75
Vilken, Lieutenant, 129, 138
Villa Alwine, 85–87, *117*, *118*, *119*. *See also*
  Novogeorgievsk Estate
Vitgeft, Vilgelm, 136, 138
Vladivostok: American Consulate, *121*, *122*;
  Amur Bay, 47, 50, 194, 201, 214; attitudes
  toward Chinese, 17; Bay of the Golden
  Horn, 47, *111*, *116*, *120*, 126; Bloody Sunday (1906), 154–59; bombardment of
  (March 1904), 133–36; Chichagov's beau-
  tification project, 65; city landmarks
  and cultural attractions, 47–48, 53–56,
  234n1, 236n13; as city of contrasts and
  complexity, xxi–xxii, 49; coat of arms,
  113; Danish House, 41, 233n3; duty-free
  port status, 234n9; Eagle's Nest (hill),
  133; ELP's stubbornness to remain in,
  196–97; European colony in, 5; famous
  visitors to, 75–83; as feast for the senses,
  48–49; fiftieth anniversary celebration,
  56, 236n19; geological expeditions from,
  16; import duties in, 33; Japanese occupation of, 180–86; natural setting of,
  47, 48; November Riots (1905), 147–54;
  outings and picnics, 49–53; panoramic
  views of, *111*, *116*, *120*; remoteness and
  international connections of, xxiv–xxv;

Sedanka Reservoir hydrocomplex, 232n8;
  Sodom Street and Sodom Hill, 231n2;
  street vignettes and human interactions,
  56–63; Svetlanskaia Street view, *110*;
  Ussuri Bay, 47; walking in, 49–50, 52–
  53, 127, 129, 183. *See also* Dom Smith
  (home); *specific people and events*
Vladivostok squadron, 66, 125, 133, 136,
  244n27. See also *Bogatyr*; *Gromoboi*;
  Rurik
Volkenstein, Liudmila Alexandrovna, 158,
  244n7
Volunteer Fleet, 64
Voronezh, 12
Voronko, Mikhail, 188–89

Wagner, Mr., 205
walking in Vladivostok, 49–50, 52–53, 127,
  129, 183
Walldén (Valden), Axel Kirillovich, 14, 73,
  228
Walldén (Valden), Franz, 228
Walldén (Valden), Selma Augusta, 228
Walsham, John (Jack), 43, *105*, 228
Wang-sama (dog), 228
war. *See specific wars*
washing-day, 18, 93
weather and climate, 50, 51–52, 53, 200–201,
  208, 212
weddings, 57–58
Wedekind, Mr., 76
White, Mr., 78
Whittier, John Greenleaf, 78, 239n26
Williams, Therese (Mika), 97, 224
Wilson, Woodrow, 169, 245n17, 246n18
Winslow, Mary (née Macgowan), 226
Winslow, Rollin, 226
Wissing, Anna (Ännchenlieb), 86–87, 91,
  228
Wissing, Nicolai Lauritz, 87, 228
Witte, Sergei, 143, 144
Wohlfahrt, Rudolph, 28, 228
Wohlfahrt, Sophie: biography, 228; children
  lost by, 28; at Novogeorgievsk, 85; pho-

CPSIA information can be obtained
at www.ICGtesting.com
Printed in the USA
BVHW082111020119
536919BV00003B/11/P

9 780295 994536